THE LIFE OF
GEORGE MATHESON

D.D., LL.D., F.R.S.E.

BY

D. MACMILLAN, M.A., D.D.

MINISTER OF KELVINHAUGH PARISH, GLASGOW

NEW YORK

A. C. ARMSTRONG AND SON

3 & 5 WEST EIGHTEENTH ST·

1907

THE LIFE OF GEORGE MATHESON

D.D., LL.D., F.R.S.E.

Rev. George Matheson, D.D. LL.D.

TO
HIS SISTER
J. G. M.

PREFACE

I DESIRE to express, in a word, my indebtedness to
the many friends who so readily responded to my
appeal for help in the preparation of this volume.
To Miss Matheson in particular I owe much.
She unreservedly placed in my hands the Literary
Remains of her brother and all the materials in her
possession that might aid me in my work. She
gave me, besides, much information regarding his
early life, and cleared up many points of doubt
and difficulty. My cordial thanks are also due to
the Rev. John Anderson, B.D., and the Rev. W. S.
Provand, M.A., for revising the proofs ; to the Rev.
R. S. V. Logie, M.A., for preparing the index ;
and to my friend, Dr. William Wallace, for
again placing his invaluable literary experience and
judgment at my service.

D. M.

October 11, 1907.

CONTENTS

CHAPTER I

CONTENTS

CHAPTER VI

PAGE

CHAPTER VII

CHAPTER VIII

CHAPTER IX

CHAPTER X

CHAPTER XI

CHAPTER XII

CHAPTER I

EARLY YEARS

GEORGE MATHESON was born in Glasgow on March 27, 1842. The Church of Scotland, of which he was to be so distinguished a minister, was on the eve of its greatest trial. The forces which for the past ten years had been concentrating into opposing camps were now almost ready for the conflict that was to break up the Church into two bodies. A year after his birth the Disruption took place. His parents kept by the Church of their fathers, but the ecclesiastical division and strife into which young Matheson was born were not without their influence on him. They touched him, however, in a manner greatly different from that in which they affected most men. In place of embittering they would seem to have sweetened his temper. They set him in the ecclesiastical sphere the problem which in theology he all through endeavoured to solve. From the very first the question faced him : How can opposing differences be reconciled? In the realm of religious thought he did his best by his writings to

1

answer that question ; and though he took no part in Church politics, his catholicity of spirit and practice did more to soften the acerbity of ecclesiastical life, and to bring about a kindlier feeling between different communions, than the active and well-meant proposals of those who framed definite schemes of union.   True brotherhood does not depend upon outward uniformity.   The love of a common ideal, which in reality is the true bond of perfectness and peace, is independent of all external barriers.   It treats them in relation to Christian fellowship as non-existent.

It was at 39 Abbotsford Place, on the south side of the river Clyde, that Matheson was born.   A walk through the district tells of its former glory. There still is the wide street with its blocks of solid masonry, giving the houses an air of substantiality which time has not destroyed ; but the ever extending city has laid its hand on the once fashionable suburb, and by its smoke and tread of busy commerce has reduced it to the type of an artisan quarter.   Its roomy dwellings still command tenants who prefer comfort to external appearance, but the rising merchants who fifty or sixty years ago chose it as a quiet, airy, and genteel locality, have long since migrated far beyond its boundaries.   It offered, however, a sufficiently attractive residence for Matheson's parents at the beginning of their married life.

George Matheson, the father, after whom his eldest son was named, was a fine type of the

successful Glasgow merchant of two generations
ago; shrewd, kindly, and God-fearing. He shared
to the full in the old ideals of Scottish religious
and social life, which wealth, in place of destroying,
fed and fostered. The Church, with its time-
honoured services and sanctities, was to him what
it had been to his fathers, and he found his
recreation in the kindly ministries with which it
leavened public life. The old beliefs still stood
unshaken; and Church and State constituted to
him a time-honoured union on which the prosperity
of the country depended. His personality, after
the lapse of years, stands out clear and strong.
His memory is fondly cherished by the remaining
members of his family, and by many who knew him
through the intercourse of business and social life.
He was a native of Dornoch. When quite a
lad he was taken to Glasgow to be educated and
launched upon his career. Dr. Matheson used to
refer with pride to his Highland ancestry, and he
ever regarded this happy chance in his father's life
as the making of their fortunes. Had it not been
for his father's response to the voice which called
him thither, the land of promise, of intellectual and
spiritual conquest, might never have been his.

Dornoch has charms of its own. As a summer
resort it is full of attractions. Its golf course is of
ancient renown. So far back as 1630 Sir Robert
Gordon wrote of it: "About this toun, along the
seacoast, there are the fairest and largest linkes or
green fields of any part of Scotland, fitt for archery,

goffing, ryding, and all other exercise; they doe
surpasse the fields of Montrose or St. Andrews."
Professor Blackie, who wandered thither in 1881,
while having a characteristic fling at the town itself
as "an old-fashioned, outlying, outlandish, grey
nest," speaks of it as " interesting, with a splendid
beach for sea-bathing, a fresh, breezy, and dry
atmosphere, and a golfing course second to none in
Scotland." It offered little inducement, however, to
ambitious youth. Cut off from the commercial life
of the country, and with few or no resources in
itself, Dornoch practically compelled its sons to
look elsewhere for success. Still it gave them
what the more populous and wealthy centres could
not bestow, and prepared them for those conquests
which were in store for many of them. The robust
health, the latent talent, the tireless energy and
ceaseless enterprise of the Glasgow merchant, are a
heritage from ancestors who ran on the "braes" of
the Scottish Highlands and Lowlands. They were
denied the opportunities which their sons enjoy.
They received not the promise, some better thing
having been reserved for those in whose life their
own is perfected.

The elder Matheson on coming to Glasgow
looked, to begin with, to the ministry as his future
career. This was natural. To country lads in
his day, who were fired by youthful ambition, the
Church seemed to be the only sphere in which
their talents could find scope. The two men of
importance in the parish were the laird and the

minister. The position of the one was beyond
them, but that of the other was within their reach.
The intellectual joys of such a calling also appealed
to them, apart altogether from the spiritual ideals
in which its true significance is found. Accordingly,
on leaving school he entered the University and
became a proficient Latin scholar; but his career as
a student was of short duration. By the advice of
friends his course was diverted into business, and
after a time, along with Mr. William Wilson, afterwards so well known as the genial and popular
"Bailie Wilson" of Glasgow, he started the firm of
Wilson & Matheson in Glassford Street. The
business prospered exceedingly, and under his
second son, Mr. John Matheson, as its head, it
still continues to prove successful. Mr. Matheson's
early enthusiasms never left him. If he was not
to be a minister of the Kirk, he at any rate could be
an office-bearer in it. While he lived at Abbotsford
Place he attended St. David's Parish Church (the
Ramshorn), during the ministry of Dr. Paton.
When he removed to the West End of the city he
became one of the first promoters of Sandyford
Church, and he was deputed, along with a few
others, to hear the Rev. Mr. Macduff, then minister
of St. Madoes in Perthshire, who became the first
minister of Sandyford. Mr. Matheson continued
during the whole of Dr. Macduff's ministry to take
the deepest interest in church and parish, and he
proved himself a loyal supporter and friend. Dr.
Macduff on his deathbed dictated a letter (March

18, 1895) to Dr. Matheson, in which, among other references quite pathetic in their nature, he thus recalls his old office-bearer and friend : " My two strongholds in Sandyford, for genial kindness and wise direction, were that dear, great-hearted George Matheson of Glassford Street and James Ritchie."

Dr. Matheson's parents were second-cousins. His mother was the eldest daughter of Mr. John Matheson of the Fereneze Print Works, Barrhead, and her brothers were Mr. John Matheson, Junr., of Messrs. William Stirling & Sons, Turkey Red Dyers in the Vale of Leven, and Sir Donald Matheson, K.C.B., of the United Turkey Red Co. Ltd. She came of a talented family. Her brother John was one of the foremost business men of his day, full of enterprise and energy. He possessed many of the qualities which afterwards distinguished his brilliant nephew. Cultured and versatile, a patron of art and literature, specially fond of music, a capable public speaker, and an author of considerable reputation, his sudden death in the prime of life was a distinct loss to his native city. Sir Donald was for many years the head of the volunteer movement in the West of Scotland. His services were repeatedly recognised, his final reward being a knighthood in 1887. The outside world might have said that Mrs. Matheson's special gift was song. Music certainly was the art she cultivated most ; as a pianist she was striking and brilliant, but her talent was many

sided ; and if it was from his father Dr. Matheson
inherited that sane view of worldly matters and
power of managing business affairs which frequently
surprised even intimate friends, it was certainly
to his mother he was indebted for his gift of
imagination and spiritual insight. He was quite
aware of this himself. " I was brought up on the
most traditional theology," he once remarked.
" My father held by the old paths ; my mother had
an inquiring mind, and doubtless much of my
speculative spirit comes from her." He thus united
in himself, and in a unique degree, the special
qualities of both his parents, and their joint
influence on him accounts much for the man that
he afterwards came to be. Young Matheson had,
therefore, in the character and culture of his parents,
the most valuable asset with which a child can be
blest. He had also the advantage of a full family
life. The Mathesons were eight : five sons and
three daughters. George was the second eldest,
coming next to that sister with whom his life was
to be inseparably linked to the end. That touch of
nature which marked him all through was early
developed. It was fostered by his home environment, and grew through the contact and conflict of
the domestic circle.

As a child he was inquiring and sensitive.
His nurse used to be annoyed by his stopping
her in her walk to ask, for instance, how masons
built houses. The memories of childhood lived
long in his mind. Towards the close of the remark-

able address which he delivered a few years before his death, in proposing the Immortal Memory at the Edinburgh Ninety Burns Club, he refers to the following youthful recollection: "I remember how in the days of my boyhood, in the midst of a crowded street, the scene of bustle and traffic and commerce, there lingered the trunk of an old tree. There it stood; amid the din and the roar and the rattle, proclaiming the survival of the country in the town, like the touch of a vanished hand and the sound of a voice that is still." Another memory of his boyhood flashed upon him once when preaching a sermon in St. Bernard's to children, the day after the Sunday-school trip. The experience was one with which he would be familiar after his family had removed to St. Vincent Crescent in the West End of the city. The town had evidently been making encroachments upon Abbotsford Place, as one can gather from his reference to the "trunk of an old tree." In their new abode they would be secure from the "din and the roar and the rattle" of the city's commerce. From the windows of their house there was an unimpeded view of the upper reaches of the river; nothing intervening but green fields. In preaching to the Sunday-school scholars on that occasion, he chose as his subject "The children playing in the streets of Jerusalem," and in the course of his sermon he told them how, as a boy, he had watched the different steamers on the Clyde. To each steamer a name had been given by the children of the Crescent, and one which was always behind was christened "Sure to be Late." He had also, like his favourite poet Burns, an eye not only for natural objects but for the dumb creation as well, and a heart that felt for their suffering.

It will thus be seen that, in his early years, he had the use of his eyesight; not by any means the full use, for at the age of eighteen months his mother made the melancholy discovery that his power of vision was impaired. The cause of the defective sight was found to be inflammation at the back of the eyes. Dr. Mackenzie, the leading oculist in Glasgow at the time, was consulted, but he could do nothing. He held out the hope, however, that if the boy lived to be an old man he might see well. Other specialists were consulted, one of whom declared that he had a perfect organ of vision; but no operation was proposed, and no means could be recommended by them for effecting a cure. The fact of Dr. Matheson having what appeared to be a perfect organ of vision, struck more than the oculist referred to. There were times when his friends thought that he not only saw them, but saw through them. This must have been Mr. Eric Mackay's experience, for when visiting Dr. Matheson, along with his foster-sister Marie Corelli, he suddenly paused in the midst of his conversation and remarked, "You have a penetrating eye, Dr. Matheson."

The failure of his eyesight was gradual. Dur-

ing the greater part of his school-life he was able
to see sufficiently well to read and to write, and
to acquire a competent knowledge of the Classics
and of French and German. He used powerful
glasses and availed himself of large type, and was
permitted at school to sit near a window with
a southern exposure so that he might get the
full benefit of the sunlight. But from the time
that he entered the University until the end he
was dependent upon others. There is indeed a
tradition of him, while in the Humanity Class,
construing at times from the pages of his own
book, but there were occasions when he was
unable to do so. A fellow-student remembers
young Matheson listening eagerly to a companion
reciting, at the door of the class-room, the lesson
for the day; it was a chapter from Ramsay's
Roman Antiquities. It was only by having it
read to him that he could learn its contents. By
the time he entered the Logic Class his eyesight
for all practical purposes was gone; he was then
in his eighteenth year. It never could be said
that he was totally blind; he had his moments
of vision. Looking out from his windows at
Innellan Manse, across the Firth, he sometimes
caught a shadow of the steamers as they flitted
up and down. Walking along one of the main
streets of Glasgow, he at times could discern the
sign-boards above the shop doors and windows.
Indeed, it would almost seem as if Dr. Mackenzie's
prophecy was to become true, for in the autumn

in which he died, while driving in North Berwick
with his two sisters, opposite to whom he sat,
he remarked that the one had no veil while
the other wore a thick black one ; which was the
truth. A correspondent recalls the following
incident :—

During the summer of 1869 I was on a visit to my
father and mother at their seaside quarters at Innellan.
One day Mr. Matheson took afternoon tea with us. The
conversation turned on his great deprivation. My father,
who had snow-white whiskers, and who was seated near
him, asked, " Have you never lucid moments of sight, Mr.
Matheson ? " " Yes," he said ; " for instance, I observe that
you have very white whiskers." In the same connection
a lady related to me an incident which seemed to have
had rather a touch of romance about it. She was a young
widow, and a member of his church. One day she sailed
with him in the steamer to Glasgow, when it happened
that she wore a bright new brooch. They were standing
together in the cabin, the lady closer perhaps than she
would have ventured if her young minister had had his
eyesight. She was looking at his face with a yearning
sympathy, when a sudden flood of sunlight came through
the adjoining cabin window, illuminating them both. " I
think, Mrs. ——, you have got on a new brooch," said Mr.
Matheson. " And didn't I get a red face," said Mrs. ——.

The occasions, however, on which there were
such luminous breaks in the darkness that shrouded
him were few in number. It is possible that if
the medical knowledge of his day . had been
equal to what it is in ours, the disease might
have been cured in its initial stages, and then
we would have had even a greater George
Matheson ; for those who knew him in his early
schooldays, before his defective eyesight grew

so bad as to make him dependent upon others, were conscious of the splendid use he could have made of the faculty of vision. It has, however, been remarked that his loss of eyesight was in a sense the making of him. This may be true, if we reflect on the moral heroism which he displayed in rising superior to the physical calamity which would have crushed most men, and making it a stepping-stone to spiritual triumphs. I am aware that those who speak thus are of opinion that his natural defect threw him back upon himself, compelled him to meditate upon Divine things, and thereby enabled him to produce those works which by their depth, insight, and suggestiveness have been the joy and comfort of many. That touch of mysticism in his preaching and writing, in which consisted much of their charm, they hold, might have been wanting if Matheson had been distracted by those sights which disturb or absorb the thoughts of most men. There may be a measure of truth in this, but only, after all, a very limited measure. George Matheson was cast by nature in the mould with which we are familiar, and his education, environment, profession, and impaired eyesight may each have had its share in his spiritual and intellectual development; but his own personality was greater than them all, and they and the other circumstances of his life were utilised by it in forming and perfecting his character and finishing his work.

Hearers of Dr. Matheson's preaching, readers

of his books, and even members of his congregation, seldom thought, perhaps, that there was a
time in his life when the awful tragedy of the loss
of his eyesight all but overwhelmed him. He was
such an optimist, so buoyant and inspiring, that it
would not occur to them that he was blind, or that
there was an hour in his life when he all but
succumbed to the deep despondency into which his
threatened loss threw him. Yet there was such an
hour. He had as a boy the happiest of natures ;
he took unaffected delight in every pleasure that
was innocent; he was companionable, and shared
the interests, the pastimes, and the joys of his
family and schoolfellows. He had a mind that
reached forward to the boundaries of knowledge,
a soul that yearned to be in touch with everything divine and human ; he took a natural zest
in life, and was ambitious of probing its depths
to the full. And yet at the very opening of his
manhood the appalling fact faced him that he would
have to go through life maimed, crippled in that
very faculty by whose means the world of knowledge, in which from his earliest years he took
supreme delight, could be gained ; and debarred
from sharing in those human interests in which his
soul rejoiced. He felt more than a momentary
shock when he knew that a cure was impossible.

It was now that he entered upon the great
struggle of his life and encountered the trial which
tested his character to the utmost. It has always
seemed to me that there is more than a reminiscence

of this period in his study of the Book of Job. The problem which this profound poem raises had a singular attraction for him. It formed the subject of the sermon which he preached before Queen Victoria at Balmoral, and he dealt with it on subsequent occasions in the pulpit and through the press. It was the very problem which he himself, in the first blush of eager manhood, had to solve, not only theoretically but practically, by a veritable agony and bloody sweat. Why should the innocent have to suffer? Why should a catastrophe altogether unmerited befall him? Why should his career, through no fault of his, be blasted on its very threshold? Why should he be denied those natural and intellectual joys for which he was so well adapted? These and similar questions that test a man's faith recurred to him with overwhelming force at this time; and his after life, from that very moment to its close, was a proof that he answered them in the only way by which peace is possible. In the spirit of his Master he conquered through submission. Thus early did he enter into the very Holy of Holies, and discover the secret of Christianity.

His education began at a very early period. A tutor at first came in to teach him. Afterwards he went to a school in Carlton Place, conducted by a Miss Hutcheson, and then to Mr. Buchanan's in St. George's Place. Something more than a tradition remains of this pedagogue. Many men who afterwards became famous passed, in their youth, through his hands. He had considerable reputation as an educationist, and excelled as a teacher of elocution. It is not at all unlikely that Matheson's oratorical gifts received their first impetus from his early schoolmaster. Buchanan, after retiring from his profession, resided at Port Bannatyne in Bute. He was in the habit of entertaining his friends with a rehearsal of his triumphs in the teaching art, boasting of the distinguished men whose early genius he had inspired, and taking not a little credit to himself for Matheson's gifts as a preacher.

It was when George was about ten years of age that the Mathesons removed to the West End of the city. The district which they chose for their residence was quite in the country. Those who know Glasgow only as it now is can hardly believe that St. Vincent Crescent could ever have been in the country. It is now surrounded by docks, railway lines, and public works. Like Abbotsford Place, it has had to yield to the pressure of the city's industry. The Mathesons took up their abode first in No. 60 and afterwards in No. 30, and it was in these two houses that the foundation of their son's education was laid. They were fortunate in having within an easy walking distance one of the two best schools in the city. This was the Glasgow Academy, recently erected. It was at that time situated in Elmbank Street. After the passing of the Scotch Education Bill it was bought by the School Board, and to it the High

School was removed from its old premises in John Street, the Academy migrating westward to handsome new buildings across the Kelvin, in Hillhead. Young Matheson's first session in the Academy was in 1853; he remained in it altogether four years, and his record was one of unbroken distinction. The close of his first year at the school saw him Dux of his Class. He in addition gained the prize for History and Religious Knowledge. His second year at the Academy was his first in Latin. On this occasion he won the second prize, and carried off the prizes in History, Geography, and English Composition. In his third session he resumed his former place as Dux of his Class, winning all the other special prizes, and in addition the prize in Science. Had he completed his full course he would no doubt have been in his last year Dux of the School, but he left at the close of the Session 1856–7, and never took the fifth Latin Class, which at that time was the highest. One of Dr. Matheson's old schoolfellows, Mr. James Hotson of Glasgow, gives the following reminiscences of those far-off days :—

My first acquaintance with Dr. Matheson would be about 1853, when my father's family removed to No. 31 St. Vincent Crescent. George Matheson and his next brother attended the same school with some of us,—the Glasgow Academy,—and my younger brother Hamilton and myself came, after a time, to be in the same class with him. It happened thus that we frequently walked to and from school together. The usual route was along Kent Road, then a real road, with deep hollows, called "orchards," on both sides. There were orchards also behind the Academy playground, so that when a football happened to be kicked over the paling it frequently took some time to recover it. There were at that time two headmasters in Classics, Dr. M'Burney and Mr. Currie. Matheson was at first under the former, but in 1856 he changed to Mr. Currie's, under whom my brother and I had been all along. Mr. Currie, to judge by his *Cæsar for Beginners* and *Notes on Horace*, both used in his classes, must have been a man of considerable scholarship, but I cannot say he was much of a teacher. He conducted the class usually after a sleepy sort of fashion, alternating with periods when he made things just a little too lively. Our principal other teachers were Mr. Bell (English), Mr. Reid (Arithmetic and Mathematics), Mr. Gow (Writing and Book-keeping), and Mr. Finlay (French and German). I cannot remember anything of Matheson's appearances in Mr. Bell's or Mr. Reid's class. Both were pleasant men generally, although at times they could be stern enough. Mr. Gow was good-natured even to softness. Matheson and I had a seat next each other, at a desk facing a window, and the circumstance that, with such light as he would thus get, he could practise a kind of half-text, shows that at that period his eyesight was not nearly so defective as it afterwards became. He and I were then engrossed with Byron's "Corsair," and I regret to say that I occasionally carried the book in my pocket and read bits of it to him when we ought to have been attending to our copy-books. Mr. Finlay was also extremely good-natured. When he set us to recite a portion of some amusing French Comedy, which he frequently did, and laughed himself as heartily as any of the boys, it seemed more like a dramatic entertainment than a school lesson. I remember Matheson, James Carlile, and my brother taking part in one of these recitals. But our principal class was Mr. Currie's, in which, besides Latin and Greek, we had lessons in History, Geography, Religious Knowledge, and English Composition. Matheson from the first distinguished himself in all these, but it was chiefly in English Composition

2

that he excelled.   In this, however, he had a keen rival
in John Ronald, who had long been acknowledged first
in this department, and was bitterly jealous in consequence.   Matheson composed a poem " Bethany Tears,"
and the boys subscribed and had it printed.   It began
thus :

> Once when the world in pomp and pride swept by,
> And " Raise up Mammon " was its ruling cry,
> When man in sin's embrace had fallen asleep,
> The God-man Jesus was constrained to weep.
> Time has flown on with wings of speed arrayed,
> Empires have risen, flourished, and decayed ;
> Great kings and warriors in oblivion lie,
> But those embittering tears can never dry.

Without delay Ronald came out with a lampoon on
Matheson, commencing :

> In sparkling Clutha's verdant vale,
> A verdant Homer chants his tale,

which though not printed was quickly circulated throughout the class.   Towards the end of the session Matheson
wrote and recited another set of verses, the refrain of
which was :

> Up, up and rejoice, the vacation is nigh,

which showed that his good spirits were not much
affected by Ronald's rivalry.   Of the other leading boys in
his class, which numbered about eighty, I need scarcely say
anything.   There was one, however, who afterwards highly
distinguished himself in the literary world as poet,
novelist, and playwright—I mean Robert Buchanan.   He
made no figure to speak of in any of the classes.   I
suppose he was too much occupied with Shakespere,
then his favourite author, to do justice to his lessons.
Although he also lived in St. Vincent Crescent, and must
frequently have walked to and from school with the
other Sandyford and Partick pupils, I don't think
Matheson and he ever got intimately acquainted.   My

brother and I knew him quite well, and spent a good deal
of time in his company. The most remarkable feature in
his personal appearance was his enormous head. I could
give some reminiscences of him, but "that is another
story." Matheson at school was well liked and very
popular. He was always in good spirits and full of
laughter.

One at the first blush must feel surprise at the
high spirits of young Matheson and the success
of his schooldays. Credit him with the most
cheerful nature and the most brilliant talents that
ever a youth possessed, the portrait of him that
has thus been drawn by an old companion surely
calls for some explanation. This will be found in
his home life. No youth could be more happily
situated in this respect than he was. His parents,
on discovering his talents, gave him every encouragement, and having ample means at their
disposal were quite prepared to spare no expense
on his education. But the difficulty faced him how,
with the increasing loss of eyesight, he could
acquire a knowledge of subjects which were
necessary for a scholastic career and continue
abreast of the progress demanded of any who
aspired to a University degree and a learned profession. It was when this need became apparent
that the members of his family rallied round him
and began to show that devotion to his interests
which continued to the very end. The home of
the Mathesons at this period affords a picture of
a "Scottish Interior," equal in beauty, on its own
lines, to that which Burns gives in the "Cottar's

Saturday Night." We see the father and mother
with the other members of the family gathering
round the budding preacher, who at the early age
of seven improvised a church and congregation,
and standing on a chair which for the occasion was
dignified into a pulpit, and with a pair of paper
bands on his breast, astonished his hearers by
delivering sermons which showed an ability and
an eloquence far beyond his years. While still a
schoolboy he wrote a play with Theseus as its
hero. This play was frequently acted in his
mother's drawing-room; his brothers and sisters
taking the leading parts, with a select number of
relatives and friends as auditors.

It was, however, in relation to his studies, and
the necessary preparation of them for school and
University, that the devotion of his family comes
into the boldest relief. Latin, Greek, and Hebrew
do not as a rule commend themselves to the minds
of women. It is only within recent years, after
the gates of the Universities were thrown open
to them, that the gentler sex began to show any
special interest in these subjects. Yet in this
"Scottish Interior" we see two of Dr. Matheson's
young sisters labouring earnestly to acquire a knowledge of these languages, so that they might be able
to read them to their brother and thereby assist him
in his career.

It was at an even earlier stage than this that
his eldest sister began to forge those links which
joined her in so close a union with her brother,

and which grew in strength as the years passed
by. It was she who taught him to read, and
she still remembers the childish delight with
which she one day announced to her mother that
George was able to spell. The interest of the
other members of the family might flag or vary,
but hers knew no change. She was in very truth
his *alter ego*, and it was touching to notice the
way in which he leaned upon her. Her sympathy
and companionship had become indispensable to
him, and the one great dread of his life was
that she might be taken first. It is impossible
to measure her literary labours, especially during
the earlier period of her brother's life. His college
exercises and essays are in her hand-writing.
It was she, too, who to his dictation wrote his
earlier sermons. It was not until he had entered
upon his ministerial career that the services of a
permanent secretary were secured, and she was in
a measure relieved. This, after all, was but giving
up one task to undertake another, for after he
became a parish minister, and his rising fame drew
crowds of admirers to his door, upon her largely
rested the burden of guiding her brother through
the quicksands and pitfalls of congregational and
parochial life, and of tempering those social relations into which his position naturally drew him.
In a scrap-book, which dates from 1868, there is
to be found on its very first page a sonnet by the
Archbishop of Dublin on a " Brother and Sister "
who died at the same time. It was evidently

selected for preservation because of the singular
manner in which it expressed not only their affection but also their wish :

Men said who saw the tender love they bare
Each to the other, and their hearts so bound
And knit in one, that neither sought nor found
A nearer tie than that affection rare—
How with the sad survivor will it fare,
When death shall for a season have undone
The links of that close love ; and taking one
The other leaves to draw unwelcome air ?
And some perchance who loved them, would revolve,
Sadly the sadness which on one must fall,
The lonely left by that dividing day.
Vain fears ! for He who loved them best of all,
Mightier than we life's mysteries to solve,
In one fire chariot bore them both away.

CHAPTER II

STUDENT DAYS

DR. MATHESON's early interest in intellectual pursuits clearly marked him out for a professional career. His impaired eyesight, with every indication of its final loss, necessarily limited his choice. His own inclinations pointed to the Bar. Indeed, in after years, he used to declare that if he had been without any physical impediment, this is the profession he would have chosen. One can readily understand the reasons which would weigh with him in preferring such a choice. He possessed in a marked degree the qualities necessary for success in such a career. He had natural ability, mental alertness, and the gift of speech. His buoyancy of nature and indomitable perseverance would have enabled him to surmount the preliminary drudgery, and to wait for his first great opportunity. It may be profitless to forecast his success in such a profession, but it is surely not too much to say that, all things being equal, he would have risen to eminence and become one of the most distinguished advocates of his time.

How striking a resemblance exists in this respect between the opening years of his life and
those of Robertson of Brighton? Robertson's
early ambition was to be a soldier; Matheson's,
a barrister. An unseen Hand intervened in both
cases and led them to the Church; but as
Robertson's early pieties marked him out for the
career which he in the end was to follow, may we
not see in young Matheson, preaching, at the age
of seven, sermons to his family which caused them
to wonder, that his choice had already been made,
although at the time he was altogether unaware of
it.

The young scholar was singularly fortunate in
the place of his birth. He had at his door not only
one of the best schools which his native country
could provide, but a University whose roots were
deeply imbedded in the past, and whose steadily
growing fame gave an impetus to the student who
was ambitious of scholastic success. The University of Glasgow was founded in the Middle
Ages, when the city, of which it was afterwards to
be so distinguished an ornament, was little more
than a village. It was subjected to many vicissitudes, especially in its early years; and immediately
after the Reformation it had all but vanished.
New life was put into it by Andrew Melville, its
first great Principal, and from his day till our own
it has never, with the exception of one or two
pauses, looked back. It has within recent years
entered upon a period of hopeful expansion, and its

future promises to be more than worthy of its past. Since Matheson left the University, only forty years ago, it has, however, undergone so many changes, almost amounting to a revolution, that the young student of to-day can have no idea of what his *Alma Mater* was half a century ago. Her home is now on Gilmorehill; it was then in the High Street. The house in which she dwelt was begrimed with the city's smoke; her new abode shines resplendent.

The ancient College of Glasgow, as it appeared to the men and women of the eighteenth or nineteenth century, is now a thing of the past. Every stone of it has been carried away; and with the exception of the lodge at the main entrance to the present University, and the stairway that leads from the professors' court to the quadrangle, not a vestige of it remains. In a few years very few will be alive who studied in the old place, and it will be difficult for future generations to believe that the site of the present unsightly railway depôt was once dedicated to learning and to the Muses. The old buildings, with which Matheson and his contemporaries were so familiar, were begun early in the seventeenth century, and a hundred years elapsed before they were quite completed. Glasgow was proud of them in their day, and Sir Walter Scott writes in *Rob Roy*, with not a little enthusiasm, of the "old-fashioned buildings," "the college yards," and "the solitude of the place"; "the grounds opening in a sort of wilderness, laid out in the Dutch taste with clipt hedges and one or two statues." Other writers, from "Jupiter" Carlyle to A. K. H. Boyd, have exercised their gifts in describing the ancient University and College life in Glasgow. Carlyle had not a very sharp eye for externals; he is for the most part silent about the buildings themselves. He was much more interested in the human beings that inhabited them, or who, at any rate, found in them the centre of their existence. Nothing that has since been written can be at all compared to his vivid sketches of Glasgow society and Collegiate life in the year immediately preceding the '45. Principal Campbell, Professors Leechman, Hutcheson, and Simson, still live in the pages of his famous *Autobiography*. But it was the Principal's daughter, "Miss Mally," who was the chief personage, in the estimation of young "Jupiter," of all the brilliant set in which he mingled. "For on asking," he says, "my friend James Edgar, afterwards a commissioner of the Customs, for a letter of introduction to someone of importance and influence, he gave me one to Miss Mally Campbell, the daughter of the Principal; and when I seemed surprised at his choice, he added that I would find her not only more beautiful than any woman there, but more sensible and friendly than all the professors put together, and much more useful to me. This," he adds, "I found to be literally true."

Lockhart, Scott's son-in-law, in *Peter's Letters*

to his Kinsfolk, and Captain Hamilton, brother of
the famous Sir William, in *Cyril Thornton*, give
descriptions of the College and College life in their
day, but the account which affords the best idea of
the external appearance of the University buildings
as they existed in Matheson's time is A. K. H. B.'s,
who himself was a student of Glasgow University.
It will be found in his *Leisure Hours in Town*, and
refers to the period when Matheson was still an
undergraduate :

The stranger in Glasgow who has paid a visit to the
noble cathedral, has probably, in returning from it, walked
down the High Street, a steep and filthy way of tall
houses, now abandoned to the poorest classes of the
community, where dirty women in mutches, each followed
by two or three squalid children, hold loud conversations
all day long; and the alleys leading from which pour
forth a flood of poverty, disease, and crime. On the left
hand of the High Street, where it becomes a shade more
respectable, a dark, low-browed building of three storeys
in height fronts the street for two or three hundred yards.
That is Glasgow College; for here, as also at Edinburgh,
the University consists of a single College. The first
gateway at which we arrive opens into a dull-looking
court, inhabited by the professors, eight or ten of whom
have houses here. Farther down, a low archway, which
is the main entrance to the building, admits to two or
three quadrangles, occupied by the various class-rooms.

There is something impressive in the sudden transition
from one of the most crowded and noisy streets of the
city to the calm and stillness of the College courts. The
first court we enter is a small one, surrounded by
buildings of a dark and venerable aspect. An antique
staircase of massive stone leads to the Faculty Hall or
Senate House; and a spire of considerable height sur-
mounts a vaulted archway leading to the second court.
This court is much larger than the one next the street,

and with its turrets and winding staircases, narrow windows and high-pitched roofs, would quite come up to our ideas of academic architecture; but unhappily, some years since, one side of this venerable quadrangle was pulled down, and a large building in the Grecian style erected in its place, which, like a pert interloper, contrasts most disagreeably with the remainder of the old monastic pile. Passing out of this court by another vaulted passage, we enter an open square, to the right of which is the University library, and at some little distance an elegant Doric temple which is greatly admired by those who prefer Grecian to Gothic architecture. This is the Hunterian Museum, and contains a valuable collection of subjects in natural history and anatomy bequeathed by the eminent surgeon whose name it bears. Beyond this building the College gardens stretch away to a considerable distance. The ground is undulating—there are many trees, and what was once a pleasant country stream flows through the gardens; but Glasgow factories and Glasgow smoke have quite spoiled what must once have been a delightful retreat from the dust and glare of the city. The trees are now quite blackened, the stream (named the Molendinar Burn) became so offensive that it was found necessary to arch it over, and drifts of stifling and noisome smoke trail slowly all day over the College gardens. There are no evergreens nor flowers; and the students generally prefer to take their constitutional in the purer air of the western outskirts of Glasgow.

The other changes that have taken place are even more far-reaching than those which have affected the external appearance and locality of the University. In Matheson's day students of all ages, from twelve to forty years, might be found sitting on the same bench. No conditions were exacted as to scholarship. Anyone who could pay his fees was entitled to admittance, and to all the advantages which the University could

confer. It was a strange sight in those days, not
so very far distant, to see "the shepherd's son
from the banks of the Teviot take his place in the
class-room with the son of the Lord of Session, or
of the country squire, with nothing to mark his
social inferiority." This may still be found, but
it is the exception to see the greybeard sitting
side by side with the youth on whose chin the
incipient signs of manhood have not as yet begun
to appear.

There is a final change which deserves to be
noted in passing. The struggles which many a
Scottish lad, who determined to graduate at one
or other of the Universities of his native land,
had to face have become a national tradition.
Scott has immortalised them in his sketch of the
early career of Dominie Sampson. That their
son "might wag his pow in a pulpit the poor
parents pinched and pared, rose early and lay
down late, ate dry bread and drank cold water."
Sampson himself, as the representative of a type,
is described as slinking "from College by the
most secret paths he could discover, and plunging
himself into his most miserable lodging, where
for eighteen-pence a week he was allowed the
benefit of a straw mattress, and, if his landlady
was in good humour, permission to study his
task by her fire." There may be some exaggeration in all this, but, making every allowance, a
fair proportion of Scottish students of the olden
time had to fight hard for the means which would

enable them to keep body and soul together while attending the University. Private teaching in winter while the College was in Session, and manual labour in summer during the Long Vacation, was the order of the day for many. The self-sacrifice of the parents, and even of brothers and sisters, gave a pathetic interest to the student's struggle, and helped not a little to form that special type of character for which Scotland is famous. Many causes have arisen during the last half century to change all this. The country itself has increased vastly in wealth; bursaries and scholarships have been greatly multiplied; Mr. Carnegie has stepped in with his princely benefaction to abolish class fees and to endow research; Societies and Churches are founding hostels for the cheap and comfortable housing of the students, so that learning, which in past days a Scottish lad had to fight for, so to speak, with the naked sword, is being now administered by a silver spoon. What effect this may have on the future of the national character time alone can tell.

The Scottish University system in vogue in Matheson's day, as will readily be seen, afforded a good training for character. It was free, independent, and gave room for the mingling together of many varieties of social rank and mental attainment. Types, as far asunder as the poles, were brought together in a common centre, and the battle of life, which the youthful com-

batants would have to wage to the end, was there
and then begun, under the conditions that would
prevail all through. Matheson threw himself
heartily into University life, and his bright intellect
and undoubted powers, which would have gained
him distinction under any circumstances, were
enhanced in the estimation of his fellow-students
by his constant cheerfulness and hopefulness,
which to them seemed nothing less than marvellous
in view of the physical disadvantage under which
he laboured. No student of his time was more
popular than he, and fond memories of him are
cherished to this day by surviving contemporaries.

It was fortunate for young Matheson that he
began his College life under the most favourable
circumstances. There was no need for him to
struggle for existence; he had every comfort in
his home. Had it been otherwise the world might
have been so much the poorer, for we cannot
conceive how it would have been possible for him
to struggle at one and the same time against
poverty and the loss of sight. The fire of his
genius might not have been quenched, but his
intellectual training would in all likelihood have
had to be sacrificed. It would have been better
perhaps if he had remained a year longer at
school, but it was the custom then to enter College
at a comparatively early age. He more than made
up for whatever loss he may have sustained
through not taking the last year at Glasgow
Academy by attending for nine sessions at the

University. This embraced a period of eight years and a half, and during that time the eager student subjected himself to the most rigorous mental discipline, and laid the foundation of his future distinction.

It was in the autumn of 1857 that he first matriculated as a student of Glasgow University, and enrolled himself in the classes of Junior Latin and Junior Greek. His professors were William Ramsay and Edmund Law Lushington. Even the students of to-day are familiar with these two names, so deep a mark did the possessors of them make on the University. They were both eminent scholars and distinguished teachers. Matheson was only fifteen years of age at the time, and notwithstanding that for the study of languages the heaviest handicap is imperfect eyesight, he gained an honourable place in the prize list of the Latin Class, and in the following year as a Senior Student he won the third prize for general eminence. One of my earliest recollections is Matheson's appearance, during his first year as minister of Innellan, at the annual examination of the school, which in those days was conducted by the Presbytery. I was among the few scholars who had been prepared by the teacher to appear for the Latin examination, and I remember distinctly Matheson's intervention and correction of some mistake unchecked by the schoolmaster. His knowledge of the ancient language had not been allowed to grow rusty, and the

impression which he made upon the pupils of the
Parish School by his command of the Latin tongue
on this memorable occasion was perhaps more
profound than that made on their parents by his
eloquent preaching.

It was in the Philosophical Classes, however,
that his special gifts displayed themselves in their
full power. It was in Session 1859–60 that he
became a student in the Logic Class under Professor Robert Buchanan, fondly and familiarly
known by his pupils as " Logic Bob." Buchanan
was from all accounts one of the ablest and best
teachers that Glasgow University ever possessed.
He more than divided the honours of his day with
William Ramsay, the Professor of Humanity. He
was a minister of the Church of Scotland, and had
filled the charge of Peebles for eleven years when
he was appointed assistant and successor to Mr.
Jardine, the Professor of Logic in Glasgow
University. Buchanan occupied this chair from
1827 to 1864, when he resigned. As an author
he cultivated the drama, and published, among
other works, *Wallace: A Tragedy*. It appeared
in 1856, and six years later it was performed in
one of the theatres in Glasgow by a number of the
students of the time. Not a few of those who
received instruction at his hand are still to be found
in Scottish manses, and, without exception, they
speak with the highest praise of his ability as a
teacher, and of the charm of his character. A
fellow-student of Matheson's, the Rev. Thomas

3

Carruthers, minister of the United Free Church at Bridge of Weir, and himself a prizeman in the Logic Class, gives the following account of Buchanan's course and method :—

He lectured from the beginning of November till Christmas on Psychology, or, as it was called, Metaphysics. He treated the subject like Reid in his *Intellectual Powers.* The lectures were not influenced by Sir William Hamilton or German philosophers, yet so great was Buchanan's fame as a practical teacher, that Sir William Hamilton sent his sons to study under him. His lectures were exact and clear, and in questioning students he was very sympathetic. He would frequently say to a student who answered his question imperfectly, "Follow up that idea." From the new year · to the end of March he lectured on Logic. Most of the time was spent on the deductive logic of Aristotle, but the inductive logic of Bacon was also clearly expounded. No students could be more thoroughly drilled in Terms, Propositions, Syllogisms, etc., than those who studied under this prince of teachers. At the close of the session, for about a fortnight, he gave lectures on Rhetoric. That was all the teaching Matheson got in English Literature, for the Chair of English Literature, with Professor Nichol as occupant, was only instituted when he was finishing his Arts Curriculum. Though he became so eminent as an English writer, his degree did not include English Literature; but the orator, like the poet, is born not made.

Buchanan's influence over his students did not depend entirely upon his lectures, excellent though they were. He possessed in a high degree the power of drawing out whatever knowledge the students may have had, by his method of oral examination. "The perfect quiet of his manner," remarks Professor Stewart, in his *University of Glasgow,*

Old and New, "the clearness of his thinking
and expression, and the occasional rapier thrust
of his wit, made him master in the class-room
without effort; and though averse to original
speculation, he had a wonderful power of awakening in his students an interest in the problems
of intellectual philosophy. The veneration and
gratitude of his former pupils," he adds, "have
preserved his memory to succeeding generations
in the Buchanan prizes, which, founded in 1866,
are annually awarded to the most distinguished
students in the classes of Logic, Moral Philosophy, and English Literature." Distinction in the
Philosophical Classes has been invariably regarded
by Scottish students as the test of intellectual
eminence. However successful a man may be
in Classics or Mathematics, the blue riband of
the University is, in the estimation of his fellow-
students, gained by him who carries off the chief
prizes in Logic and Moral Philosophy. Glasgow
University has from the days of John Cameron
been noted for its freedom in speculation, and for
the distinguished men who have occupied its
Philosophical Chairs. Among them have been
Gershom Carmichael, Francis Hutcheson, Adam
Smith, Thomas Reid, Robert Buchanan, and
Edward Caird. It may be said that it was when
he joined the Class of Logic that Matheson experienced his first real intellectual awakening. He
proved himself to be easily head and shoulders
above every competitor, and was unanimously

voted by his fellow-students the first prize in the Senior Division for general eminence, and a like honour was conferred on him by his professor for an essay on the best specimen of Socratic Dialogue.

Three of his contemporaries, who have favoured me with reminiscences of this period of his life, testify to the strong and lasting impression which he made both on his professor and class-fellows. He shone particularly in the oral examinations and in the essays set by the professor and recited to the class by the students when called upon. These essays, which formed a special feature of the work of the session, did not occupy more than eight minutes in their delivery. In the case of Matheson they were necessarily committed to memory, and the command of English style which he, at that early age, displayed, together with his inborn gifts as an orator, took the class by storm. " My recollection of his appearance," says an old fellow-student,

in the Logic Class in 1859–60 is vivid. He was far and above any other student. I often made up to him on the road to the Old College, as he would be going along George Street and into Albion Street and College Street. He knew one's voice, and having seized his arm he would say, "Oh, is that you, Young?" His talk was always interesting, nothing pedantic; and he gave a most hearty laugh as one told him some fresh story or joke. We had as students to stand up when "Logic Bob" would examine us orally. Matheson was always ready, and never appeared to be without an answer. His memory was magnificent. More than once he recited the contents of his essay. The subject on one occasion was the "Association of Ideas as illustrated by Milton's *Paradise*

Lost, First Book, 'Satan's Palace of Pandemonium.'" The professor asked Mr. Matheson to give his essay, which he did, and he held the class spellbound by his beautiful diction and eloquence. He excelled in imagery, and often borrowed illustrations from nature. The class broke into frequent applause. At the end, the ruffing of the feet was so great that the dust of centuries was disturbed and one could hardly breathe. The professor characterised the essay as the finest he had listened to in his experience of thirty years, and then pictured the various famous men who had sat in the class-room. One, I remember, he referred to with feelings of pride, was Archibald Campbell Tait, Archbishop of Canterbury, who had sat as a student in bench xvi., the same, I think, which Matheson occupied. He made various complimentary remarks, and wound up by prophesying that, if health were given to him, Matheson would adorn the calling to which he aspired.

Mr. Carruthers, who has already been quoted, would seem to have been impressed by another of Matheson's essays. "One day," he remarks, " Matheson was called upon to give his essay on the ' Acquired Perceptions of Sight.' He did not read but delivered it from memory. Two impressions in that oration cling to me. He described the babe learning to distinguish distance by light and shade as the 'infant philosopher,' and he illustrated a certain point by saying, 'You do not despise the rose for the thorn that lurks underneath.' These expressions showed the boy, at College, to have been father to the man, in the pulpit."

It was, however, on the closing days of the College, when Buchanan, according to custom, invited his students to engage in a great debate, that Matheson made his most brilliant appearance.

"A charming April day," writes the Rev. Thomas Gordon, minister at Edgerston,

in the session which extended from November 1859 to the Kalends of May 1860, rises to my recollection, as we came down to the Logic Class in the mediæval Quadrangle of the Old College in the High Street, where Robert Buchanan gave students their first lesson in Logic and Rhetoric. The professor had prescribed an oration to last no more than eight minutes. Each student was to come prepared to take his place, if called on, in the arranged discussion, which was to be carried over two or three days. The subject was an imaginary debate in the Canadian Senate as to whether "Canada being now ready for a Constitution, ought that Constitution to be a Limited Monarchy, with one of the sons of the British monarch as sovereign, or ought it to be a Republic?" As a Junior Student I remember having taken the Republican's side, and was thereby perhaps all the more forcibly impressed by the oration of Matheson, who took the opposite side. He charmed his professor, and carried away his youthful audience until we almost seemed to forget where we were. When the deafening rounds of applause had ceased, Buchanan said: "Your oration, Mr. Matheson, is not only creditable to yourself, but it is an honour to the class of which you are a member"; and turning to the class, he said: "I do not wonder you are pleased with *that*, Gentlemen."

This essay still remains in the original form in which it was written. The paper is of the finest quality, with the leaves tied together with a blue ribbon. It bears the title, "Oration delivered in the Logic Class on Friday 21st April 1860," and is signed "George Matheson." Mr. Gordon quotes a part of it with wonderful accuracy. We shall give an extract from the manuscript itself, as a specimen of the young orator's method. One can well understand, on reading it, how, when delivered with all the fire and enthusiasm of which Matheson was capable, it left so indelible an impression on his audience :

It has been said, Gentlemen, that the word Republic means fraternity, but ask history in what Republic fraternity is to be found? Ask the United States, and the chains of three million slaves shall answer: Not here! Ask the France of last century, and the Reign of Terror will respond: Not here! Ask the Florence of the Middle Ages, and the wandering Dante shall respond: Not here! Ask ancient Rome, and the exiled Scipio shall respond: Not here! Ask Carthage, and the banished Hannibal shall respond: Not here! Ask Athens, and the dying Socrates shall respond: Not here! It has been said, Gentlemen, that the word Republic means liberty. It may be so, but it is the liberty of the planet that has broken loose from its centrifugal force and is rushing on through space into annihilation. It is the liberty of the mind that has burst the restraints of freedom and is borne along to ruin by a current of angry and contending passions. It is the liberty of the ship that has lost its rudder and is drifting with the winds and the waves to destruction. It has been said, Gentlemen, that the word Republic means equality. But I say that the constitutional monarchy is the only sphere of true equality. There is not a citizen of Britain this day who cannot stand up and proclaim himself an equal part of its Government, an indispensable item of its Constitution. If the King have a sovereign power to act, it is from the community that this power emanates. If there is boundless wealth at the disposal of royalty, it is the community that furnishes it.

Matheson's other chief success in the Logic Class, and perhaps his most remarkable one, was his specimen of the Socratic Dialogue on a subject set by Buchanan: "The Volunteer Movement:

Ought Britain to Arm?" His essay was awarded the first prize. It took the form of a Dialogue between Mr. Disraeli and Mr. Bright, and is prefaced by the following Explanatory Note:—"It is here presumed that Mr. Disraeli, being aware that Mr. Bright is opposed to the Volunteer System, and being also conscious of certain very sensible opinions entertained by that gentleman, draws him out for the purpose of refuting him by his own sentiments, and touches such springs of thought as are calculated to elicit a declaration of them." This essay is much more matured in thought than the speech in support of a monarchical form of government for Canada, and more chaste and moderate in expression. Taking the two together we find in Matheson the born artist. He adapted both his matter and manner to his subject and audience. He carried away his youthful hearers by an oration set on a key suited to their eager spirits, and in the dialogue he reasoned out his thesis in a way to enlist the sympathy and to secure the approval of his learned professor. It is a capital specimen of the Socratic method, as the two following extracts will show. Bright had declared, in reply to Disraeli, that a well-regulated imagination is the most useful of all our intellectual powers, mainly for the reason that it develops a most commendable self-esteem. This thought is elaborated as follows :

There are individuals of the race of Adam who have never known themselves; to whom praise and censure,

honour and disgrace, exalted excellence and moral de-
gradation, are terms as insignificant as colours to the
blind. Born in a low sphere, breathing from childhood
a pestilential vapour, and looking around them upon
nothing but squalidity and beggary, these wretched out-
casts of society have, from the earliest dawn of reason,
learned to loathe themselves. To them the word man
is associated only with certain physical peculiarities,
but the ideas of rationality, of nobility, of grandeur and
progress, have never once been annexed to it. Famine
has hunted them down; the higher and middle classes
have ignored their existence, and they have always imagined the commission of crime to be their vocation.
And yet how little has been achieved by the contempt
of their superiors. They still swarm in our streets, crowd
our highways, and infect our very atmosphere. But
could you by any language convey to these miscreants
a definition of the human mind, could you make them
know, not the nature of legal punishment, but the latent
good in their own natures, I am convinced you would
effect more than all the proscriptions, ignominy, and scorn,
which have for ages been heaped upon them by a
censorious public.

Disraeli all through contented himself by putting questions to Bright which would elicit the
very answers that he desired; and after having got
the "tribune of the people," as he called him, committed to certain propositions, he turned the tables
upon him, and wound up the dialogue as follows :

Enough, Mr. Bright. I was previously made cognisant
that such were the sentiments entertained by you, but I
wished to elicit them from your own lips. And how, then,
can you, who hold such manly principles, reconcile them
with your opposition to the Volunteer System? If I ever
had any doubts on the subject, your conclusive reasoning
would have convinced me that it is a social, moral, and
commercial good. You have admitted the frequency of

crime amongst the lower classes, and you have held that nothing can tend so much to eradicate it as a conviction of self-dignity, importance, duty, and responsibility. The country has acted up to your wise suggestion. It is about to put arms into the hands of the artisans and the working populace, to let them feel that they are citizens of the land and bound to protect its rights and privileges. Inasmuch, then, as this is an elevation of honest pride, and consequently a comparative restraint from the commission of enormities, you must admit it is a legitimate inference, from your own premises, to be a social good. Again, you have stated that the poor are held in contempt by the rich, and you have affirmed that the best alleviation of this contempt would be the mutual dependence of all ranks. Once more, Mr. Bright, has the country acted on your suggestion, for by putting weapons into the hands of the populace she is about to make the middle classes feel that they are in a measure indebted for their safety and their prosperity to the brawny arms and the dauntless hearts of the sons of toil. Nay, more, you have said that the secret of all security is confidence in our own strength, and that the absence of this confidence engenders jealous anxieties. Inasmuch, then, as it is the cure of pride, and the promoter of tranquillity, you have admitted the Volunteer System to be a moral good. And, finally, you have affirmed that the true cause of flourishing trade in France during the Napoleonic struggles was the consciousness of impregnability. Our land has been recently visited with severe commercial panics; at every breath of war the funds have fallen fifty millions in a day. But you, Sir, have pointed out a remedy: Let us be impregnable, you say, and not tossed about at the mercy of every wind. A third time, Mr. Bright, has the country acted on your suggestion, and it only remains for experience to prove the justice of your reasoning when you desire social comforts, moral benefits, and mercantile advantages from the Volunteer Movement.

The closing day of the session, when the professors, students, and their friends were present in the Common Hall at the distribution of prizes, took place on May Day, and the scene is thus described in Hamilton's romance of *Cyril Thornton* :

The first of May is the day fixed by immemorial usage in the University for the distribution of the prizes, a day looked forward to with " hopes and fears that kindle hope" by many youthful and ardent spirits. The Great Hall of the College on that day certainly presents a very pleasing and animated spectacle. The academical distinctions are bestowed with much of ceremonial pomp, in the presence of a vast concourse of spectators, and it is not uninteresting to mark the flush of bashful triumph on the cheek of the victor, the sparkling of his downcast eye as the Hall is rent with loud applause when he advances to receive the badge of honour assigned him by the voice of his fellow-students. It is altogether a sight to stir the spirit in the youthful bosom, and stimulate into healthy action faculties which but for such excitement might have continued in unbroken slumber.

Matheson, on going up to receive his prizes, met with a perfect ovation, which was heightened by the memorable eulogium passed upon him by Professor Buchanan. The wild assemblage was hushed as his aged teacher quoted with deep emotion Milton's famous lines on his own blindness, comparing the youthful scholar to " Blind Thamyris and blind Maeonides " :

Those other two equalled with me in Fate,
So were I equalled with them in renown.

This was the red-letter day in Matheson's career as a student. He met with equal distinction the following year in the Moral Philosophy Class, in which he took the first prize; but the Professor, Dr. William Fleming, was not the equal of his colleague Robert Buchanan. He was incapable of creating the same interest in the work of his class, and the students treated him with an easy tolerance. Matheson graduated B.A. in 1861, the last occasion on which this degree was granted with " Honourable Distinction in Philosophy," and M.A. in 1862. His Arts Course was now finished, and in the same year he entered as a student in the Divinity Hall.

This was John Caird's first year as Professor of Divinity, and by him a fresh direction was given, and a new spirit imparted, to the teaching of Theology in Glasgow University. The Divinity Faculty was strengthened at this time by the founding of the Chair of Biblical Criticism ; its first holder being Professor Dickson, a ripe scholar, whose wide and accurate erudition was the marvel of succeeding generations of students. He was admired for his knowledge, and beloved for his kind heart. Dr. Duncan Weir was the Professor of Hebrew and Oriental Languages. He was a born teacher, and although he published little his opinion was frequently sought by workers in his subject, and greatly valued. He combined with his duties as Professor those of Clerk of Senate. This was perhaps necessary, for it enabled him to add to the salary of his chair, which at that time was modest in the extreme. Dr. Thomas Jackson was the Professor of Church History. He taught his subject on philosophical principles, but very few had the patience to understand what they were; and the hour spent in his class was more frequently given to wild frolic than to serious study.

Caird was the man who at that time riveted the attention of the students. He came with a great reputation as a popular preacher, and he had already given one or two indications that he did not intend to be bound by the traditional methods of his chair. He succeeded Professor Hill, who practically reproduced his father's, Principal Hill's, lectures, and anyone who wishes to know the kind of teaching that for several generations prevailed in the Divinity Faculties of the Scottish Universities will find it embodied in the Principal of St. Andrews' published volumes. There he will find the high-water mark of Scottish theology previous to the new trend given to it by contact with the speculative theories of German philosophy. Caird while at Errol, and afterwards as minister of the Park Church, Glasgow, had been turning his mind towards the new light that was shining from the Continent. He had been gradually working his way into the speculative ideas of the great German thinkers. He was beginning to be influenced by Hegel, and after a time he accepted him as his master, and was in the habit of humbly regarding himself as his interpreter. There can be no doubt that the Hegelian method has a wonderful fascination; it charms, especially the youthful mind; and in a few years afterwards, when

Caird's brother, Edward, subsequently Master of
Balliol College, Oxford, became Professor of Moral
Philosophy in Glasgow University, the spirit of
Hegel dominated the whole place, for Edward
Caird had no rival as an exponent of the Hegelian
philosophy, and his eloquence of thought impressed
the students quite as much as his more famous
brother's eloquence of speech.

If there be any virtue, and if there be any
praise in this speculative standpoint, then George
Matheson was John Caird's debtor.   It is almost
certain, however, that an eager mind like his would
have discovered the Hegelian philosophy for itself.
The great writers of the day were busy disseminat-
ing German ideas.   Carlyle, and Coleridge before
him, had done their part, and there were other
workers in the field.   In any case the first period of
Matheson's life as a writer was strongly influenced
by the spirit and method of Hegel.   He came
afterwards to doubt the absolutism of the system.
"Facts are chiels that winna ding," and however
attractive the rhythm of the Hegelian philosophy
may have been to a poetic mind like his, he, like
many others, found that there are "more things in
heaven and earth" than were dreamt of even by
the great Teutonic thinker.

Matheson had as contemporaries in the Divinity
Hall not a few who afterwards rose to distinction
in the Church.   They must have been a very able
set of students.   Among the prizemen of his year
were Matheson himself, Professor Stewart of

Glasgow University; Rev. Dr. M'Lean, St.
Columba's, Glasgow; Rev. Dr. Blair, St. John's,
Edinburgh; Rev. Robert Thomson, Rubislaw,
Aberdeen; and the Rev. Dr. D. M. Gordon,
Principal of Queen's University, Kingston, Canada.
One of them, the Rev. Mr. Thomson of Aberdeen,
who was afterwards, when minister of Rothesay,
Matheson's co-Presbyter, has favoured me with the
following reminiscences of him when a student in
the Divinity Hall :—

Among the students of my time at the Glasgow
Divinity Hall, no one stands out more prominently in
the retrospect than George Matheson. It would be
about as difficult to recall the professors without thinking
of Dr. Caird, as to recall the students without thinking of
Matheson. Not only was he a distinguished student in
the sense of taking prizes,—others were distinguished in
the same way who have left no abiding impression on the
memory,—his distinction lay in the uniqueness of his
personality. Students have their groups and coteries, but
you could hardly rank him with any of these. He was
quite unlike the rank and file, quite unlike the ordinary
prizeman. There was a something that marked him off
from all the others. It is difficult to say precisely in
what this uniqueness consisted; many things probably
were contributory. One of its obvious features was an
unmistakable exuberance of emotional and intellectual
life. His laughter was the biggest and heartiest in the
College quadrangle, being equalled, however, by his
tenderness and sensibility. One was not surprised at any
flight of eloquence in which he might indulge, or indeed
at any intellectual exploits ever so far remote from the
conventional routine. That a sober-minded professor
should attempt to keep him within bounds suggested, in
a small way, an attempt to harness Pegasus. When, on
a certain occasion, word was passed round that a poem
by Matheson was actually published in one of the

magazines—the *Sunday Magazine*, if I mistake not—no
one was surprised. That he should write a poem, and
have it accepted and published by a recognised magazine,
so far from being incredible, seemed in his case the most
natural thing in the world, and quite in keeping with all
we knew of him. Though he was undoubtedly ambitious,
in the best sense, he never sought to gratify his ambition
at the expense of others; however conspicuous his success,
no feeling of jealousy was left behind in the breasts of
any of his fellow-students. Theirs rather was a just pride
in the exploits of their gifted class-fellow; everyone had
a share in the reflected glory that fell on the class of
which he was a member, and on the whole Divinity Hall.

He was, of course, as we all were, fortunate in his
professors. One and all, they were eminently qualified to
act as guides. Those were the days when we sat spell-
bound under the vivid and inspiring teaching of Dr.
Caird, then newly appointed to the Divinity Chair. We
students felt ourselves of no small importance when the
appointment was made, and we realised that the great
preacher who drew enormous crowds Sunday after
Sunday to the Park Church, among which every Divinity
student, I suppose, squeezed his way inside the doors, was
now to be our very own, and that we should have him all
to ourselves. Great things certainly were expected, and
we were not disappointed. The teaching itself was
supremely instructive. The methods of the modern
science of history were brought to bear on theology.
The best things in Schleiermacher and Hegel shed fresh
light on eighteenth-century maxims. In Dr. Caird's
luminous presentation, theology seemed to us a veritable
Queen among the Sciences. Even more than the matter
of the teaching was the manner of it. Earnestness and
fervour were always present; so also the spirit of reverence,
"the angel of the world," against which did the audacity
of even the most brilliant student transgress in the
slightest measure, prompt suppression followed. Above
all there was the supremacy of Christ, "of Him, and
through Him, and to Him, are all things," in the forefront
of all Dr. Caird's teaching. That One was their Master,

even Christ, was burned into the minds of the students
with a power which they can never forget.

The influence of such a teacher on a nature so sensitive
and high-strung as that of Matheson, everyone can see.
Matheson used to listen with rapt attention to the fervid
eloquence of his teacher, drinking it in with avidity, and
silently assimilating it. So thorough was the assimilation
that long years afterwards, when listening to Dr. Matheson
at the height of his fame, and in his most original excursions, one seemed now and again to hear faint echoes of
the old teaching which had been our inspiration in the
Divinity class-room.

It so happened that during Dr. Matheson's ministry at
Innellan he and I were co-Presbyters. It was hardly to
be expected that he should attend meetings of Presbytery,
nor do I remember ever to have seen him present. It
was well known that he was engaged in systematic study.
His co-Presbyters understood that he was simply biding
his time, and that in due course he would emerge from
the seclusion of Innellan and fill a wider sphere—a forecast
which the event amply justified.

I have received the following account of
Matheson's first sermon from one of his fellow-
students, the Rev. Dr. Somerville, of Blackfriars
Parish, Glasgow. The discourse was delivered
while he was still in the Divinity Hall, and the
account is so interesting that I have great pleasure
in giving it in full :

In our day we had to prepare in the first session of
our Divinity Hall course the Homily, a discourse on a
text given out by the professor. And no sooner had we
finished the Homily, and rehearsed it before our teacher
and our fellow-students, receiving his criticism in public
and their observations in private, than we looked round
for a suitable place of worship in which to deliver it.
Matheson, like the rest of us, was desirous to let his light
shine. The opportunity came when he was in his second

4

session ; his friend David Strong, now the Rev. Dr. Strong, of Hillhead Parish, Glasgow, was then acting as College Missionary, and it was his duty to have evening service in the Parish schoolroom of the College Church in High Street, of which I became in later years the minister. He had occasion to be away, and he asked Matheson to take his place. It was also the custom for the associates of each student to go in a body to judge of their friend's effort.

Matheson duly intimated to the fraternity the coming event, and we turned out in full force to hear him. We expected the Homily which had been delivered in the Hall, but we did not get it. Matheson had made special preparation, and had chosen as his theme the text "Precious in the sight of the Lord is the death of His saints." Young as he was, and young as I was, I have never forgotten the sermon. It had the freshness and originality that were characteristic of him in the after days. Darwin's book on Evolution had been published a short time before, and Matheson's sermon instead of rehearsing, after the stereotyped fashion, the joys of the believer, and the victory in the last act, was upon spiritual evolution. Death is the gate to a larger sphere and a higher service. One of his illustrations was so vivid that I have never forgotten it. "Death is the gate to higher work and purer joys. Here on earth everything ripens except man. The fruits ripen every year. A longer season would make them no bigger and no better, but what man ever came to full maturity. Even in the most saintly there are faculties not fully developed, affections not applied to the highest objects. Are these never to ripen or to do their highest work? Is there no sphere where the good and the gifted shall come to the perfection of their full power? The saints, as we term them, those who have grown in grace and knowledge, are as the plants of promise removed by death from this cold world to another, more congenial, in which they will grow in beauty and in strength, and find sweet exercise for each function. Life, long or short, is but a waiting to be born into a higher sphere, and death is the birth-angel."

I can only say that if before we had thought that Matheson would be a great poet, but would not be a great preacher, because of his physical defect, we were converted to a different view. We went to criticise, but we returned deeply impressed. "Yes," said one now gone to his rest, "George is to be the Caird of the next generation."

The sermon still remains among Matheson's papers, and its theme was the burden of his thought to the end.

CHAPTER III

RECESS STUDIES

GEORGE MATHESON was a thoroughly representative student. He was not a mere bookworm who confined himself constantly to his desk and refused to take part in the social side of University life. He had a big heart, and felt in sympathy with everything human, even with those animal spirits which now and again broke forth. They, too, served their purpose; they prevented the youthful competitors who strove for class honours from having their friendship broken by too keen a rivalry, or from degenerating into mere "intellectuals." Both at home and at College he entered fully into the side interests of life, and no one enjoyed more than he the pleasures of poetry, of music, of literature and society. "When a student," writes his brother, "he was very fond of hearing a good play in the theatre, and when a distinguished Shakesperian actor like Vandenhoff came to Glasgow he never missed the opportunity. Music was one of his favourite pastimes, and many a night saw him at the opera when the great stars,

Titiens, Giuglini, Grisi, Santley, and others, were in the ascendant. His school-friend, Mr. James Hotson, whom we have already quoted, gives the following reminiscences of this period of his life and of this phase of his character :—

Meanwhile, and after he had gone to College, I saw a good deal of him in private life. My father had a pretty large library, and I frequently read to Matheson or talked with him of books and kindred subjects when he came down to smoke with me. Byron was our first idol. Later on we came to prefer others, such as Wordsworth, Tennyson, and Longfellow. Matheson would recite pieces from these authors with great expression. In particular I can recall "Tears, Idle Tears," portions of *In Memoriam*, and the "Ode on Immortality," as also the closing stanzas of *Evangeline*. Among novelists we ranked Bulwer Lytton high above either Dickens or Thackeray. This was, I remember, owing to his wide range of subjects, his scholarship, and the philosophical trend of a number of his novels. I remember one evening we were expressing our views to this effect when my late brother William struck in and maintained that there was nothing in all Bulwer to equal *Pickwick*. He also enjoyed humorous writers. I remember how hugely tickled he was with the student's "Fox Song" in Longfellow's *Hyperion*, with its "Sa, Sa, Leathery Fox." Our final favourite was Carlyle, to whom Matheson took from the very first reading. He became so familiarised with the Carlylese style that one evening at a meeting of a literary society, criticising an essay which had just been read, he remarked that the essayist appeared to have had Carlyle in view as a model. This society would probably be "The Clifton Literary," which met weekly in the smallest of the Queen's Rooms. It was started by a number of Academy boys who had just left school and gone into offices, and our patron was no less a personage than Dr. Pritchard, afterwards the celebrated poisoner. Even then, from the "Münchausen" flavour of some of his adventures, as he related them, we began to "smoke" him. After he had made his exit from the world no successor was appointed. It would have been awkward to have had to minute that "So-and-so was elected as patron, *vice* Dr. Pritchard *suspended.*"

My late brother William was a law student while Matheson was in Divinity, and, it being election time, they became in some measure associated, both belonging to the Conservative side. The Conservative candidate for the Lord Rectorship was Lord Glencorse (Inglis), and his opponent was the Lord Advocate (Moncreiff). There was great enthusiasm among the students, and Matheson became a very popular speaker among his party. I remember of him being present at a small gathering of young folks at our house one evening, when William and another student, John Fraser, came in, and said there had been a great meeting of students, and Matheson had been loudly clamoured for. A verse of one of the election songs ran—

> Confound the Radicals in a heap,
>   Hurrah, Hurrah!
> Their candidate to pot we'll sweep,
>   Hurrah, Hurrah!
> But prosper every bonnet blue,
> And Johnny Inglis our Rector new.

The prophecy of the song came true, Inglis was elected.

Matheson always seemed to enjoy life thoroughly and to take an interest in all that was going on. He once remarked to me, "I don't know how it may be with you people, but we of the Establishment see life whole, and as a consequence, I think, more truly." This philosophic, and indeed religious, standpoint conditioned his outlook, and enabled him to relish a good song or a good story quite as much as a good book or a good sermon. Although, as I have heard him admit, he knew nothing of music theoretically, he could appreciate it, and himself sing with true expression. The best songs of the more sentimental class were probably "The Harp that once through Tara's Halls," "Believe me if all these endearing young charms," and the "Irish Brigade"; while among humorous ones he excelled in "Three Jolly Post-Boys" and "Agus O!" the latter being a Highland woman's lament for her child; but better, perhaps, than any of these were his imitations of a young lady's singing. He had a command of the falsetto register such as I never knew equalled, rendering an entire melody in it with the greatest of ease, and the result was extremely comical. I have seen some of his auditors almost in fits, and he himself, when the performance was finished, seemed to enjoy it quite as much as anyone. His two principal songs of this class were "A Father's Love," and "Sweet Spirit, hear my Prayer." It is hard to say which of them was first favourite. He also told a good story; he had any number of them about the clergy, some of them not very complimentary to that body. Perhaps as entertaining as any was "the late Rev. Mr. Davidson of Arran's Courtship, as narrated by himself."

Matheson was a born actor; the histrionic faculty was strongly developed in him. He could, single-handed, entertain an audience for hours; and while a student, and even after he became a minister, he occasionally gratified a select number of friends with an exhibition of his gifts. He was also a wonderful mimic. He naturally dropped the practice of this harmless accomplishment as he grew older. Experience taught him that even the greatest can be touched to the quick, when the gifts on which they pride themselves are caricatured by others. Matheson relieved the strain of study by other means. The stated course of reading which his class work demanded was supplemented by another, which was even more congenial to him. He delighted from his earliest years in poetry. Indeed, he was a poet

before he was a philosopher or a theologian, and
although his professional studies in the end got
the upper hand, his gift of song was never quite
silent. Not only did it occasionally burst forth,
but it gave a special note to all he wrote.
Even his most thoughtful and serious works
are touched by his native gift, and lifted into a
sphere in which those who may not be able to
follow his reasoning find themselves in a congenial
atmosphere. His appeal to their imagination is
effective, although his demand upon their logic
may fail. It is difficult to say at what age he
first began to write poetry. From the specimen
already given of his powers, his first flight in song
must have been before he reached his teens. The
poem which his class-fellows at the Academy
admired so much, and caused to be printed, shows
a knowledge of the technique of the art which
could not be acquired in a day. A very considerable quantity of these youthful efforts are still in
manuscript; many probably were destroyed, but
enough remains to show the direction in which
his early genius flowed.

It was during the summer holidays chiefly
that he wrote verse. His family were in the
habit of spending the greater part of each summer
at one or other of the seaside resorts on the Firth
of Clyde. Dunoon, Skelmorlie, Row, and Innellan
were visited in turn, and young Matheson took
every advantage of the opportunities which these
charming places afforded. He responded to their

beauty, took extreme delight in their many
attractions, gave free expression to his nature,
and enjoyed himself to the fullest. Boating was a
favourite pastime; and sailing in one or other of
the many steamboats that plied up and down the
Firth was a source of great pleasure to him. He
was well known to captain and crew, with whom
he was a prime favourite. They showed him
every courtesy and attention; and being overwhelmed one day with their kindness, he said, " I
might be ——" (mentioning some great man), "you
are so kind to me"; and the reply was, " We are
fonder of you than of him." He loved to walk by
the seashore, and to stand on the pier watching
the boats coming in; and to test his power of
vision, then, alas! steadily failing, he would tell how
many funnels they had. He was keenly sensitive
to his surroundings; and even to the last he
selected the place for his summer holiday on the
ground of its natural attractions. He was more
alive to the beauty of land and sea than the vast
majority who have their power of vision.

It was during one of those summer holidays
that the first of his *Sacred Songs* was written.
They were gradually added to as the years rolled
by, but many of them, his sister thinks, were composed while he was a student, and particularly one
summer while they were resident at Row. An old
manuscript volume of certain of these *Sacred
Songs* still remains, and at the top there is
inscribed the words "Written in Boyhood." One

or two of them are equal to anything that he wrote
of the same kind afterwards,—with the exception
of course of his famous hymn,—in particular a poem
on the "Withered Fig-tree." It bears as a heading the text—

"How soon is the Fig-tree withered away."

Not because the fruit was clinging
To thy branches, withered tree,
Came the awful sentence, ringing,
"Grow not henceforth aught on thee."

'Twas not time for thee to render
What required the ripening hours,
And that Heart so kind, so tender,
Sought not what surpassed thy powers.

But amidst the sunshine gleaming,
Thou didst proudly rear thy head,
And thy boughs with foliage teeming,
Falsely to the traveller said:

"Nature fruit to me has given,
Earlier than the other trees,
And the beams of day have striven
To exalt me over these."

Many trusted in thy story,
Hopeful hearts thou didst delude,
And the very King of Glory
Came to see thy vaunted good.

Thy pretentious leaves extending,
Far and wide in empty show,
Kept the sunshine from descending
On the humbler plants below.

Thine was but the specious beauty
That attracts the stranger's gaze,
Lustre more was prized than duty,
Virtue less desired than praise.

Therefore fell those words that blighted,
Like the fleecy winter's breath;
And the charms that once delighted,
Withered in the grasp of death.

He composed about this period two long poems,
of about one thousand lines each, the one dealing
with a sacred and the other with a classical
subject. They are both written in blank verse.
On reading over these two poems one can see,
at a glance, how blank verse was a much more
effective measure in Matheson's hand than the
different forms of metre afterwards chosen by
him in writing his *Sacred Songs*. The form of
versification which hymn-writing demands would
seem to have cramped his easy flow of thought
and freedom of expression. This was entirely
owing to his blindness. It is easy to perceive how
difficult it would be for anyone without the faculty
of vision to conform to an artificial and intricate
measure. In epic verse this difficulty is considerably lessened, and that is, perhaps, the reason
why it was chosen by blind Homer and blind
Milton for their great poems. It seems a pity,
with the specimens which he has left us, that
Matheson did not persevere in this form of verse.
The following account of his poetic labours at this
time may not be without interest :—

The poetical genius of George Matheson culminated
in that beautiful hymn "O Love that wilt not let me
go," but there were many previous excursions into the
field of poesy, most of which he strangely suppressed.
He was a poet before he became a preacher. Some of

us who knew him in early years expected that he would
become famous as one of the great poets of our day.
I remember that in the summer of 1862 there was a
company of students resident in Dunoon: D. M. Gordon,
now Principal Gordon of Queen's University, Canada;
C. M. Grant, now the Rev. Dr. Grant of Dundee; Finlay
M'Donald, late minister of Coupar-Angus; and Jas.
Fraser, now minister of Rogers Hill, Nova Scotia. We
were at a lodging in the East Bay, which came to be
known as the "Bears' Den." We regularly walked out
together, and talked on all subjects in heaven and earth.
Matheson was resident with his parents in one of the
grander houses of the West Bay, but his spirit of comrade-
ship was strong, and he always endeavoured to join us
as we passed towards Morag's Fairy Glen and to the
Innellan shore; and he had nearly always a new addition
to a great poem on which he was then engaged. The
subject was "Zillah, or the Life before the Flood."
But strangely enough he would not recite the lines until
we led him into what he considered suitable surroundings.
His favourite spot was an opening in the grove under
Ardmillan, then the residence of Professor Buchanan
(Logic Bob). We had to lead him to the exact spot
where the opening Firth could be seen. He was most
particular about the pose and the outlook, though blind;
and then he would begin to recite with all enthusiasm.
The picture of the youthful Zillah sitting beside the aged
Methusaleh asking strange, imperious questions, I still
remember vividly. Some of the lines I remembered
for many years, and I often wondered why "Zillah"
did not appear in print. She was one of the factors in
my literary being.

The poem to which Dr. Somerville here refers
bears in its final recension the title "The Last
of the Antediluvians." It would have been better
perhaps if Matheson had stuck to his first choice
and called it "Zillah," for she is the central figure
of the poem. The subject, as its title suggests, is

the Flood, and it is treated with much dramatic power and poetic insight and grace. We have on the one hand Lamech and his three sons, who represent the Spirit of the world; and on the other, Noah and his three sons, who represent the Spirit that is above the world. These characters, in their various intercourse, bring into prominence the conflict of thought and aspiration which justified the Flood. As a mediating influence is Zillah, the daughter of Jubal, and the beloved of Japheth, who would save her from the impending doom. The story of her fate, the descriptions of the Flood, with the emotions and passions that filled the hearts and distracted the minds of the proud spirits that defied and denied Jehovah, are strikingly graphic. The young poet traces his characters with a firm hand; and there is passage after passage which show how well in his early years he used his eyes. Many in after years were often surprised at the minute knowledge which he possessed of natural objects. Anyone who reads this poem will notice how clearly he saw and how closely he observed. If genius consists in the power of seeing, Matheson surely possessed it; and what he did see in his youth left an image on his mind that time could never erase.

Our first glimpse of Zillah is when she attracts the notice of Methusaleh, who is sitting at the door of Lamech's tent, to which he had been carried by Jubal, who thought that in this way he would avert the calamity of the Flood; for Methusaleh, being a

good man, God would surely not destroy him. If
he were prevented from finding shelter in the ark
the threatened deluge would be stayed. This
stratagem the sons of Lamech thought would at
once throw discredit on Noah's prophecy and save
themselves. Methusaleh, sitting sadly at the door
of the tent, longs to return to his own people :

> He turned his eyes upon the endless deep,
> Which mirrored back the radiant smile of morn,
> And on the margin of its shore descried
> A child, intent on that unfathomed world ;
> A girlish form, more ripe in thoughts than years.
> She caught his eye, with timid steps drew near,
> And naïvely asked : "What lies beneath the sea ?
> Surely some land as beautiful as ours,
> For nature here has tried to mimic earth ;
> And when the moon is lighted in our sky,
> In the great sea another moon is hung,
> And there are voices like the sounds of song,
> And sometimes tones like those of human grief.
> Perhaps we too dwell down below a sea.
> Is not yon heaven like a great ocean, blue,
> And on its surface may not spirits float,
> And wonder who are we that dwell beneath ?

Japheth, in pleading with his father for liberty
to take Zillah into the ark, thus describes her :

> My father, I must go.
> There is a well-wrought scheme within my brain,
> Jubal, the son of Lamech, has a child,
> A little girl, whose beaming countenance
> Mirrors the beauty of a spotless soul.
> 'Tis like a sky, where night is never seen,
> Where twilight shadows never meet the eye,
> Where sombre clouds love not to linger long,
> For happiness looks sunlight from her eyes,

Shedding the lustre of unchequered day.
She has not heard of God, yet has her soul
Sought some exalted worship; and in sun,
And moon, and stars, in tempest and in cloud,
In rippling stream, and far-resounding sea,
In pensive evening, and majestic night,
She sees some greatness which she may adore,
And deifies the garments of our God.

The first threatening of the deluge is thus described :

Up from the hollow caverns of the earth
There comes a rushing sound like the great hum
Of some far-distant ocean; yet ere long
The murmur rolls more loudly, and at last
The ground begins to shake beneath their feet,
As if the very heart of the vast world
Were palpitating with an awful dread.
They stand aghast, each scans his neighbour's face
And finds no comfort there.

Zillah, who had been brought by Japheth into the ark, in her anxiety for her father's safety climbs to its top, and whilst scanning the waters for his form, is thus impressed by the terrible desolation around her :

She heard the thunder roll,
A peal so loud that all the mountains shook,
And threaten'd to fall headlong on the plains.
Then came a frightful crash, the earth was rent,
And, bursting open wide, disclosed a gulf
Whence the imprisoned waters from beneath
Darted, with lofty leap, into the air,
And the great sea, made mightier by the rains,
No more restrained itself, but burst its bonds,
Bounding to meet the subterranean flood,

As host advances to encounter host,
And in a moment, like a fleeting dream,
Terrestrial objects vanished from the eye,
Not as the summer gently fades away,
But rather as is ravished from the view,
A sunny peak, where sudden clouds alight,
Extinguishing its glory. The vast plains,
The modest valleys, the oak-studded woods,
The stable rocks, and the stupendous hills,
All dipped beneath the unrelenting waves ;
The lights went out in the celestial halls,
All space put on her funeral attire ;
The chambers of the universe were dark ;
Their walls were lined with drapery of black,
In tribute to the earth that was no more.

If the theme of this poem was inspired by
Milton's *Paradise Lost*, the second undoubtedly
owed its origin to Byron, who was, as we have
seen, one of those who influenced Matheson during his College career. Its title is "The Blind
Girl's Retrospect." The scene is laid in Greece,
and the hero is a corsair. It is not necessary to
give a sketch of the plot, for the author, in a
foreword, declares that his aim was purely
a "philosophical one." "It is not so much
designed," he says, "to depict any adventures
peculiar to a blind girl, as to ascertain two things :
First—With what imaginary analysis one born
blind might associate the descriptions of visual
phenomena ; and Second—How far the imagination
could extend without the aid of the visual faculty."
It is interesting to note that this poem was written
by Matheson in his eighteenth or nineteenth year,
just at the time when the failure of his eyesight had

become almost complete. It is pathetic to find him taking up such a theme and spending his full strength on it. It is a strong testimony, at the same time, to his cheery optimism and unconquerable faith. He did not take his misfortune lying down. He attempted, on the contrary, to turn it to a glorious use.

It is remarkable how, many years afterwards, when, as minister of St. Bernard's, he gave an address to the inmates of the Blind Asylum, his theme was the very one which formed the subject of this early poem. Reverting, afterwards, to the subject, he remarked to a friend :

I hold that the training of the blind has been greatly neglected in one respect, that of the higher imagination. They have been taught any amount of cyphering and manual work, but it seems to me that they have not been taught what they most need, namely, how to conceive the thing which has been denied to them. The blind cannot conceive sight, as sight, but I hold that they may be made to conceive it by analogy. Experiments have convinced me that hearing is as much a revealer of form as sight. We know that originally sight has no more to do with form than hearing has. Touch, alone, gives the idea of extension of form. The only thing which is originally given by sight is colour, not even distance. I hold that sound is simply a colour of the ear, and that it is possible to conceive figure by the ear. For instance, by ringing a bell at three points, you convey to the ear a distinct impression of a triangle; and, after all, there are only a very few forms in the universe. Begin by representing lines, and you may go on representing the very sky to the blind. When I went to the Blind Asylum, and described the sun rising, they said it was a revelation, and you would have rejoiced to hear their

5

exclamations.   Never before, they said, had anyone
broken the dark cloud.

"The Blind Girl's Retrospect" is an illustration
of Matheson's views on this subject.   He attempts
to show how, by her other faculties, particularly
those of hearing and of touch, and also by her
imagination, she is able to conceive to herself the
visible world.   As a matter of fact, Matheson
himself carried out his principles.   He was never
without a picture in his mind of his surroundings,
and he created an image of the natural scenery in
which he moved.   The images in his mind were
quite as distinct and glowing, and in many respects
more vivid and accurate, than those which affected
the retina of ordinary observers.   He thus constantly lived in a world of reality.   It was framed and
filled by his imagination, aided by his other senses,
which had been carefully trained by a lengthened
experience.   He always formed to himself a portrait of the individual with whom he might be
conversing, and he sometimes amused a friend by
describing him to his face.   An instance of this
kind is recorded by the Rev. James Cunningham,
an old fellow-student of Matheson's, and now
minister of the Presbyterian Church, Wandsworth.
Cunningham had paid Matheson a visit, in the
summer of 1898, at Craigmore, Rothesay, and
among other interesting topics that he refers to,
Mr. Cunningham says: "After lunch, and, full
time to take what Mr. Fawcett used to call 'a good
look of his man,' when Matheson began to describe

my appearance, as he conceived it, in a series of queries, his sister and I ·delightedly responding, 'Yes, yes; Right, right,' it was my turn to clap hands, but nearer crying than laughing." To such a man the loss of sight was not the calamity which it would have been to others less endowed with intellect, imagination, and Christian faith. More than most, he was the habitant of two worlds, both intensely real and living.

The poem opens with a soliloquy by the Blind Girl as she sits by the seashore :—

> Art thou not weary, music-breathing sea?
> Is thy great voice not yet worn hoarse with time?
> Storms rend the breast of man and scatter strife,
> Thy tempest is but high-toned harmony.

After a pause she breaks forth in the following invocation to Light :—

> O Light! thou unknown object of my search,
> Too much a spirit to impress the touch,
> Thou art the oldest of created things,
> And heaven delights to be compared with thee,
> For God has called Himself "Light of the World."

In the following passage we find an illustration of his theory, that the objects of vision can be conceived by the other senses with the aid of the imagination :—

> One day the winds ran loose along the deep,
> And high in space the storm-king blustered by;
> In rocky cradle, moaned the restless sea,
> And nature, sorrowful, began to weep,
> Pouring down tears of rain upon the trees.

·   ·   ·   ·   ·   ·   ·

As nature wept, the rude and burly blast,
With wanton mirth, scattered her tears away,
The sea birds' cry shivered the air in twain,
Dragging behind it echoes from the hills.

        .   .   .   .   .

The lowliest chorister that cleaves the air
Can revel in an enviable joy,
Yet these I envy not, for I can feel
How beautiful is light by its effects.
For I can judge the parent by her child,
And light is parent of all happiness,
And tunes the lark to song when sleep dissolves.
Yet there are times when man complains of light,
And speaks as one deserted by his guide;
I never knew them, never felt their power.
Whence is it so with me the blind Greek girl?
Perhaps as one on whose familiar ear
The ticking of the clock has fallen long,
Grows passive, and forgets the tuneless sound,
So has the habit of this darkness grown,
That I in vain would find where it abides,
And cannot feel the horror it involves.

The reflections which these poems—with Matheson's own thoughts on the power of imagination working upon the deposits of memory and on the other senses, particularly that of hearing—suggest, is finely expressed in a reference to the subject by Dr. David Sime, who for ten years (1872–1882) practised in Innellan, and who during the whole of that period was on the most intimate terms with Dr. Matheson.   He remarks :

His memory of the light of nature, and of sunsets, and of the green earth and its flowers, and of the stars in the infinite depths of sky; the memory of the faces of man and woman, of mother and father, of sisters and brothers, remained with him, and grew purer, more choice and sweeter every year. The same kind of sifting, burnishing process of the sweets of recollection is to be seen in Milton's superb description of sunrise in Paradise. The poet was blind, and had been so for years in the heart of a great city's crowded life, when he wrought in undying poetry this vision. But it was the memory of a thousand sunrises, and lingering so long, and becoming more and more perfect in such a mind, it became all the more fitted for a sunrise in Paradise itself. Dr. Matheson's memories of the loveliness of sea, cloud, and sky, and of the earth in its seasons which were now shut out from him for his life on earth, became idealised, and at times his talk of the visible universe was like that of a spirit, and always with emotion. It is the memory of pleasures and highest joys that alone lingers in the mind. Pain and suffering of even intensest degree, when once over, as in toothache, neuralgia, colic, are, thank Heaven, soon forgotten. So, likewise, are disappointment, misunderstanding, persecution, failure. Even the misery, the corrupt injustices and sufferings, the depravity of the Middle Ages, are well-nigh obliterated in their sanctity, worship, and work. Complete as it was, Dr. Matheson's blindness was not revealed so much in his brown laughing eyes, which were expressive, and had a light of their own which was from within and not of the world, as perhaps in the use of his delicate hands. When he laughed heartily, as he often did, and he had an unrestrained flowing laugh, full of thrilling delight—he would sometimes flutter his hands like wings, as if still he were a wondering wee boy. And to the end he had much of the sweet spontaneity of a child.

CHAPTER IV

PROBATION

MATHESON was licensed by his own Presbytery, that of Glasgow, on 13th June 1866. The register is signed twice in his own handwriting. The penmanship is round, clear, and bold; in later years, from lack of practice, there was a marked falling off in his caligraphy, but up to the very end he was in the habit of freely appending his signature, and sometimes, as a mark of very special favour, he would pen a whole letter with his own hand. Very few young men ever appeared before a Presbytery to receive their commission to preach the everlasting gospel more fully equipped for the task than George Matheson. He had spent nine years at the University of Glasgow, five in Arts and four in Divinity. He had entered with zest into the work of the different classes, gaining the highest honours in many of them. The summer vacation was industriously employed in studying the great masterpieces of English Literature, in maturing his mind and perfecting his style, and generally, in broadening his culture. He did not

enter the ministry as a bread-and-butter profession; it was his early choice. From his youth
upwards he had a passion for preaching. The
sphere which the Church could afford him for
exercising to the fullest his rare gifts of thought
and speech he highly valued, and one of the great
regrets of his closing years was the fact that his
failing health compelled him to relinquish his
charge, and to decline the many pressing invitations which he received to address, in different parts
of the country, the large crowds that were eager to
hear him.

It was not, however, till the following year
that he entered upon his professional duties. The
summer and autumn months that intervened were
employed in preparing himself for his new vocation,
in writing sermons, and in travel. There are still
in existence a number of his early productions,
some of them College exercises, and others written
for future use. They are inscribed on loose sheets
of paper, and do not belong to the professional
period of his life proper. From the time that he
preached his first sermon as an assistant, to the
day that he delivered his farewell as minister of
St. Bernard's parish, he was careful to have his
sermons written in large and well-bound notebooks.
Each notebook is numbered, and so is each sermon.
At the end of every notebook there is an index
giving the date on which the sermon was written
and the churches in which it was preached. And
at the close of each sermon that was written out

in full there is a brief summary, a skeleton of its contents, which, should he have occasion to preach it again, he could easily carry in his mind to the pulpit. One is greatly struck by the care displayed, not only in the preparation, but in the penning of these sermons. There is hardly an erasure, and they could be printed from beginning to end without a correction. This regard for exactness characterised all his work, and his different secretaries testify to his having suffered more agony in the correction of his proofs than in the composition of his works. I remember meeting him on one occasion at a private dinner-party; it was at Christmas-time, and he had just posted the final revision of a volume that was not to appear till the following autumn. He had failed, or thought he had failed, to make a correction; it was a single word, and an outsider could not understand how even with the desired correction the sense or style could be improved. He, however, was differently affected, and now and again the thought of this omission disturbed his enjoyment of the evening.

Matheson was never much of a traveller; he detested railway journeys. This can be easily accounted for. Had he been able to travel alone with his secretary, all might have been well, for he could then have enjoyed being read to, which was one of his greatest pleasures; but in the company of fellow-passengers this was impossible. Latterly, also, he had a repugnance to being all

night from home, and he preferred to make preaching engagements which would enable him to return
the same evening. Before harnessing himself,
however, to what was to be his life's work he made
a trip to London and another to Paris. He was
accompanied on the latter occasion by his brother
John, and his sister declares that they were amazed
at the interesting account which George gave of his
trip. "Few," she remarks, "who had good eyesight
could describe things and places as he did." Have
we not in this a proof of his own contention that the
faculties of hearing and of touch, aided, as in his
case, by memory and by a powerful and well-trained
imagination, are able to represent to the mind the
world of vision. This was the only foreign tour in
which he indulged, but blind as he was he probably
learned far more from it than do the modern globe-
trotters, who career through Europe at the rate of
a country a day, from their incessant travelling and
constant sight-seeing.

There can be no doubt that Matheson on
starting his ministerial life was determined to be a
great preacher. It was his ambition to do with all
his might any work to which he might put his hand.
Whether he succeeded or not he always aimed at
being first, not that he might outstrip rivals, for no
man that attained to his supreme position ever
provoked so few jealousies. It was a healthy
boyish instinct that possessed him, and all who
knew him intimately were at once disarmed by
this youthful element in his nature; and, when he

hit the mark in a sermon or a book, they shared his joy just as much as if he had been a young fellow who had made the highest score in a cricket match or won the game at football. It will, then, go without saying that he formed to himself an ideal of preaching, and took advantage of hearing the most renowned exponents of the Art within his reach. He was singularly fortunate in this respect, for Glasgow at that time possessed several preachers who left their mark on their generation. It will be enough to mention five : Caird, Norman Macleod, Charteris, Pulsford, and Macduff. It is no disparagement to present-day pulpit oratory to say that no city in Scotland can now boast of such a combination. They were men who profoundly impressed, by their thought, eloquence, and life, not only the city which boasted of their ministry, but the country as a whole. Indeed, the fame of some of them travelled far beyond the limits of their native land, and their names are still cherished by many as household words. There can be no doubt that Matheson was much impressed by them all, and in a sense he was the representative of all their special qualities. The speculative genius of Caird, the humanitarianism of Macleod, the mysticism of Pulsford, the fervour of Charteris, and the poetry of Macduff, may all be said to be reproduced in Matheson, but in such a way as not to dominate but to make them tributary to his native genius, which incorporated and transformed them into its own likeness. Nor was he slow in acknowledging his indebtedness to two of them at least. He was in the habit of declaring that he owed his spiritual awakening to William Pulsford, the thoughtful and saintly minister of Trinity Church, Glasgow. "The man of all others," he once declared, "that shaped my personality, was Pulsford. I met him only once, but I never heard a man who so inspired me; he set me on fire, and, under God, he was my spiritual creator." Dr. Pulsford was told this on his deathbed, and it was a great joy to him.

Trinity Church is situated in the Sandyford district of Glasgow. It was within a stone-throw of Matheson's residence as a student in St. Vincent Crescent. It was also within a few minutes' walk of Woodside Terrace, whither the family had removed before George's University course was completed. Matheson would, accordingly, be a frequent worshipper in Trinity Church, drawn thither, like many other students, by the winning personality and suggestive preaching of William Pulsford. The minister of Trinity Church was not a popular preacher in the ordinary acceptation of the term. He did not strive nor cry; he made no attempt to attract crowds by any of those methods with which we in these times are only too familiar. He was content to be himself, and to give of his best in his own quiet but effective manner. I have heard him in Trinity on a Sunday evening. There was no crowd, indeed it might be called a small audience, but one felt the inspiration of the man. His very

appearance was a benediction.   As a pastor he was
a true son of consolation; he was surrounded by
a spiritual atmosphere which gave comfort and imparted peace to the afflicted.   One of his greatest
friends and admirers was Principal Caird, who frequently invited him to preach in the University
Chapel.   It is now twenty years since he died, but
the remaining members of his flock regard his
memory with the profoundest reverence.

The other preacher to whom Matheson has
publicly owned his indebtedness was Dr. Macduff
of Sandyford Church.   He was what may be called
a sweet preacher, an exponent of the devout life,
a gentle radiance that brightened the path of
Christians on their pilgrimage from earth to
heaven.   He was the author of books that had a
phenomenal circulation; some of them reaching
the unprecedented figure of three millions.   Such
volumes as *Memories of Bethany, Grapes of
Eshcol, Memories of Olivet, Morning and Night
Watches, Palms of Elim,* and many others, found
readers in every part of the world, and no name
was so universally known and respected by the
Christian public of his day as that of Dr. Macduff.
He was the minister of Matheson's boyhood and
early manhood.   He was the first incumbent of
Sandyford Church, and his congregation was one
of the largest and wealthiest in the city.   Between
the two there was formed an early friendship, which
continued unbroken until the end; and it said much
for Matheson that six months after he was licensed

as a probationer of the Church he was invited by Dr. Macduff to become his assistant. The young licentiate naturally shrank from the position to which he was thus invited. He felt a reluctance to assume ministerial duties in the church in which he was brought up, and among a people who knew him so intimately, and who represented the culture and the influence of the city. He also felt his unpreparedness for the task, and pled with Dr. Macduff to excuse him on the ground that he had hardly any sermons. "How many have you?" asked Macduff. "Only thirteen," said young Matheson. "Ah, then, you are rich," was the rejoinder, and the appointment was made on 8th January 1867. I have been favoured with the following interesting sketch of this period of Matheson's life by Dr. Macduff's daughter, who has inherited much of her father's literary talent:

George Matheson did not come amongst us for the first time when he began his ministerial duties. His parents had (I believe from the date of its opening) been members of Sandyford Church, and had for years enriched the heart and life of its minister by their valued friendship. From early boyhood their eldest son grew up in our sanctuary as in a spiritual home, and its holy and beautiful services were familiar to him long before he occupied its pulpit.

Thus, when the time of his appointment arrived, he became all at once the teacher of those who had watched his development from childhood. Some, who listened with a thrill of pride and joy to his first public utterances, had known him from earliest years, and in other homes besides our own he was still affectionately and familiarly spoken of simply as "George," as if there were but one

George in the world to us. If this very fact might in
some ways be supposed to add to the difficulties of the
young pastor's task, the warmth of the friendly atmosphere
by which he was surrounded must at the same time have
proved an inspiration and a joy.

At the period in which he became my father's helper,
Dr. Matheson was still very youthful in appearance, retaining an almost boyish contour of countenance, and
was, I can well remember, in spite of difficulties connected
with his sight, specially characterised by a peculiar
buoyancy of step and movement as he went about his
pastoral duties, his arm linked in that of his secretary.

In spite of the marvellous attainments of his school
and University career, there was nothing about him which
suggested the traditional student, "sicklied o'er with the
pale cast of thought."   He had no affinity with the
recluse, but was in its truest sense a man of the world,
finding his inspiration in life's human contacts and
sympathies, seeking not so much to renounce as to
reclaim the world, regarding our earth less as a wilderness
or a battlefield than a garden in which man might still
trace God's footsteps, and feel His touch. His was a
genial and a joyous nature, and the brilliant intellect was
ever warmed and softened by the glow of the kindly
heart.   It was possibly because he was so intensely
"human," giving sympathetic response to the joys and
sorrows of existence, that he was able so soon to take the
place of pastor as well as preacher to my father's flock,
for, as will still be remembered by some, almost as soon
as his dear friend and spiritual son was appointed to the
assistantship, Dr. Macduff left on a tour to Palestine
and the East, leaving him as his representative.   It must
have been a hard test to one so new to the ministerial
office not only to keep the threads of church life and
organisation from entanglement, and to exercise the
wisdom and tact often learned only in the school of
experience, but Sunday by Sunday to hold that great
congregation together by the charm of his intellect and
eloquence.   But he passed through it with victorious
success. Certainly in his case the proverb failed of its

truth, "A prophet is not without honour save in his own country."

I was, it may be, too young at the time to form any reliable estimate of his pulpit gifts, but my impression is that while the poetry of his nature lent its aid, while his command of language enriched and adorned, while his eloquence stirred, and his power of memory astounded, it was his individuality and originality of thought which gripped his hearers. Of course, from the very first, not only the sermon, but all the chapters, psalms, and hymns were committed to memory, and I can remember no instance of even a hesitancy in this respect. I do not know what may have been the habitude of his later days, but at that time Dr. Matheson was always seated in the pulpit before the congregation assembled. It appears to me that his manner was a quiet one. As he rose to give out the first hymn, or at the beginning of a fresh paragraph or division, the head would be well thrown back with a motion peculiar to him, but he used very little action, his words being usually emphasised only by a uniform and slightly persistent forward movement of one delicate hand. In my childish and girlish days his great deprivation always, in ordinary life, pathetically appealed to me, but I have no consciousness of this being the case when he occupied the pulpit. I only mention the fact, because it goes to prove how completely his mental and spiritual qualities overcame and outshone physical disabilities.

At the time it all appeared to me perfectly natural, but, looking back, it seems almost phenomenal that so young a man should at once have achieved the position he took as a preacher and a power; not less so that my father, ever scrupulously anxious for the well-being of his people, should without hesitancy or anxiety have committed them to his care. Doubtless much that others learn gradually in the discipline of life, he had already mastered in that of early trial, his own affliction putting him at once in touch with the sorrows of others, his deprivation with their losses, his victorious struggles with their hopes.

I feel that no reference, however slight, to any portion of Dr. Matheson's youthful life would be complete, did it not suggest that, while his own genius secured his rank as preacher, and his early trial conduced to his success as pastor, there was one external influence and aid without which he would not have been what he was. It was, in those Glasgow times of long ago, an open secret that one stood by his side in the school and college days which led up to the pulpit and the pastorate, who was indeed "eyes to the blind," and often, as in the old story of David and Jonathan, "strengthened his hand in God." To that gentle and gifted lady all those who have been inspired by Dr. Matheson's teaching owe a deep and lasting debt. From early morning till night's last shadow fell, she was the good angel of his life.

The most happy and sympathetic relationship between my father and his young and valued coadjutor was dissolved by Dr. Matheson's translation to the church and parish of Innellan. But though the bond of close personal intercourse and mutual work was all too soon broken, the golden links of friendship were only riveted more closely by the lapse of years, and severed alone by death.

Now both have passed away to that land where kindred souls are reunited in kindred service. Of the afterglow of that beautiful friendship which, because I was my father's daughter, Dr. Matheson from the warmth of his generous heart bestowed on me since he left us who was, as he wrote, "also to him a father," it is not for me to speak here. I can only in thought twine with his memory a wreath of amaranth and forget-me-not, and write, " *Mine own friend and my father's friend.*"

That Miss Macduff in her closing paragraphs had good grounds for emphasising the close relationship that existed between her father and Dr. Matheson, until death divided them, will be seen from the two following letters, written when Dr. Macduff was on his deathbed. On hearing

of his friend's serious illness, Dr. Matheson wrote
to Miss Macduff as follows :

19 St. Bernard's Crescent, Edinburgh,
March 14, 1895.

I cannot tell you what a shock I received this morning
on hearing of the illness of one who has been to me
associated with life itself. Your dear father is the one
who gave me my first sense of literary beauty, my first
impression of oratory, my first idea of sanctity, my first
real conviction of the beauty of Christianity. The tones
of his voice are even now unconsciously reproduced in my
own. I have retained more of his pulpit influence than
that of any other teacher. I am myself slowly recovering
from a sharp attack of influenza, and I am still so weak
that writing is extremely difficult, but I would not feel
happy if I did not speak out the grief that is in me.

To this Dr. Macduff dictated the following
reply :—

Ravenswood, Chislehurst, Kent,
March 18, 1895.

God bless you ! I am very ill, and can still only speak
in a whisper, but I cannot resist telling you how at this
season of great infirmity you have strengthened, encouraged, stimulated, by assuring me that the echoes still
linger of these dear old Sandyford days. I was proud of
you as one of my flock. My days are numbered, but you
have a great future before you. May you live to inherit
its crowns and encouragements.

It is important to mark his theological standpoint during this early period, and to trace the
stages in his religious growth. To enable us to do
this I cannot do better than give a synopsis of, and
an extract from, his first sermon. The text is the
37th Psalm, 6th verse : " And He shall bring forth

6

thy righteousness as the light," and the subject is
" The Manifestation of Practical Christianity."   At
the close of the sermon there is this brief summary
of its contents :

Has not God been kinder to matter than to mind?   Why
does He not say to the latter as to the former, "Let there
be light"?   Because He wanted from man precisely what
the previous creation could not give—a life ruled not by
law, but by the voluntary choice of love.   Yet while they
are different in their origin, they are one in their manifestation.   Light is at once the most heavenly and the most
secular object; above other things, yet gaining its beauty
from reflecting them.   Compare it with the life of Christ
and with spiritual life in general.   Worldly diffusiveness
does not degrade God's Spirit.   The spirit of poetry in the
heart manifests itself not merely in grand works, but unconsciously in the most commonplace acts.

Here is a passage in the sermon, in which he
compares natural light to the light of Christ in the
soul :

Perhaps the most prominent feature of resemblance is the
idea of a permeating power, of a capacity to blend with
all scenes and with all circumstances.   For I ask you to
consider for a moment how close is the point of analogy
between the glory of the Father above and the glory of
the Son within.   Of all physical existences light is at
once the most heavenly and the most secular.   It comes,
indeed, from a height which imagination cannot measure.
No astronomic power has ever soared so high as to trace
the source of that wonderful essence.   Away beyond the
farthest star, beyond the utmost flight of fancy, lies its
hidden, its mysterious seat.   Its going forth is from the
remotest heaven, and its circuit is unto the end of it.   And
yet how it descends to the commonplace, how accessible
it is; how practical, universal, all embracing is its
influence.   It goes forth into the rough, rude, everyday

world; it visits the meanest haunts of men; it gilds the mart of commerce and the scene of toil, the exchange, the counting-house, and the workshop. It touches the most prosaic objects and converts them into gold. It blends with the smoke and dust of the great city, dispelling its dense mists and chasing away its gloomy vapours, yet gathering not a stain upon its spotless beams. And there is no parallel to its boundless catholicity; unconscious of all partiality it looks up as proudly from the lowly vale as down from the haughty hill; it rests as brightly on the desert wildflower as on the palace dome.

Now compare this description for a moment with the outward course of that mysterious Being who was emphatically the external embodiment of evangelical religion; that true Light which more than eighteen centuries ago flashed through this little world. He came from far heights of majesty, yet His rise was not a sudden glare of noonday, but the morning beam of childhood; soft, gentle, unpretentious. No rustling in the folds of night announced the coming of the dayspring from on high. Unseen, unknown, He rose into youth amidst the hills of Galilee, and even when He entered on His grand career, He spread like the sun through earth's most common ways. For mark how broad a path was His; how to every heart He brought warmth and peace and comfort. How every affection of our nature went out to meet Him. Joy with its marriage bells; sorrow with its sickness, its bereavements, its poverty; intellect with its scribes and pharisees; love with its alabaster box of ointment; friendship with its house at Bethany; penitence with its poor desolate Magdalene,— He had an affection and a word for all. Every pulse of His spirit reverberated to universal humanity; to laughing childhood and thoughtful manhood; to festive happiness and to overwhelming sorrow; to the dear delights of kindred and family and home; to the social intercourse of a Lazarus and the benign companionship of a John. No gloomy, ascetic, narrow, circumscribed religion, but a piety whose gladness was another's joy, whose grief another's pain, and whose mightiest impulse that universal charity beneath whose heaven all nature is made bright.

One can see at a glance in this brief extract the exuberant style of youth. Subsequent years brought restraint, but the interest, for us, lies in the theological standpoint. It is that of half a century ago. The young preacher struck the note with which he had been familiar in Sandyford pulpit and elsewhere from his boyhood. The tone of the discourse is thoroughly evangelical. Matheson had not as yet begun to reflect seriously upon the contents of the Gospels, or to interpret their meaning for himself. The speculative theories with which Caird and his own reading had made him familiar were not to bear fruit until a later day. The other sermons which he wrote during his probationer days are cast in much the same mould as this one. There is undoubtedly an originality and freshness about them which must have distinguished them from the productions of his youthful contemporaries. They also possess that beauty of style which was to characterise all his subsequent writing. There is no mistaking his meaning, his thoughts are distinctly conceived and clearly expressed, and a logical sequence links together each step in the argument, which is brightened up by apt and telling illustrations. We have in these early sermons the talent necessary for the making of a great preacher ; all that is wanting is the spirit. We feel that once the author begins to think for himself on the great problems of religion, there would be revealed a pulpit orator of the first order. Tradition after having played its part must yield to reflection.

That also came; and when it did, the shell was
burst, and Matheson soared forth fully fledged, and
in his daring flights carried his hearers to heights
before undreamed of.

It is important to observe that from the very
first day of his ministerial life he was determined
to shrink from no duty which his profession imposed
upon him.   He resolved to be the pastor as well
as the preacher.   During Dr. Macduff's absence
in Palestine, the whole care of the congregation
devolved upon him.   In a flock which numbered
a thousand members, there must have been much
sickness and sorrow.   He could not have been
an admirer of Pulsford or of Macduff without
possessing the pastoral touch.   His sympathy at
all times was quick and overflowing, and he never
failed to render those services which are due to
the house of affliction.   Nor did he neglect his
parochial duties.   Within a stone-throw of Sandyford Church there is a large working-class population.
At that time it was still in the Barony Parish.   A
few years afterwards it was disjoined and erected
into the parish of Kelvinhaugh.   During a part
of Dr. Macduff's ministry he and his Kirk Session
relieved Dr. Norman Macleod, of the Barony, of
the charge of this district, and it was customary
for the Sandyford assistant to conduct a prayer-
meeting in one or other of the houses in Kelvinhaugh.   This duty Matheson also discharged; and
I remember him, a few years before his death,
asking if a family, which he named, still resided

in the only main-door in Teviot Street. On my replying that they did, he said that he was in the habit, when a probationer, of conducting a prayer-meeting in their house. His position as an assistant in Sandyford Church was, however, to be of short duration. Events soon happened which transferred his services to a new sphere, and promoted him to a charge of his own.

CHAPTER V

MATHESON OF INNELLAN

THE minister of Sandyford had but newly returned from his tour in Palestine and the East, when his promising young assistant was elected minister of Innellan. The new appointment might not on the first blush be regarded as a great step in advance, for Innellan, at the time of Matheson's election, was only a Chapel of Ease in the parish of Dunoon. Some years had to elapse before it was erected into a parish, giving to its incumbent the status of a parish minister of the Church of Scotland. It, however, had this advantage, that the members of the congregation had the right of election, and in this respect they occupied a position of greater power and privilege than the members of the Parish Church of Dunoon, of which they formed, in a way, a dependent part. The Act of Disraeli's Government which abolished patronage in the Church of Scotland had not yet been passed, and the original parishes, numbering between nine hundred and a thousand, had to accept, subject to certain ecclesiastical conditions, the nominee of some patron. It is futile to discuss whether this was a better system than the one which now generally prevails. It had its advantages and its disadvantages, like everything that is human, but it says much for Matheson that, blind as he was, the first important step in his professional career did not depend on the patronage of any influential man, but on his own ability and efforts. He was elected to Innellan on his merits. In spite of his physical disadvantage, he was chosen the minister of the congregation by a popular vote.

It was most important, in his case, that he should be appointed to a charge at the earliest opportunity. There was naturally a strong prejudice in the minds of people against having placed over them, as their minister, one whose eyesight was so seriously impaired as to render him practically blind; and the congregation of Innellan were not superior to a feeling which was so general. There was very strong opposition to his appointment, and the contest was so keen that Matheson's supporters only managed to secure his election by a very narrow majority. The successful candidate was admitted by everyone to be by far and away the ablest and most eloquent preacher of all the competitors. But he laboured under one great disadvantage, which the older members of the congregation had not the courage to ignore. Matheson was the chosen of the younger section of the church, who thought less of what was expected of a minister, out of the

pulpit, than in it. His approved talents and
preaching gifts were to them of far more consequence than the discharge, according to use and
wont, of the petty details of ministerial duty. As
after events proved, Matheson fulfilled these duties
with a promptitude, a grace, and a success that
ministers with the most perfect eyesight would
have difficulty in excelling. That, however, had
still to be shown, and while giving our cordial
support to his youthful admirers, we cannot altogether blame those who experienced some hesitation
in welcoming him as their minister.

There was one element in the election which
must have had some weight in producing the final
result. Matheson was no stranger to many of
the people. His family had been in the habit of
making Innellan their summer quarters for some
years. Their genial and kindly relation to the
villagers had made them popular, and this helped
to break down to a large extent the prejudice
that prevailed. It is not at all unlikely that, had
Matheson appeared in the pulpit of Innellan for the
first time as an absolute stranger, his transcendent
talent and eloquence might have been of no avail.
Those who are accustomed to the ways of Scotch
congregations at election times know how little
turns the scale. Anything in the personal appearance of the candidate, in his tone of voice, in his
gesture, even in his dress, may make or mar him.
He may come before them with the most powerful
credentials, he may preach like another Chrysostom;

but if a slight peculiarity tickles the fancy, or offends the taste, of his rustic hearers, his fate, for weal or woe, is sealed. No one knew this better than Matheson himself, and he was in the habit of telling some stories in illustration. On one occasion he was introducing a friend to his new congregation. The church was crowded, even the passages and pulpit stairs were lined with people. Matheson, on leaving the pulpit at the close of the service, had some difficulty in piloting his way to the vestry. An aged lady, and a warm admirer, seized him by the hand, and whispered so loudly in his ear as to be heard by many others : " I voted for Mr. P." (naming the new minister) " not because I thought he was the best preacher, but I kenned he was a puir widower wi' four mitherless bairns." He was also in the habit of telling the following story. The minister of an Ayrshire parish secured his appointment for the following reasons (narrated by a representative farmer, who, after the election, was discussing the matter with a friend) :— " In giving out the psalms and hymns, he repeated the number and the verse twice; we liked that. In the middle of his sermon an old woman was hoasting badly, and he stopped until she was done ; and we liked that. Then, again, when the congregation skailed and he passed us on the road frae the kirk, he did not haud his head in the air, like some of the other young upstarts, but he bowed, lifted his hat, and bade us guid-day; and we liked that : and for these three reasons we voted for him." Such are the whimsicalities of popular election ; and the choice of a candidate, who under the present system has to engage in a preaching match over his less fortunate rivals, is no guarantee whatever that he is the abler minister or the better man. Should any certificate of merit have been necessary in Matheson's case, his ability to subdue, by his preaching, the strong and not unreasonable prejudice that prevailed against him may surely be regarded as a sufficient one.

The young minister left Sandyford with the heartiest good wishes on the part of minister, office-bearers, and people, and with the following extract of minute from the Kirk Session records :—

At a meeting of Sandyford Church Session held in the vestry on Monday, November 4, 1867—

Inter alia,—A letter was read by the Moderator from the Rev. Mr. Matheson, intimating his appointment to the Church of Innellan, and resigning his situation of assistant and missionary in connection with Sandyford Church.

The Kirk Session, while accepting the same, beg to enter on their minutes the expression of their high satisfaction with Mr. Matheson's labours, and especially desire to record their warm appreciation of his pulpit services during the Moderator's absence in Palestine and the East.

Extracted by
WILLIAM BROWN,
Session Clerk.

Innellan Church was built fifteen years before Matheson's appointment to the charge. It was opened in the autumn of 1853 by the Rev. Dr. M'Culloch of the West Parish, Greenock, one of the most eloquent preachers in the Church of

Scotland. It was a modest building, pretty much in the form of a chancel, but, so far as it went, correct in design and form. It was at the time, however, quite large enough to hold the congregation, for Innellan was then in its youth. A generation earlier it was in its infancy, and a generation earlier still it was as a residential district non-existent. Anyone sailing up the Firth of Clyde at the beginning of last century, and looking towards Innellan, would have his outlook arrested by a line of bleak hills, fringed on the foreshore by a few green fields and clumps of wild wood, with here and there a primitive farmhouse or a shepherd's shieling. It might strike the wayfarer as a place possessing great possibilities, but its day had not come. It had not long to wait, for with the prosperity of Glasgow came its opportunity. That rapidly growing city made every year fresh and increasing demands upon the shores of the Firth of Clyde, for accommodation for its inhabitants, during the months of summer. The smoke, and dust, and din, amid which the citizens had to work and live during the greater part of the year, drove them, when the spring-time came, to seek purer air and recreation at one or other of the watering-places within reach of the city. No town in the United Kingdom is so fortunate in this respect as Glasgow. Thirty miles from the Broomielaw are to be found as sweet retreats for the jaded man of business as can be found, not only in any part of Scotland, but in any other country in the world.

The shores of the Firth of Clyde seemed to
have been devised by a special Providence for the
recreation of the Glasgow merchant and his family.
And soon there began to be erected along them
pretty villas, which, year after year, attracted to
them those who sought refreshment and respite, for
a few months, from the labour and strain of their
business life.   By the middle of last century one
of the most popular of these summer retreats
was Innellan.   Nor will anyone who has resided
at it feel any surprise at its popularity.   From
the lawn in front of the manse, which, with
the church beside it, crowns the hill that over-
looks the village, one's eye rests on a scene
as bright and winning as is to be found in
Scotland.   Looking to the left, due east almost,
the hills of Cowal are seen merging into the
mountains that guard the entrance to Loch Goil
and Loch Long; and the shores of Kilcreggan
seem to close the mouth of the Gareloch and the
estuary of the Clyde.   In front, and straight south,
one looks on Skelmorlie and the Ayrshire coast.
The most inspiring view is to the west, where the
broad waters of the Firth flow into the Irish
Channel ; the far-stretching sea broken by the Isle
of Cumbrae, Toward Point, the low hills of Bute ;
in the distance the high peaks of Arran and, standing solitary as a sentinel in mid-channel, Ailsa
Craig.

The first minister of Innellan was the Rev.
Robert Horn, who after a brief stay was elected

to the charge of Slamannan. He was succeeded
by the Rev. Martin Peter Ferguson, who also
remained but a short time. In a few years he
was chosen to be minister of the Presbyterian
Church, Buenos Ayres. The first who made a
distinct impression on the district was the Rev.
William Porteous. He came in 1862. One of the
earliest recollections of my childhood is being sent
to inquire for the minister, who at the time (1865)
was on his deathbed. He had been the subject of
a ruthless persecution. The young minister of
Innellan won the hearts of the people by the
transparency of his character and by his generous
and enthusiastic interest in all that concerned them.
He had a striking appearance; his tall spare form,
pale countenance, and jet black curling hair, would
have made him a conspicuous figure anywhere.
He was full of nervous energy, and in the pulpit
his matter and manner were attractive in the
extreme. A vacancy happening at the time in
Bellahouston Church, in the parish of Govan, he
was chosen its minister by the votes of the congregation. Bellahouston at that time occupied in
relation to the Parish Church of Govan much
the same position as Innellan did in relation to
Dunoon. The ministers of both parishes had
certain rights over the subordinate charges, if they
cared to exercise them. This the parish minister
of Govan, the Rev. Dr. Leishman, determined to
do in the present instance. He objected to the
appointment of Mr. Porteous on the ground, it was

generally supposed at the time, of a preference for
a friend of his own. The charge which he made
against him, however, was one of plagiarism, and
he prosecuted the young minister through the
various courts on to the General Assembly. The
case, if I mistake not, came up before two General
Assemblies. The final result was a victory for Mr.
Porteous, but it was a Pyrrhic victory; it was
worse than defeat, for before the day of induction
to his hard-won charge he was dead. The strain
and the odium connected with the prosecution so
affected his sensitive nature and his delicate frame
that he succumbed and died. Never was a congregation so affected by the death of a minister as
was that of Innellan. There are still living those
who cannot speak of the sad event without deep
sorrow, in which there is a feeling of bitterness and
resentment against him who did so cruel a wrong to
one who was innocent, and who promised to be a
bright and leading light in the Church of Scotland.
Mr. Porteous was succeeded in 1865 by the Rev.
James Donald, now Dr. Donald of Keithhall.
He was also most successful and much beloved,
and under him the church prospered so greatly
that it had to be enlarged. The work was
carried out in the winter of 1866-67, and was
so arranged that, while the extension was taking place, the congregation was able to worship
in the church as usual. Dr. Donald was translated to his present charge in the summer of
1868, when he was succeeded by Matheson, under

whose ministry the fame of Innellan reached its climax.

There are three events in connection with the settlement of a Scottish minister to his charge which are of supreme importance to him and to his people. These are the ordination, the ordination dinner, and his formal introduction to the congregation on the following Sunday by his most trusted friend. It is rather sad, in looking over the list of the members of the Dunoon Presbytery who took part in the ordination service on the 8th April 1868, and who were present at the subsequent dinner, that all of them, with one exception, the Rev. Mr. Bain of Duthil, are dead. I question if any of the laity who were present are still living. But the occasion was one of deep interest, and a united and hearty welcome was offered to the new minister. At the dinner in the evening, at which the Presbytery with numerous friends were entertained, the young minister in replying to the toast of his health spoke as follows :

There are moments in the lives of all in which we seem to pause between the past and the future, preparing to advance yet looking back to bid farewell; and such a moment has now arrived for me. Behind there is a background of vivid memory; before there is a prospect of stern responsibility. I will not meet the new without a closing glance at the old. The retrospect I speak of is cast in no distant scene. It is within hearing of your ever sounding shore, within sight of your perpetual hills. It seems but yesterday since you and I met together in a very different relationship, not as the pastor and the people, but only as mutual friends, prepared to render to another the honour you have conferred on me. When last I stood in this apartment it was to celebrate the ordination of my esteemed and able predecessor, now minister of Keithhall. To you, whose sympathies have followed him to his new abode, the coincidence must be a pleasing one, and the association with this night's proceedings will come like a last ray of the past summer which has wandered back into our April showers.

Perhaps, too, there are some here to-night whose memories are travelling further back still, to the ministry of one who, though outwardly dead, is yet living and breathing in the hearts of all; whose life, so short in its duration, was yet so long in its intensity, so brief and yet so crowded, so unfortunate and yet so fraught with lasting power; sealed, too, by a fate so untimely and so sorrowful, has rendered him for ever devotedly beloved. I do not call back these shadows from the past that I may contrast them with the present, but rather that I may catch the mantle which falls from the vanished years. My predecessors have left indelible footprints, and these footprints I would like to make my guide. And, Gentlemen, never was there an age in which the preacher had more need of a guide, whether from books or men. From every grade of rank and station, from every sphere of profession and calling, from every tinge of character and life, alike from the palace homes of luxury and from the rudest hamlet on the mountain-side, there is going forth the one united voice—the demand for intellectual enlightenment. Reason, recognising that bread is her birthright, refuses any longer to be satisfied with a stone. They tell us in these days that the pulpit has declined, say, rather, that the laity have advanced. The beach has not receded but the waves of the great sea have rolled up and covered half its glory. The candle is not more dim, but the surrounding sunshine has absorbed its brightness. The Church has not lost its pristine power, but the spread of universal power has robbed it of its contrast.

The preacher of our day must be a man not only of universal knowledge, but, to some extent, of universal nature too. In him must be blended something of the lives of all men. There must be the depths of the

7

philosopher's thought, with the simplicity of the child's expression; the inquiring mind of manhood, with the pensive faith of declining years; the speculative strength of youth, with a hallowed, chastened, humble sense of feebleness. There must be argument for the doubting and confirmation for the trustful, encouragement for the fearing and approbation for the brave, gentleness for the erring and sympathy with the strong, and boundless, deathless charity for all. He who has entered the Church has become a student of the noblest academy; not the mere college of sciences, but the university of souls. His books must be selected, not merely from the dead letters of a printed page, but from the living indelible epistles of a myriad of human hearts. Gentlemen, in you I recognise the subjects of my future study. It is said by them of old time that the minister is the teacher of the people; I think that in all which is worthy to be known the people are the teachers of the minister. But little acquainted, as yet, with the personal cares of life, young in years and younger in experience, I come to find in your cares that power which is perfect through suffering; to gain in your experience that wisdom which grows in favour alike with God and man; and if in long time to come my maturing mind shall give back to you the fruits you lent it—if the bread you shall have cast on the waters shall return to you again after many days—I will deem that, with all its frailties and shortcomings and imperfections, my ministry in Innellan shall not have proved in vain.

It will be evident from this brilliant speech that Matheson had now reached that maturity of mind which characterised, for the most part, all his subsequent utterances. The first thing that strikes one in his address is its perfect taste. The graceful allusions to his two immediate predecessors are a proof of that generous recognition of the worth of others which was one of the most notable traits in his nature. The spontaneous manner, again, in which he throws himself upon the forbearance of his new congregation, and the humble attitude he assumes towards them as their teacher, won at once that confidence and loyal support which never failed him. In fine, his outlook upon the intellectual and religious needs of the day, which called forth all that was highest and best in the modern pulpit, showed that he was thoroughly alive to the signs of the times, and was determined to spare no effort in proving that the resources of the Christian religion were able to supply the spiritual needs of every man in every age. Add to all this, the charm of style and the power of delivery which even then he possessed in a marked degree, and it will require no straining of the imagination to conceive the effect which his oration had upon his hearers. Everyone felt that, whatever his future among them might be, there could be no doubt of his brilliant gifts of head and heart and utterance.

The last of the three supreme events in Matheson's settlement at Innellan had still to take place. This was his formal introduction to his congregation on the following Sunday. To whom should this honoured duty be assigned but to Dr. Macduff, the friend of his youth and his revered pastor, whose pulpit too he had, as assistant minister in Sandyford, recently filled? Macduff's name in those days was one to conjure with. He was one of the most popular preachers in Scotland, and his reputation in the west of Scotland was second only to those of Norman

Macleod and John Caird. The occasion was a
great one for Innellan. The seaside village held
its head high on that beautiful spring Sunday
morning, when the hour of service drew the people
from far and near to listen to Dr. Macduff and to
celebrate the introduction of the young minister to
his flock. The little church was crowded to the
doors by a congregation representing the wealth
and culture of the city and the simple rustic life of
the village itself, and the interest reached its
climax when, at the close of the sermon, Dr. Macduff addressed the congregation as follows:

I appear here to-day to discharge a pleasing and
interesting duty. It is a time-honoured custom in our
Church, on the Sabbath succeeding the solemn service of
ordination, to introduce the new minister to the flock over
whom in God's providence he has been placed. This, I
need not say, in the present case is almost, indeed in one
sense, entirely superfluous, as he who now occupies that
sacred and endearing relation is one with whose voice and
with whose friendship you are already well familiar. I
do not regret, however, that it has been deemed fitting
that there should be no departure on this occasion from
use and wont, as it gives me the opportunity of expressing
my unfeigned gratification that the day has arrived when
my excellent young friend stands before you and the
Church fully equipped for his great Master's service, and
for the career of usefulness and blessing which I trust he
has before him. If I dared mingle personal feeling with
a public duty, it would be to say that I hail the advent of
this hour with all the pride and affection of one who has
watched with tender interest the development of your
pastor's mind and character from early and precocious
boyhood. It would be alike unnecessary and unbecoming
in me in this place to dilate on the combination of natural
gifts with which he has been endowed, or on that manful

and heroic struggle achieved over difficulties which to most would have been insurmountable.

Intellect and genius have in these days many ready outlets, and had literary success been his only aspiration few would have more easily secured it than he. But I rejoice that with unwavering resolution he has adhered to his early formed purpose of consecrating himself to the service of the Redeemer, casting the gifts of nature, sanctified by grace, at the foot of the Cross, and enrolling himself in that honoured band who are embarked in that angel-work of promoting God's cause and glory.

I have spoken of intellectual acquirements; these are undoubtedly a vast possession, but they are only, after all, the part of a great whole. The greatest mental gifts are incomplete without the complement of higher, nobler qualities. The head is nothing without the heart. I would rather have the humblest mediocrity of talent, combined with tender, genuine, unselfish kindness and sympathy, than all the intellect of the schools. I know that in my dear friend the didactic or preaching power of the pulpit will be accompanied and followed by the keen and kindly sensibilities of a warm and affectionate heart in his daily intercourse with his people. If, indeed, there is one attribute of his nature more conspicuous than another, it is his constant and unvarying cheerfulness, as if the dimming to him of the outer world were compensated by a gladder and brighter inner sunshine. And there is yet one other diviner gift, which to those who are engaged in the work of the ministry is more precious still either than intellectual power or human kindliness; and this is the influence radiating from the spiritual, regenerated being, the celestial unction of vital piety. This glorifies all else. As it has been beautifully said, in illustrating another subject, it is the figure standing before the other ciphers which invests them with untold significance and value. I believe you will come soon to know that, in the case of him who is set over you in the Lord, there is no absence of this crowning gift.

While what may be called the young pulpit of Scotland is too often in these days characterised by unprofitable disquisitions, giving heed, in the words of St. Paul, to "what minister to questions, rather than godly edifying which is in faith," your young minister will, I think, give you proof and evidence that he values above all the teaching of the Cross, and that profound and vigorous thought and apt illustration are not incompatible either with simplicity of style and language, or with evangelical fervour.

May the Great Head of the Church, with His own abundant blessing, hallow the relation which from this day onwards connects pastor and people. May this continue to be the end of his conversation—"Jesus Christ the same yesterday, to-day, and for ever." May he long be spared to be a polished shaft in his Master's quiver, and after a laborious and honoured ministry receive the crown which awaits the good and faithful servant.

The young minister was thus launched upon his new sphere under the happiest auspices. Whatever opposition existed soon died away; his frank and friendly attitude towards the people, apart altogether from his commanding ability in the pulpit, speedily won the confidence and affection of all ranks and classes. Indeed, it is a minister's personal relations to his congregation, his unaffected welcome of them when they call, and his kindly interest in them when he visits their homes, that give him an influence which his preaching, however excellent, would never enable him to secure. Innellan was an ideal place for a man like Matheson to begin his ministry in. He was quite aware of this himself, for while he was a student he declared on visiting it that he would like on some future day to be its minister. The population numbered a few hundreds only; for

eight months in the year there was only one service,
and during the other four months he had the
stimulus of a crowded, intelligent, and thoroughly
appreciative congregation. This made the burden
of the second service easy, and during the long
winter months the anticipation of the summer
services kept him, if that were necessary, up to the
mark. But he very soon found that among the
natives there were brains quite as capable, and
hearts as quick in their responsiveness, as among
the Glasgow merchants and their families who
composed the bulk of his hearers in the summer-
time. Norman Macleod was in the habit of saying,
that even in the editing of *Good Words* the man
that he always kept in his eye and wrote up to
was the level-headed engineer. Dr. Matheson in
his preaching had much the same aim, and if at
any time in his flights he soared over the heads of
his congregation, there were always present some
who could follow him, though it were at a distance,
and catch his meaning, even if they could not
fully understand all its bearings and significance.

One is able to describe, in a word, the tenor of
Matheson's life, in its ministerial aspect, during
the whole of his eighteen years' residence in
Innellan. On the Sunday afternoon, when the
day's work was over, he would select the text of
his next sermon, and for a few days following he
would ponder over it. Towards the middle of the
week he would begin to dictate it to his secretary,
and by the Saturday morning it was done. As he

himself was in the habit of remarking: "At the beginning of the week it was without form or void, but at the end he was always able to pronounce it to be very good!" This was his habit, week in week out, and even when he was on holiday he wrote his sermon, so that he was well in advance of any emergency. In the summer-time he preached in the evening one of the sermons that he had delivered to his congregation during the preceding winter. This was a prudent practice, for, as this service was attended almost entirely by strangers who had never heard the sermon, it would have been a work of supererogation to have composed a fresh one specially for their use. Besides, as in those earlier years, the discourse was written out in full, and committed verbatim,—the composition and memorising of two new sermons every week would have been subjecting himself to an unnecessary and unwise strain. He was in the habit at first of reading, after the ordinary manner, portions of Scripture as a part of the service, but after a time he substituted for this a brief exposition of certain passages of the Old and New Testaments; and having discovered, both to himself and to his people, his wonderful faculty in this respect, he, to their delight and profit, continued this practice to the end. His favourite book for these addresses was the Book of Psalms, and I have before me, as I write, several manuscript volumes which embrace the whole of the Psalter and other sections of Holy Writ, filled with these expository notes.

They are so carefully done that a man with a touch of Matheson's mind and genius could easily reproduce them.

It may be of interest to picture Matheson as he appeared in the pulpit of Innellan Church on any Sunday morning during these memorable years. Take a Sunday in the month of July or of August, when the little place was full of visitors, every villa and cottage along the shore, from the Bullwood to Toward Point, being occupied by families drawn from far and near, but chiefly from the great city of the west. It was a gay sight, and also an impressive one, filling the mind with what was best in Scottish Sabbath - day observance, to see whole families emerging from their doorways and gradually concentrating on the little kirk that crowned the hill. The murmur of the wavelets as they broke upon the shore, the song of birds, and the humming of bees that clustered round the limes that led to the sanctuary, were nature's sympathy with the service of human hearts and voices that was soon to be engaged in, and seemed to beckon the worshippers to the house of God.

After the congregation was seated there appeared from the vestry, through a door immediately behind the pulpit, the young preacher, whose fame, already fast spreading, had drawn to hear him that day as representative and eager a body of hearers as could be found in any church in Scotland. As he stood up one saw that he was above the middle height. He had a spare form and a pleasant ruddy countenance,

and his eye, albeit unseeing, had that penetrating
look which seemed to read the secret thought, and
gave one the notion of any other quality than that
of blindness.   There was a buoyancy, a cheerfulness,
a hopefulness in his very appearance and attitude,
and a self-confidence, the farthest removed from
self-assertion, which put everyone at his ease.   In
a clear ringing voice, which one would characterise
as a rich baritone, he gave out the Psalm to be
sung, repeating the first verse, and then sitting
down.   The opening prayer was a thing to be remembered.   It consisted, at that time, of appropriate
selections from the English and other prayer-books,
with additions of his own, but the manner in which
it was offered up was altogether his own; he
breathed into the ancient words the breath of a
fervent spirit, and made the eternal desires of the
human heart an offering, for the day and hour, for
himself and those who heard him.   In later years
he broke loose from the trammels of liturgical forms,
and led his congregation in those original prayers
which came to be regarded as a unique part of his
ministry.   The other psalms and hymns were given
out in the same fashion as the first, and the inter-
cessory prayer was quite as impressive as the prayer
of confession and thanksgiving.

The beadle on taking the books to the pulpit,
before the appearance of the minister, always left
the Bible open on the book-board, so that when
Matheson gave out the portions of Scripture to be
read or expounded, or when he announced his text

for the day, he could look down upon the open page, and without any pretence to deceive he could foster the illusion that he was reading. In this we see a touch of true art, not only permissible but commendable, for it prevented the minds of his hearers being distracted from the service and the message he had to deliver by reflections on his blindness. Indeed, to my knowledge, many have heard him preach and gone away with the impression that he could see like other men. Accordingly, when he came to read the lessons for the day he did so as if he were really reading them. The chapter and the verse were announced, and then followed the repetition of each word and sentence. Sometimes the passage was a long one, but never on a single occasion was he known to make a slip or a mistake.

It was, however, when he came to his sermon that the interest of his hearers quickened and deepened. His discourse in those days seldom lasted more than twenty minutes, but it was almost always a gem of the first water, perfect in thought, in form, in diction, and in delivery. He usually seized the mind of his hearers in the first sentence. He struck a note which they never thought of before, but which they felt to be true. He even then displayed his rare gift of setting old texts in a new light, and giving a reading to a well-worn passage which was at once startling in its freshness and impressive for its truth. He opened up his subject by a brief and luminous introduction, and

by what seemed a logical necessity his theme presented itself under three heads or aspects.   These
he would develop in detail, enforcing his points by
argument and illustration, each paragraph leading
up to the climax of thought and impassioned utterance, which swayed all breasts.   The peroration
was usually followed by a brief application of the
principles which his theme inculcated.   All this was
done without the slightest straining after effect : his
gestures were few, an occasional raising of the right
hand and a slight movement of the body ; but one
felt that the preacher's heart and mind were on fire,
that behind all there was a restraining will and a
commanding personality.   The man, after all, was
felt to be more than the preacher, and the oftener
he was listened to the more convinced were his
hearers that there was a reserve of thought and
strength which could only be exhausted by death.

It was not long before he came to be known as
"Matheson of Innellan," and by the close of his
ministry there his name was as closely identified
with the place as Frederick William Robertson's
was with Brighton.   Summer after summer many
families came to Innellan for the purpose mainly
of hearing Matheson preach.   There was one man
in particular who for his sake visited the seaside
resort for thirteen years in succession.   On Matheson's departure he came no more.   This made the
preacher a valuable asset in the finances of Innellan.
The prosperity of the place depended entirely on
its popularity as a summer quarter, and it was of

importance to the people, who made their living
largely by house-letting, to have as their minister
one who proved so great an attraction. The
demand for houses was unprecedented; the rents
were proportionately high, and the season corre-
spondingly prolonged. It is not surprising that
Mr. Charles Turner, banker and session clerk, the
one man in the place who understood this aspect
of the life and interests of the people better than
any other should declare that "it was a great loss
to Innellan when Dr. Matheson left, and the people
knew this well. He was our one and great attraction. Visitors have often told me that the reason
why they came, summer after summer, was that
they might sit and listen to him."

It would be as unfair to the people of Innellan
as it would be untrue to fact to say that this was
the only reason why they valued him. They
admired his preaching, respected his character, and
were proud of his reputation. He gave them a
new ideal of religion; he opened up their minds,
and made them impatient of anything in the way
of preaching that was inferior or even commonplace.
I remember, as a boy, being sent to the pier on the
Saturday evening to watch the arrival of the last
steamer. My commission was to see whether it
was Matheson himself, or a substitute, that landed
for the purpose of conducting the service on the
following day. This would very likely be in the
late autumn, towards the close of his holidays. The
report soon spread, and if it was a stranger who

was to officiate very few of the villagers found their way to church that morning.

He soon began to be much sought after on special occasions. Whenever a liberal collection was desired by the office-bearers of a church, the minister of Innellan was approached, in order that he might give his services. Large congregations gathered to hear him, first in the west, and, as his fame spread, in almost every part of the country. His name became a household word all over Scotland. Indeed, it speedily began to be known far beyond the borders of his own country. Searchers after truth, men whose faith was distressed, and others who were interested in spiritual and theological matters, found their way to the seaside village, their sole purpose being to hear Matheson. Not a few of them gave an account of their impressions in one or other of the periodicals of the day. It is thus that one such visitor writes of a Sunday service in Innellan Church :

I have a delightful recollection of the day on which I first heard him, several years ago now, when he was minister of Innellan. It was my privilege, one delightful Sunday morning, to hear him preach in his little well-filled church, and I shall never forget the freshness, power, and eloquence of his words on that occasion. I went expecting to see a venerable man, with "countenance sicklied o'er with the pale cast of thought," and was not a little surprised to see a man under forty, strong, ruddy, possessed of a voice of great compass and power, and whose every movement in the pulpit suggested a personality of vast energy and commanding force, yet blended with wonderful tenderness and graciousness. He seemed to be looking the congregation full in the face, so that it was difficult to believe that he had been, in early life, deprived of the great gift of sight. I left the church that September morning wondering how it could happen that a man of such splendid parts had never been drawn away to some larger sphere. I thought of the pulpits in Glasgow, Edinburgh, London, and other great cities, often so inadequately filled, and it seemed to me that a moral wrong was being inflicted on the Christian Church, for the services of so remarkable and powerful a man to be confined to so limited a sphere.

Another visitor to Innellan, writing a few years later, says :

I have heard Dr. Guthrie and Principal Caird, Norman Macleod and Principal Tulloch, and, in the English Church, the Bishop of Wakefield, the Master of the Temple, Stopford Brooke and Professor Momerie, and while not depreciating any of those distinguished divines, I say that there is a power of eloquence wielded by Dr. Matheson which places him on a level with any or all of them, while in originality of conception, and forcible, quaint expression, he excels them all.

There was a pastoral and practical side to Matheson's character which found scope in Innellan, limited though its opportunities were. He visited his people, he was most attentive in cases of sickness and sorrow, and he discharged the other duties of his calling with unfailing promptitude and punctuality. His prayers at the bedside inspired sufferers with a fresh courage and a new hope, and the outpouring of his soul at funerals bridged the gulf which separated the Here and the Hereafter, and confirmed the faith of the

mourners in the blessed truth of immortality.
Every baptismal service was to him the promise
of a new birth. He was passionately fond of
children, and won his way to the mother's heart
when he tenderly inquired for the "wee things."
Marriage bells were ever to him bells of joy,
ringing in the larger hope for the individual and
humanity. The humblest member of his flock
was received at the Manse with a genial welcome,
and he honoured the social customs of his people;
himself setting the example of moderation in all
things. During the winter months he heartily
fell in with any scheme that might be proposed
for the brightening of that dull season. He frequently presided at social gatherings and delivered
lectures, doing his best at all times to inspire the
minds of his people with an earnest quest after
the higher things of the intellect and the heart.
Nor did he neglect the summer visitors. He was
frequently seen in the afternoons, accompanied by
his sister or his secretary, calling upon those who
attended his church and supported it by their
liberality; nor was he loath to receive them at his
own house, and to entertain them with that
hospitality for which he, then and afterwards, was
so well known.

Matheson had not been more than two or
three years at Innellan when steps were taken
for the building of a manse, and for the erection
of the charge into a parish. This necessitated
the raising of a capital sum by the congregation

and their friends of something like three thousand pounds; and it says much for their enthusiasm and energy that by the end of 1873 the twofold object was accomplished. A few years afterwards the spire of the church was completed, a bell presented, and, in the year of Matheson's translation to St. Bernard's, plans were prepared and arrangements completed for a further extension of the church. All this reflects, in the highest degree, not only on Matheson's popularity, but also on his practical foresight and power of leading his congregation. He had the faculty of conducting the meetings of his office-bearers in such a way as to secure their hearty co-operation in everything that concerned the good of the church. "One thing I greatly admired in Dr. Matheson," writes one who acted for some time as his session clerk, "was the able way in which he conducted the meetings of office-bearers. He trusted them, and everyone was more anxious than another to do all he could for him and the church." The following letter, written to his old friend Mr. William Stevenson, who was his right-hand man in every scheme that was initiated for the good of the church, shows at once Matheson's tact, business faculty, and generous handling both of men and of money matters :—

> MANSE, INNELLAN,
> *October* 2, 1879.

I yesterday received the sum of two pounds sterling from Mr. ——. It was given gratuitously out of his own pocket to liquidate the spire debt. As I have promised

8

to give other two, the debt is now reduced to three pounds
and a few shillings. I had a call yesterday morning from
Mr. ——. He insists that he shall be informed of the
date of our Annual Meeting, and that to suit him it must
be held during the day ; in whatever part of the country
he is, he will come to it. He wants any overplus funds
of the church to be appropriated to certain projects with
which his head is on fire. I would like you, when the
meeting comes, to try and prevent any encroachment on
what was done at your instigation last year. Beyond
this I would be disposed to humour ——. I do not desire
any more money, and I do think there are required by
the church certain improvements which would require
all the spare funds, if not more. I merely want to hint,
meantime, that I see something like a storm signal for
next meeting.
    Believe me, etc.

    The phase of Matheson's life and work at
Innellan that has now been dealt with may be
summed up in the following reminiscences by one
who knew him well, and who was closely associated
with him during this period of his ministry ; I mean
Dr. J. B. Watt of Ayr :—

    During the College summer vacation of 1867 I had
the delight and privilege of becoming associated with the
Rev. Dr. George Matheson as reader and amanuensis. At
this time he had been left in charge of Sandyford Church,
during the absence of Dr. Macduff in Palestine. He had
been suddenly appointed ; and his work, it having been
changed from that of a probationer to that of a pastor,
for the time, of a most important Glasgow congregation,
necessitated very active study. Reading had to be done
in all fields of theology and other allied departments of
knowledge. Sermons had to be composed and written
out, psalms and lessons committed to memory, besides
the visitation of all ranks had to be undertaken ; but his
master mind showed itself in every detail, and when work

was over for the day he greatly enjoyed his evening's recreation. What struck one first was his amazing ability to commit to memory sermons and lessons after one or two readings. At first the active work was somewhat of an effort, which, however, he steadily overcame. It has been said that "without music man is but half complete." Matheson fulfilled this conception of the finished man, and his singing of "John Peel" and other songs delighted all who were privileged to hear him. Story-telling was another of his great delights, and no matter how often he told his tales, his own enjoyment was so transparent, and his hearty laugh so infectious, that one always welcomed them again. The summer ended, work at College had to be resumed, and we were parted for a period of some years. But, as good fortune would have it, after visits at rare intervals at Innellan, where he had now gone, I became settled in practice there in 1871, for a year, and our friendship was renewed, became closer, and our meetings were as frequent as our duties would allow. Entering fully into his life there, I became the secretary of his flourishing church, and experienced great pleasure in co-operating with him in the schemes that were then on foot for the building of the Manse and the endowing of the charge. During that summer he and I took a holiday to London for a couple of weeks, doing the sights, and meeting many friends of previous College days, and not a few of the well-known writers and poets—G. A. Sala, H. S. Leigh, etc.—in whose company his rich personality found genial expression. At this time nothing important had appeared from his pen, but his preaching was entrancing. His extraordinary flow of poetic language, and his vivid descriptions, held one spellbound till the end of the service. During the brief year of my life in Innellan our intimacy was one of most unreserved confidence; and though I was the familiar repository of, I believe, his most secret thoughts, such was the transparency and purity of his nature that death itself could do little to enhance the sacredness of the affection with which I regarded his character, and now revere his memory.

Two important changes took place in Matheson's preaching while he was at Innellan. They radically affected both its matter and manner, and had far-reaching results. In Dr. Watt's reminiscences there is a tribute to Matheson's remarkable memory. Two readings of a sermon, of a psalm, or of the lesson for the day, were sufficient to enable him to repeat it without a mistake. For the first twelve years of his career he was in the habit of committing his sermon to memory. As this involved little trouble, and as he delivered his discourse with an ease which suggested extemporary speaking, neither he nor anyone else saw reason why it should be changed. He evidently enjoyed this method of preaching, and his hearers shared his enjoyment to the full. But one Sunday morning an event happened which suddenly transformed his former practice. At the time it looked like a catastrophe, but it proved to be his salvation. While in the flow of his oratory he abruptly stopped. The sudden collapse caused a profound sensation. Not only was it absolutely unprecedented, but he was never known to have been at a loss for a word or to have been subject to the slightest hesitancy. Matheson was equal to the occasion. He quietly announced to the congregation that, so far as the sermon which he had prepared for their hearing that morning was concerned, his mind was a perfect blank. He then gave out a psalm and sat down. After it had been sung, he rose, gave out a fresh text, and from it preached a sermon

with all his wonted freedom, eloquence, and
vigour.

The surprise ought to be, that a collapse of
this kind had not happened long before. It was
not due to any failing of memory, to lack of preparation, or the impairing of any faculty whatso-
ever. It was entirely due to the steady enrichment
of his mental and spiritual nature by years of constant reading and profound meditation and study.
His mind had become so full, he was so armed
with intellectual weapons, fresh thoughts were
bubbling up in his soul so irrepressibly, that in
the middle of his prepared discourse a happy
suggestion protruded itself which he felt impelled
to develop. Once he had developed this thought
he had lost the thread of his old one, or, at all
events, the words which ought to have appeared
for expression failed to be forthcoming, and he
only stated the sober truth when he declared that
so far as the sermon in hand was concerned his
"mind was a perfect blank." It cost him no
trouble to preach another sermon, his mind was
full of discourses which he had delivered on many
occasions; but it shows his complete mastery over
himself, and confidence in his own powers, that he
so quickly recovered his self-possession, which in
fact was never altogether lost, and felt his ability
to deliver another discourse without any fear of a
breakdown.

This must have happened in the year 1878,
for I find from that time onward none of his

sermons are written out in full. Up to that
period sixteen volumes are filled with his discourses,
and each one is complete, except that occasionally
the practical application at the end is simply
indicated by a note. But from this time onwards
there is a marked curtailment; the space in
manuscript is reduced to a half, and, in a very
short time, to a tenth part of what the sermon
formerly occupied. He now adopted the method
of preparing a skeleton only. Each skeleton
seldom occupies more than a page, if so much;
but the thoughts are so pregnant, the subject so
carefully arranged, the divisions so clear, the
suggested illustrations so apt, that anyone with a
power of extemporary speech and with a mind in
sympathy with Matheson's could, after a few hours'
meditation, deliver from them a sermon that might
be telling in the extreme. One can accordingly
understand what a power these notes would be in
the hands of a man like Matheson. Anyone who
listened to his conversation must have been impressed by the readiness and conciseness of his
utterance. He could put a thought into a nut-
shell; he could demolish an argument by a
quotation or an epigram. His poetic mind was
kept under the control of a strong will, which
always compelled the thought into the channel
which he had meant for it, and directed the arrow
of his fancy to the object at which he was aiming.
His logical faculty was much more pronounced
than those who are accustomed to argument by

syllogism were aware of. The truths which he enforced often soared on the wings of imagination, and his matter-of-fact hearers thought they were lost in the clouds; but those who were able to follow him on such occasions felt that there was reason in his madness, and recognised the force of his logic when the discourse was done.

For the subsequent, which fortunately was the longer, period of Dr. Matheson's ministry, his preaching gained in spontaneity, directness, and power. He came into the pulpit after hours of meditation, with his subject clearly held in his mind. He put himself at once in touch with his audience, and trusting to his marvellous power of extemporary utterance, which had been trained by long years of patient labour, he poured out his whole soul and carried his hearers captive. It was now that those who came to hear him discovered the man, as well as the preacher. He stood before them as he was, and gave them not only the best of his thought but of himself, Sunday after Sunday. This was a joy to him as to them, and although for the moment he experienced that ease and freedom which are shared by those who have the gift of extemporary speech, still virtue went out of him. The strain upon the physical frame may have been too much. The spiritual and mental nature itself only grew richer and deeper.

Of more importance perhaps than the change in the manner, was that which took place in the substance of his preaching. This change was

anterior to the other. It took place during the
first or second year of his ministry at Innellan.
It reached far down, and shook the foundations
of his faith. The result was a temporary un-
hinging, a threatened collapse, of his religious
beliefs. Nor should anyone express surprise at
this, any more than he should at the breakdown in the manner of his preaching. Both were
bound to come. One cannot conceive a man
like Matheson passing through life without being
called upon to reconsider his theological bearings.
He was brought up on the traditional beliefs of
his day. His boyhood and youth were passed in
a period of extreme orthodoxy. He was educated
under a ministry which was noted for its evangelical fervour; and even Pulsford, whom he
declares to have set his soul on fire, never
disputed the evidences which were explicitly
accepted in his day. It was the spiritual genius
of Pulsford rather than his theological speculations
which quickened Matheson's nature. It is true
that John Caird had been gradually groping his
way in the direction of a new outlook upon
traditional and current theology. He had been
bitten by the speculative methods of the German
philosophers; and his lectures, as Professor of
Divinity, were largely influenced by their spirit
and method. But the remarkable fact is that, at
the time, Caird's influence upon Matheson would
seem to have been extremely slight. It is perfectly
certain, at any rate, that he was not tempted to

assume that negative attitude towards the current
method of regarding Divine truth which was
adopted by many of those who came under the
influence of Caird's teaching.   The Professor
himself, it need hardly be said, never wavered in
his allegiance to what is truly essential in the
Christian religion.   Indeed, he was the helper of
those who had the power to follow him in his
search after eternal truth ; and the inspiration of
his teaching and character was deeply felt by
those who sat under him.   But a spirit of negation
began to possess not a few of those who at the
time were affected by the new outlook upon
theology.   Matheson never fell under its spell,
nor had he as a student become thoroughly imbued
with the positive spirit which reconstructed afresh
the forms of belief after criticism had done its work
with them.   He was evidently content for the time
being to walk in the old paths, and to light them
up with flashes of imagination and poetry.   He
could not, however, live long in a frail house of this
kind ; the crash was bound to come, and when it
did come his theological tabernacle was a mass of
ruins.

Ten years before his death, referring to this
experience, which could never be forgotten by
him, he said :

At one time, with a great thrill of horror, I found
myself an absolute atheist.   After being ordained at
Innellan, I believed nothing ; neither God nor immortality.   I tendered my resignation to the Presbytery,

but to their honour they would not accept it, even though
a Highland Presbytery. They said I was a young man,
and would change. I have changed.

I do not think that the matter ever came to so
acute a crisis ecclesiastically. There is no evidence
that the subject came officially before the court,
although he undoubtedly was quite willing that it
should do so, and had taken the first step towards
this result. I possess a letter from an honoured
minister of the Church, who at the time was a co-
Presbyter of Matheson's, which throws some light
on the question :

With regard to a resignation, certainly nothing of the
kind ever came before the Presbytery while I was a
member. Your letter, however, brings to mind a circumstance I had long forgotten. In a conversation with the
late Dr. Cameron of Dunoon, a friend of Dr. Matheson's,
and leader of the Presbytery in those days, he mentioned
that Matheson had thought of giving up the ministry,
for the reason you indicate. He spoke of it, however,
as a thing past and done with. I never heard any other
member of Presbytery refer to the subject. I do not
think they could have known anything about it. I had
forgotten it altogether until your letter recalled it. As
Dr. Matheson was in the Presbytery of Dunoon some
three years after I left it, it is, of course, just possible
that he may have taken more decisive steps afterwards.
I do not think this is probable, as I should have been
sure to hear of it in the course of my coming and
going, and meeting with his co-Presbyters. The impression left on my mind by Dr. Cameron was, that the
matter had not gone beyond the stage of conversation,
and, though grave, was but a passing phase of thought.

It is not difficult to reconcile Matheson's statement with this letter. He had never been in the

habit of attending meetings of Presbytery. Accordingly, when such a matter as the one under consideration had to be dealt with, it was natural that he should do it through a friend, who might bring it up before the court in due course. Matheson was perfectly honest at the time in his resolution, and one cannot be too grateful to Dr. Cameron for counselling him to pause before the subject should be officially communicated to the Presbytery. His friend must have known that it was impossible for a spiritually-minded man like Matheson to remain for any length of time an atheist. The darkness could only be temporary; new light was sure to dawn upon the troubled mind.

This new light came from the philosophy of Hegel. Matheson's first introduction to the system of the great German thinker was at the hands of Dr. Caird. After his induction to Innellan he took up the study of theology and philosophy afresh, and with great thoroughness and earnestness. The practical work of the ministry, the necessity of not only thinking upon religion, but of presenting it, Sunday after Sunday, in a way satisfactory to his own mind and helpful to his hearers, brought him face to face with his fundamental beliefs, caused him to search for them, and, if found, to examine them. To his amazement he discovered the search to be in vain. He had in reality no fundamental beliefs to examine. He had accepted the traditional views, and had never really inquired into their absolute truth or their living relation to his own soul. Most men are content to pass on through life without ever questioning the doctrines which they inherit. They may be reputed to be orthodox, and are among the first to cast stones at those who dare to inquire. Matheson could not possibly be numbered with this class. The day of his visitation was sure to come ; and it came to him, as it did to Robertson of Brighton, like a thief in the night. The famous Brighton preacher fled to the Tyrol, and in the solitude of its mountains and forests wrestled with his doubts until the dawn. Matheson's battle of the soul was fought in the quiet village of Innellan, and his lost faith was restored through him whose philosophy makes true to the spirit what criticism or unbelief may have rendered false to the mind.

"They," observed Matheson, referring to the Presbytery of Dunoon,

said I was a young man, and would change. I have changed. Without hypocrisy I preach all the old doctrines and use all the old forms, but with deeper meaning. My theological sympathies are in favour of breadth, but not negation. It is a great mistake to suppose that there is any advantage, or disadvantage, in being broad or narrow, long or short, high or low. The question is: What is it that is broad? Is it broadcloth or broad shoulders? Therefore I do not value an opinion simply because it is a negative opinion, and different from use and wont. I am as broad as can be, but it is a broad positive.

In this he spoke the truth. These few sentences give the key to his theological position—a position which he gained as a young man at Innellan, and which he never lost. He may in after years have deepened spiritually, but intellectually he stood fast to his profound belief in Christianity, in the ideas which it embodies. These he was convinced were from all time, and for all time. The "Lamb slain from the foundation of the world," the sacrificial element in Christianity was, he believed, the thought which God had from the beginning in His mind; and upon it the plan of the whole universe, the course of history, and the life of the individual were based. Christ, in the flesh, was the revealer and interpreter of all this. It was in the philosophy of Hegel that he found the key to the mystery; and he rejoiced with joy unspeakable when what was dark was illumined, and when his lost faith was restored in a new and living form. In a letter written at a much later date to his friend Dr. Gloag, he, in speaking of Lichtenberger's *History of German Theology in the Nineteenth Century*, which had just been translated by the late Professor Hastie, refers to this point:

I am glad you like Lichtenberger. I bought the book some time ago and I am already half through. It is truly delightful reading, full of information and replete with epigrammatic beauty. There is a chapter on Schiller and Goethe which reads like a novel. I think the author's own mind is rather French than German—more brilliant than profound. He has no adequate appreciation of the Hegelian school, nor do I think him altogether just to what he calls the reactionary party—the men of high and dry orthodoxy. But with these reservations the book is admirable, and you will thoroughly enjoy it. Regarding my own views and projects I shall at present say nothing. It is a subject on which I always like best to express myself verbally. I may say generally, however, that the man of all others who expresses most my personal belief is Pfleiderer. I am every year more persuaded that the ideal is the reality, and that the study of Church History ought to be a study of the genesis and development of the Christian ideal. I believe that the ideal of the Christian life is itself the supernatural creation in the heart of man, and that it must have existed before the historical Christ. Because without its previous presence the beauty of the Christ of History would have been unintelligible. I cannot go further here.

Keeping this expression of his position in mind, one is able to read with intelligence the long series of books and articles which he began to write a few years after his induction at Innellan; and should his sermons ever be published, their inward significance will be made plain in the light of it. His writings cover a large field; they deal with a great variety of subjects; they may be said to differ in type, but through them all can be traced his conception of the truth which this letter more than indicates, and his attitude towards the world of thought and life as a whole, which he meant by classing himself under the category of the "broad positive." The spirit of Christianity, the ideal which it embodies, and the central Figure in whom it was realised, became part and parcel of Matheson's nature. He had during that struggle at Innellan not only reconceived but relived his faith. Two extracts from his sermons may here be given. They will at once illustrate the advance made by him since his probationer days, and the way in which he expounded and enforced his reconstructed faith. Preaching at Innellan in the year 1878, on the subject of "building on the foundation" (1 Cor. iii. 12–14), he remarks:

We hear familiarly in the present day of the broad and the narrow Church.   The distinction is a real one, but it is not always what is implied.   Every church is narrow which has not Christ for its foundation, every church is broad which is built upon the Son of Man.   Every form of belief, and every form of unbelief, which is outside the kingdom of Christ, exerts a narrowing tendency over the human soul, for it tells me that I alone am right, and that everyone else is wrong.   But let a man once get his feet on the foundation, let him once stand on the all-transcending truth of the Gospel, he will find it to be an all-comprehending truth too.   It will throw light upon everything; it will cast a mantle of charity over all; it will cover a multitude of sins; it will make us see good in much that seemed hopeless evil.   It will reveal stars in many a night that appeared without a ray.   If you have reached the foundation, you have come to that charity which believeth all things, and hopeth all things, and endureth all things; for you have entered into union with the source of Infinite Love, and you have looked upon the world with His light. Thine is the boundless compassion, and the world-wide sympathy, and the endless hope.   Thine the gentleness that breaks not the bruised reed nor quenches the smoking flax.   Thine the redemptive yearning to seek and to save that which is lost.   You will go forth into the desert and gather flowers from its barren waste; you will walk among the tares and pluck from the midst of them the seeds of future promise.   When you have rested on the great foundation, "the wood and the hay and the stubble" shall alike be included in your love with "the silver and the gold and the precious stones."

If this quotation illustrates the ground on which he reared his faith as "broad positive," the following will reveal the way in which he expounded his belief that the ideal of the Christian life must have

existed before the historical Christ, and that it is in
the light of it all things are made plain.   By the
time he preached this sermon on the "Lamb slain
from the foundation of the world" (Rev. xiii. 8), he
had ceased to write out his discourses in full, but
the skeleton, although much briefer than usual, is
sufficiently explicit :

Idea is, Christ's death not an accident but part of a
system.   It also indicates that the system is one of love.
Calvary older than Eden, and the plan for redemption
precedes the fact of creation.   Divine, like human father-
hood, provides for the contingency of its children.   As
proof of this adduce the sacrificial harmony between the
volumes of nature and grace.   "The foundation of the
world," that is, the work of God in creation, prefigures
sacrifice.   All things shine by passing into the life of
others : the seed into the flower, the sun into nature, the
sea into the reflection of the light.   Each stage of human
life expands by sacrifice of self-will.   Show this in the
child, the boy, the youth, etc.   Exhibit then how Christ
was "slain from the foundation of the world."   Connect
the text with the words, "Lo, I come, I delight to do Thy
will."   When the will is surrendered the work is practically done.

There was thus to Matheson not only a Divine
purpose in the universe and in human life, but a
purpose that was intelligible to the mind and appealed to the heart.   In the light of it, all things
became new.   The dark problems of existence, the
calamities of life, the vicissitudes and trials, the
sufferings and sorrows of mortal existence, yea,
even death itself, yielded up their mystery to the
Christian ideal.   As seen through it, every effort
of the human mind and spirit, and the searchings

and strivings of natural religion, were seen to be but developments and stages in the realisation of the world plan.   The rise and fall of nations—in fact, the course of civilisation as a whole—but illustrated the truth which had now been revealed to him.   The Christian religion itself, in one sense the goal, was in another the beginning.   It revealed in full measure what had always been in the mind of the Eternal.   Its broken creeds contained fractions of the truth, and in place of being anathema one to another they ought to regard each other with that charity which believeth all things.   It was thus that Matheson could gather them all together. His intellectual and moral sympathy embraced each Church, and extended the hand to every form of Christian faith ; indeed, it could reach out to those religions that are regarded as natural, for he saw in them foreshadowings of those truths which were revealed when the times were ripe. He thus became the great reconciler of his age, and did for his own generation what Robertson of Brighton accomplished for his.   Matheson's writings, which we are to study in the following chapter, will illustrate this more fully.

CHAPTER VI

AUTHORSHIP

FOR a studious man like Matheson no better place
could have been found than Innellan. The congregational and parochial demands on his time
were slight in the extreme. The membership of
his church was never very large; there was little
poverty, and the occasions on which he had to
officiate at funerals and marriages were few and
far between. For eight or nine months in the
year his duties consisted mainly in the preparation
and delivery of the weekly sermon; the remainder
of his time was practically at his own disposal,
and it must be admitted that he made the fullest
and the best use of it. There was nothing that
he enjoyed more than being read to, and he
had, within easy distance, in Glasgow, the command of a number of libraries, particularly the
University Library, and I know from the register
of readers at the time that he perused many of
the volumes on philosophy, theology, and cognate
subjects, that it contains. His secretary was continually coming and going, exchanging a packet

of books for a fresh supply, and generally catering
for the mental appetite of his chief.

It goes without saying that most of what was
read was retained. Matheson's remarkable memory
enabled him to keep a firm hold of almost every
idea and fact that were once communicated to him.
But he did not become a mere bookworm; he had
an extraordinary power of assimilation. Whatever
appealed to his intellectual sympathy was appropriated and, with any modification necessary, became part of his own original views. In addition,
there was a method in his reading; he was by
nature and training a speculative theologian. The
poet in him contributed to the fulfilment of his
main purpose, which was to produce in speech or
by writing a fresh and stimulating view of Divine
truth. From his earliest years he aimed at authorship. As a schoolboy his efforts were printed at
the express desire of his class-fellows, and as a
student one poem at least found its way to the
press.

Nor was he long at Innellan until he con-
templated publication. The work, however, which
he intended for the world was not the one that first
appeared; indeed, it never appeared in the form in
which he wrote it. There are among his literary
remains a series of articles, or chapters, which were
no doubt intended for a volume. Including the
introduction and conclusion they number fourteen,
and would have made a very presentable book.
They bear the general title of "Conquerors by

Faith; or the Gospel of the Old Testament,"
and he evidently intended to publish them with his
own name, for on the title-page there is written, " By
the Rev. George Matheson, M.A., B.D., Innellan."
They deal with those Hebrew characters of whom
a list is given in the eleventh chapter of the
Epistle to the Hebrews, beginning with Abel and
ending with David. They bear signs of having
been submitted to some friendly criticism, and if
one can judge by the pencilled notes, the critic
was none other than Dr. Macduff. Why they
were never published I do not know. They
would have been quite worthy of any young
minister of the Church. But on the whole he was
wisely guided, for he would have forestalled the
publication, many years afterwards, of his remarkable volume on *The Representative Men of the
Bible*. The subjects are mainly the same, the
point of view not radically different. But one
misses in the earlier series the touch of the master
hand, and that knowledge of life and of character
which can only come after much thought and with
the years that bring the philosophic mind. It is
rather striking that his first conceptions were those
that were last worked out. His earliest volume
may be said to have seen the light only after
his death, for *The Women of the Bible*, just
published, was but the completion of the idea that
he formed at Innellan of issuing in book-form
sketches of the characters of the Old and the New
Testaments. He never left his first love, and there

is not a little satisfaction in the reflection that he was able to fulfil the dream of his youth before he died.

The work which he did prepare and publish within six years of his settlement at Innellan was *Aids to the Study of German Theology*. It appeared in the autumn of 1874, anonymously. It is no exaggeration to say that it came to the English public of the day as a glad and welcome surprise. There was in the mind of Britain at the time a strong and unreasoning prejudice against German theology. This, of course, was entirely owing to ignorance, or misrepresentation, of the subject. Most of what had been published in England during the first half of the nineteenth century on the speculative theories of our Teutonic neighbours was certainly not to their advantage. Our insular conceit made us impatient of anything that necessitated a reconsideration or recasting of our theological position, and the earlier writers on the subject, partly ignorant of the language, and certainly quite out of sympathy with the views which they tried to combat, presented German theology in a most unfavourable light.

All this necessarily created a reaction, and such writers as Pusey, Sir William Hamilton, Morell, and Schaff, in independent works, and the scholars who were employed to translate the German works that composed Clark's "Biblical Cabinet" and the "Foreign Theological Library," did yeoman service in breaking down this prejudice by well-informed criticism of what the misjudged authors had really said. By the time Matheson wrote, the works of De Wette, Tholuck, Neander, Rosenmüller, Lisco, and Röhr, of Hengstenberg, Keil, Delitzsch, Bleek, Julius Müller, Giesler, and Dorner had been translated; and through the "Theological Translation Fund Library" a beginning had been made with a reproduction, in English dress, of the works of Baur, Ewald, Keim, and Haus- rath.

Matheson made himself familiar with all the material in the English language that he could lay his hands on, and devoted himself to a keen and profound study of German theology. I have in my hands, as I write, a large notebook, which he used at the time, and it is full of extracts from, and reflections on, the works of Dorner, Müller, Neander, Baur, Morell, Hutchison Stirling, etc. From these and other sources, partly original and partly translated, he gathered together and sys- tematised the views of the great German writers on theology—from the time of Kant downwards. One cannot study this notebook, which bears indisput- able traces of wide and careful reading, without seeing in it the germ of all the works that Matheson produced at Innellan. It bears traces of his mental struggle at the time, gives a history to the sympathetic reader of his spiritual combat with the Giant Despair, and shows how the creative, positive, and illuminating ideas of the great German thinkers enabled him to lay hold afresh of his lost faith, and to body it forth in a new and living form. It is also evident that he had during these years, while patiently engaged in mastering the speculative theories of the new age, a steadfast purpose in view. The great names of Kant, Schleiermacher, Hegel, Schelling, Fichte, and Strauss, recur most frequently, and their views on the different problems in theology with which they deal are elaborated more or less in detail. It was during this time that Matheson gained a sure foothold, and became master of himself and the great themes with which he was afterwards to deal.

There were three features of the new publication which commended it to the religious public. These were its lucidity of style, its logical continuity, and its constructive aim. Students of German theology had previously been debarred from a sympathetic apprehension of the subject by the linguistic jargon both of the writers and their translators. Even eager aspirants were repelled. Over the portals of this temple, as over those of the kingdom of heaven, were written the words: "Strait is the gate and narrow is the way, and few there be that find it." Matheson opened the barred door. He removed the inscription, and led into the new kingdom thousands who hitherto had stood patient but disheartened at the outer gate. The fact is he had made the subject his own. The iron had entered his soul, and he spoke because he

felt and saw.   He was impatient of vagueness, and
he could never speak or write without having first
of all formed a clear conception of the subject in
his own mind.   Accordingly in his book there is a
beginning, a middle, and an end.   System follows
system, philosopher succeeds philosopher, by what
seems a necessary law of development ; and German
theology, which before was to many English
readers an inversion or contradiction of the laws
of thought, is seen in Matheson's hands to be
but the necessary historical evolution of ideas.
The style, too, was found to be charming ; clear,
light, limpid, carrying the mind along by its own
sweet music, and satisfying the most exact literary
taste.

The greatest service, however, which Matheson
rendered was his emphatic and convincing presentation of German theology as a positive and
constructive power, which in place of destroying
belief in Christianity confirmed that belief to all
doubting and thinking minds.   This is the first
note sounded by him.   In his Introduction he deals
with the subject of German Rationalism, and shows
how it was an exotic plant.   The German heart he
declares to be believing, the German mind to be
constructive ; and the late Professor Hastie, in his
excellent Introduction to Lichtenberger's *History
of German Theology in the Nineteenth Century*,
while expressing admiration for Matheson's book
as a whole, commends it in particular for the signal
service which it rendered at the time to the true

conception of German theology as a creative science.

The immediate cause of this work's inception was a conversation between him and his friend Dr. David Sime. The doctor, like others who were in the habit of hearing Matheson preach, felt that it was a pity that so much wealth of thought and beauty of style should be confined to the limited circle of his congregation at Innellan, and Sime one evening besought him to gather a choice few of the expositions of Scripture passages which he was in the habit of giving, and to publish them; or, failing this, to write out his own lucid account of the German Philosophies and Theologies; or, still better, to do both. "No man," urged Sime, "should keep to himself, or for his own set, his celestial, any more than his terrestrial work. It assuredly would not do for a heavenly flower to waste its perfume on the desert air." "Of course not," said Matheson, "but no good or beautiful thing is wasted. However, I shall think still more on what you suggest; I think that I will write, and that I have something to say." The immediate spur to his resolution came a short time afterwards, when Mr. James Sime, the well-known man of letters, happened to be on a visit to his brother. He was at that time engaged in gathering materials for his *Life of Lessing*, and the doctor having invited Matheson to meet him, the trio so stimulated each other's minds that, in a short time, all of them became authors. "Some time, probably months after this evening," remarks the doctor,

in one of my now regular, and expected, visits to the Manse, I found my friend rapidly pacing backwards and forwards through the library, and with unusual strength and determination in his usually mirthful and cheerful face. He received me with new enthusiasm, and if possible with more affection than ever. "I have made up my mind," he said; "you have broken my rock-like silence—it should have been broken long ago. I am going to write a small work on German Theology, aids to the great German conceptions, and also to prepare for the press some of the expository work to which you have so pressingly alluded. In point of fact, this morning I have finished the first three or four sheets of a small work that I am to call *Aids to the Study of German Theology*. Are you not glad? Of course you are, but whist! not a word about it."

The book appeared in the autumn of 1874, and so cordial was its reception that within two years it was in its third edition. The second edition appeared with the author's name on the title-page. The reviews were most encouraging. *The Scotsman*, for example, devoted a whole column to it, and this for a small book, and evidently the first, by an unknown author, was quite unusual, and was a proof of the impression the work had made on the reviewer's mind. It was impossible for the writer to preserve his anonymity. In a short time letters poured in upon him from leading men in the Church, full of the heartiest congratulations and encouragement. One of the first was from his old friend Dr. Macduff; and among others who wrote to him were Dr. M'Culloch, Dr. Hugh Macmillan, Dr. Jamieson of Glasgow, Professor Charteris, and

Dr. John Alison. The most valued commendation, seeing it was from a man who was particularly versed in the subject, was from Dr. Gloag of Galashiels :

MANSE OF GALASHIELS,
December 21, 1874.

MY DEAR SIR,—I have been informed that you are the author of the work entitled *Aids to the Study of German Theology*, and I cannot refrain from writing to thank you for your excellent work. Its erudition is extensive, but it is especially marvellous when it is remembered that the author had to encounter great obstacles from defectiveness of vision. I cannot understand how you have amassed such knowledge of German Theology. Although I have been studying it for nearly twenty years, yet I must yield the palm to you. I do not pretend to criticise your work, which is in all respects admirable ; written in a candid spirit, and exhibiting great judgment in weighing the different opinions. The distinction you draw between the Theology of Baur and Strauss was to me peculiarly interesting. I cannot enter into your appreciation of Hegel. To me his philosophy rests on no solid basis, and is merely an ingenious theory, without any ground of truth ; and I must confess that the Left Hegelians carried it to its legitimate conclusions. I was surprised at the statement that Ewald believed in the resurrection of Jesus as an historical fact. I thought that I had met with a distinct denial of it in one of his writings, though I cannot tell where. Nor did I know that Whitby was an Arian. His Commentary on John appears to be strictly orthodox. I am also such a theologian of the old school that I cannot agree with those who deprecate the reasoning of Paley. To me it is as convincing, in opposition to the modern forms of infidelity, as it was in opposition to the Deists.

Again thanking you for your excellent work, and hoping that it will be only an instalment and a prelude to still greater works in theology—Believe me, yours truly,

PATON J. GLOAG.

Matheson being now launched on the ocean of authorship, book after book, and article after article, followed each other in quick succession; and the remarkable feature about them all is that none bear traces of slipshod or careless work. The thought, the style, and the finish of each is as perfect as he could make them. Nor did his writing interfere with his preaching; in fact it seemed to help it. With every Sunday came a new sermon, and as the years rolled on his discourses grew in power. Their spiritual insight, richness of thought, and wealth of illustration increased with his deepening experience. Three years after the publication of *The Aids* appeared his second and his most ambitious book, *The Growth of the Spirit of Christianity.* It was in two volumes, and attracted considerable attention. It was an application of the principles of Hegel to the Christian Church; in short, it was a philosophy of the history of the Church from "the Dawn of the Christian Era to the Reformation."

The book, even after the lapse of thirty years, impresses one by its power. It is full of brilliant passages, and bristles with pointed epigrams. It is bold without being arrogant, and faces the most difficult facts with a courage that is chivalrous in the extreme. Its knowledge of the events, the movements, and the characters of that long period is most striking; and flash after flash of illuminating light is poured upon passages and incidents which make the whole period live. The author sees in the history of the world, preceding the dawn of Christianity, a preparation for the advent of Christ. The Pagan religions, as well as Judaism, serve their purpose in paving the way for Him who was to be the Light of the World. Christianity after its birth enters on its infancy. It then passes through its youth to its schooldays, and is subjected to the training, struggles, and discipline which such an experience involves. Only after it has gone through these necessary stages of development does it reach its full expansion and expression in the Reformation.

Such, in brief outline, is the plan and character of the book. It presents Christianity as a spiritual force, subject to the law of evolution, and gradually unfolding its inner purpose as the ages roll by. The leading journals, both in England and Scotland, recognised at once the importance and the significance of the new work, and it won from *The Spectator* a lengthened and favourable review. The organs of the English Church, especially of the High Church party, pointed out what they conceived to be its defects. It was easy, of course, for anyone to question the relation of all the facts to the theory by which the author strove to interpret them. In the opinion of not a few the facts were distorted to suit the theory. No one will be eager to dispute the fairness of this criticism; it is one that is constantly levelled against Hegel himself. But it is better surely to see facts in the light of some illuminating principle than to regard them as so many unintelligible obstacles in the path of a true appreciation of the course of history. The main objection to the book, however, on the part of such critics, was that it was a vindication of Protestantism, a glorification of the individual at the expense of the Church. Matheson would regard such criticism as a compliment, for he held

that individualism was the reforming centre of even collectivism; the reformation of the latter being from the unit to the multitude, not from the multitude to the unit, from within outwards rather than from without inwards. No Act of Parliament would make a drunkard a sober man, or a grasping money-lender or sensualist into a large-souled being. How often was the solitary individual the starting-point of originality, and the glowing centre of a life and light that raise all life, possibly for generations. The eternal importance of the individual fascinated him. To lose one's life in order to find it was emphatically true of one's own work and pre-eminently true of the works of great genius.

Notwithstanding the ability, learning, and fascination of this book, it never passed beyond a first edition. It is difficult to account for this. With all its defects it was a powerful and important contribution to the subject treated. Its weakness perhaps consisted in its aim, for while it may be possible to apply the Hegelian principle to the outstanding periods in the history of the world or of the Church, it is difficult, to say the least, to see this principle verified in every movement, incident, and detail, in the growth of the Christian religion, during the first sixteen centuries of its existence.

Matheson on more than one occasion expressed a desire to rewrite the work. He evidently believed in the purpose which he had in mind when composing it. No subject attracted him more than the history of thought, nor was there any other theme on which his insight and suggestiveness could find a better field for their employment.

It was now that Matheson began his numerous contributions to the religious and theological magazines of the day. He had previous to this endeavoured to find entrance to several of them, but without success. Article after article, he used to say, was rejected by the "able editors"; but once he had made a name for himself, his contributions were solicited by these same editors, who were glad to receive and publish the very articles which they had previously declined. So much for editorial insight and judgment. The very first article that appeared from his pen was perhaps the best he ever wrote. It was on the "Originality of the Character of Christ," and was published in *The Contemporary Review* of November 1878.

I have a distinct recollection of an interesting incident in connection with this article. Sparsely populated as Innellan was, it was never, in Matheson's time at least, without one or two men of intellectual ability. They naturally gravitated to the Manse, and received fresh stimulus from the young minister who was so mentally alive. With them he used to discuss current theological and philosophical topics, and they took a deep personal interest in his literary aspirations and ventures. Even at that early date he was beginning to gather round him a sympathetic band whose minds he imbued with his own spirit. One late September, or early October, morning in the year 1878, I chanced to be standing on Innellan pier, waiting the arrival of some steamer, when my eye rested on an animated group, centred round a close friend of Matheson's, who was holding in his hand a sheaf of printed slips, which at the time seemed very unfamiliar to me, but which afterwards became only too well known as printers' proof sheets. This young Mathesonian was holding forth at considerable length in an animated, and almost excited, manner to the group that had gathered round him, and on drawing near I discovered that what he held in his hand were the proofs of the article by Matheson that was to appear the following month in *The Contemporary Review*. What strikes one in reflecting upon this incident is the deep interest which these villagers took in the growing reputation of their minister. They were beginning to be extremely proud of him, and though only a few could have understood the importance, to a young author, of having an article 'accepted by so influential a magazine, they caught the spirit of the occasion and responded with hearty sympathy to the outpourings of Matheson's friend, who was expounding to them the great honour that had befallen their minister. On reading anew the article, which has now been in print for well-nigh thirty years, one feels that whatever honour may have accrued to the author, an equal honour at least befell the magazine which was fortunate enough to secure it. So deep an impression did it make that, shortly after its appearance, it was translated into French.

In the following year he formed a connection with *The Expositor* that was to last till his death. It was the magazine to which he contributed the greatest number of articles. Between him and its editor there was the closest intellectual sympathy. Samuel Cox, who at that time had charge of the magazine, was a prince of expositors—scholarly, broad-minded, original, and suggestive; and he gathered round him a band of writers who made the journal favourably known, not only in Britain but in America and the Colonies. It was only in its fifth year when Dr. Matheson joined it, and he continued his connection under the present editor, Dr. Robertson Nicoll. Even after he had, for the most part, ceased to contribute to current literature, he could not withstand the attractions of *The Expositor*, and some of his latest writings appeared in its pages. The article by which he introduced himself to its readers was on "Science and the Christian Idea of Prayer," and in its own line it was quite equal to the one that had appeared, two months previously, in *The Contemporary Review*. Indeed Matheson never surpassed, in any of his subsequent writings, whether in magazine or in book-form, these early contributions. Nothing finer of their kind had appeared from the pen of a

Scottish minister. Their originality, convincing argument, scholarship, easy mastery of philosophic and scientific thought; their suggestiveness, high spiritual tone, and literary finish, mark them out as among the best specimens of magazine writing that the age produced.

This was the year in which the first distinctive honour was bestowed on Matheson. At the spring graduation of 1879, the University of Edinburgh conferred upon him the degree of Doctor of Divinity. It might be thought that his own University should have been the first to recognise him, but he was still young; he was just in his thirty-seventh year, and he had been a parish minister for eleven years only. Think, however, of his record! He was one of the most distinguished students of his time, as a preacher he was already in the first rank, and as an author he had proved his quality. In addition to all this, there was the sad fact that he was blind. No one of his standing among his contemporaries, and with all their faculties unimpaired, had in the field of oratory or of authorship attained to anything like his distinction; and yet in spite of a calamity terrible for most men to contemplate, let alone to endure, he had achieved a reputation which was fast spreading over the length and breadth of the land. As for Matheson, the fact of a University which was not his own Alma Mater, stepping in at this early date to recognise him, was a double honour. Upon the University of Edinburgh he had no claims, except that of intellectual ability and the accomplishment of great achievements. It was these that were recognised by his degree.

It must have been singularly gratifying to Matheson that one of the men who were capped along with him on the occasion was the scholarly and saintly Dr. Hugh Macmillan of Greenock. Dr. Macmillan was an early friend of Matheson's. He was among the first to recognise his genius, and to give him every assistance and encouragement in his literary pursuits. Professor Charteris, in presenting Matheson to the Chancellor (Lord President Inglis), said :

I have also the honour to introduce the Rev. George Matheson, B.D., Minister of the Parish of Innellan. My Lord, Mr. Matheson, though young in years, and though he has had to struggle against a physical disadvantage, which would have been to most men ample reason for his enjoying a life of ease rather than of labour, has already won for himself a high place on the roll of scholars and divines. His first book, *Aids to the Study of German Theology*, is a remarkable proof of his power to present an accurate and interesting, and even lively, picture of the work of every German theologian and critic of distinction, and students have welcomed it. His next book, entitled *The Growth of the Spirit of Christianity*, passes with a scholar's sure step and a poet's eye, and the graceful ease of thorough culture, over the whole wide field of Christian history, showing the increasing power which runs through all the ages, and leading to much thought on the unequalled opportunities which are in the power of the Church of our own day. He is also the author of several well-known papers, one of which, in *The Contemporary Review*, on the "Originality of the Character of Christ," may be specially mentioned. It is not only, as in some sort, a crown for the past, but as an encouragement to other labours, that the Senatus Academicus asks your Lordship to confer on Mr. Matheson the degree of Doctor of Divinity, which he has already won so well.

Dr. Matheson received, in the following year, a unanimous call to succeed Dr. Cumming at Crown Court Church, London. It is said that one reason for his declining this call was the failure on the part of the managers to accept the condition that he should be permitted to exchange freely with the other Presbyterian and Nonconforming ministers in London. Whatever truth there may be in this, it points to a fact which cannot be gainsaid. There was no exclusiveness in Matheson's ecclesiastical views or leanings. His sympathies were sufficiently broad to include all the Creeds and Communions of Christendom. His work on *The Growth of the Spirit of Christianity* showed that he regarded every step in the history of the Church, every fresh departure and secession, as a manifestation of progress, a reaching forward to a fuller realisation of absolute truth. So keen was his appreciation of other Churches, and even of heathen religions, that on one occasion, when advocating in private, and with extraordinary force and eloquence, the cause of foreign missions, he so impressed his hearers with his fitness for the task that they urged him to go himself. They felt that he, by his intellectual presentation of Christian truth to the Hindu mind, would do more to convert the natives of India to the Christian religion than the ordinary missionary,

who depended on weapons that were outworn and
effete. "I go——!" he said, and paused. "No, I
dare not go. I am afraid I would be converted to
Brahminism."

There can be no doubt, however, that other
reasons weighed with him in declining the call to
London. It would have been a wrench to break,
even in a modified form, his connection with the
Church of Scotland, and the difficulties and un-
certainties of the situation could not be denied.
All the same, he had really nothing to fear. He
could, in London, have lived the life of the student,
and he would certainly have gathered round him a
congregation in full sympathy with his views. In
a very short time his preaching would have been
one of the attractions of the capital, and the
strangers and foreigners who crowd into it would
of themselves have filled his church. The more
likely condition insisted on by him would be, that
he should be freed from all parochial and congregational work, so that his full strength might be
given to preaching. Presbyterianism, unfortunately,
has not even yet risen to this height, and he showed
wisdom in choosing to remain, for the time being,
in Innellan.

He now began to write regularly for the press.
During the next six years, until the time that he
was called to St. Bernard's, he wrote some fifty
articles to the more important theological magazines
of the day. To *The Expositor* alone he contributed
within that period twenty-five articles. Among

them was the series on " The Historical Christ of
St. Paul," another on the "Minor Prophets,"
and a third on " Scripture Studies of the Heavenly
State." Single articles by him appeared on such
subjects as " The Paradox of Christian Ethics,"
" Christianity and Judaism," " Christianity's First
Invitation to the World," " The Outer and the
Inner Glory," " The Hundred and Thirty-Ninth
Psalm," and " Spiritual Sacrifices." He also wrote a
series of three articles to *The Catholic Presbyterian*
on " German Theologians of the Day," and another
on " The Judaic Vision of the Happy Kingdom."
His article on " The Basis of Religious Belief"
appeared in *The British and Foreign Evangelical
Review*. He wrote in *The British Quarterly
Review* on " The Christian Idea of God," in *The
Princeton Review* on " Christ and the Doctrine of
Immortality," in *The Modern Review* on " The
Religious Forces of the Reformation Era," and in
The Homiletic Magazine on " Evolution in Relation
to Miracle." Nine articles by him appeared between
November 1884 and June 1886 in *The Monthly
Interpreter*. They were on " Christ's Exaltation
in the Epistle to the Hebrews," " The Continuity
of the Sermon on the Mount," " The Three
Christian Sympathies," " The Empire of Christ,"
" Christ's Defence of his Parabolic Teaching,"
" Christ's Glorifying Work," " The Order of Christ's
Revelation," " Exaltation of Christ in the Epistle
to the Philippians," and " The Promise of Revela-
tion."

Two things strike one forcibly on reading this long series of articles. The one is Matheson's amazing intellectual fertility, and the other is the rare quality of the work which he produced. In reflecting on the former it should not be forgotten that these were but chips from his workshop. He was all the time engaged on books that demanded research and thought, and preaching sermons of the first order, the delivery of which alone must have been a great strain on his nervous energy. The last ten years of his residence at Innellan were, from a literary point of view, the most productive and important in his whole life. He experienced during that period a quickening of his mental nature which it is hard to parallel. Dr. Sime, who saw much of him during these years, bears witness to his extraordinary activity, and also to the method which utilised every hour of the day. It was this combination which enabled him to accomplish what he did. "He talked rapidly," says the doctor, "walked rapidly, thought rapidly, worked rapidly; but his work was methodical in the extreme. Every hour of the day had its allotted kind and amount of work, which was never by fits and starts, or by sudden impulses and inspirations. A more ready man of thought, for his mind was ever full, I have not ever met." Continuing, he remarks:

At certain arranged hours he read the newspapers or the monthlies, or general literature, or works of science, philosophy, and theology; or paced about the library alone, for an hour, thinking; or dictated to his amanuensis an expository gem of thought for the Sunday. As revealing his systematic method of work, it may be mentioned that whilst dictating, in full fervour and force, he would abruptly cease for the day when the time devoted for such workmanship had elapsed; sometimes in the middle of a sentence, often in the middle of a paragraph. Then on the next morning, on returning to the theme, he had the last two or three sheets carefully read over, and resumed the dictation, his whole soul in the work, fresh and animated as before. The same would occur on studying the most fascinating poem, or fiction, or piece of criticism; such as Macaulay's, Carlyle's, Professor Max Müller's, or Huxley's; not less than the most abstract German metaphysics and theology, or the most technical of scientific treatises. On coming back the next day to the study of the work on hand, here likewise a page or two would be re-read, and in full intensity and with fresh power the interest in the work would be renewed. Never did he allow himself to be fatigued, hence the amount and the variety of work he was capable of, for he was always at his best in reception and in creation. Again, at a certain hour each day he would go out with his private secretary or devoted sister to visit his parishioners, and even these with methodical preparation. He had his meals every day at the same time; at the same hour every night he went to bed; and at the same hour every morning he rose, jocund as the morn, for the work of the day, maintaining a regular, normal, harmonious life from day to day.

The most important of the articles which he published at this time are apologetic in their nature. His great aim was to commend Christianity to the times, to show that modern science and criticism had in no way impaired, much less destroyed, its foundations; but that, on the contrary, every fresh discovery in the world of mind or of matter, or in

the field of history, simply revealed its inherent
wealth, its boundless resources, and its eternal
adaptability to the needs of man. This is Christian Theism, and, having grasped the central truth,
Matheson was the very man to commend Christianity to the inquiring and thoughtful minds of
the age. His method was historical, broad, and
sympathetic. He had for years been engaged in
a profound study of natural religion. The religions
of the ancient world, in particular, attracted him.
He was also familiar with the different systems of
doctrine that had sprung out of Christianity itself,
and with the various currents of unbelief and
rationalism that had appeared during the Christian
era. He had made a very special study of English
Deism, and of the apologetic works associated with
the names of Butler and of Paley. Above all, he
had steeped his mind so thoroughly in the speculative theories of the great German thinkers on
religion, from the time of Kant, and with the works
of the theologians inspired by them, that he could
move with ease and freedom in the world of modern
thought, and apply his own fundamental principles
to existing conditions. These conditions were
beginning to be radically affected by the spirit of
science, and he bent himself with his whole force
to master the principles which underlay that spirit.
Especially did he make himself thoroughly con-
versant with the works of its great exponent and
interpreter, Herbert Spencer, and in a book which
he was to publish before leaving Innellan, and which,

to my thinking, is perhaps his greatest work, he produced an "Apology of the Christian Religion" against the attacks made upon it by that agnosticism which was the offspring of modern science. It will serve our purpose to select two or three of the more important articles, looked at from this point of view, and briefly state the thought that inspired them.

The problem which he had to face in his article on the "Originality of the Character of Christ" was the one raised by Baur and Strauss. In other words, he had to show that behind the Gospels, and behind the history from which they were supposed to have sprung, there was an element which had to be accounted for, and that was the ideal which was embodied in the historical Christ. Grant that the Gospels were the result of the conflict between the Petrine and Pauline schools of thought which arose in the Apostolic Church, and concede the contention that the ground of that conflict was the offspring of mere myth, there still remained the Christian ideal which neither the one theory nor the other could explain. Matheson then proceeds to give an historical sketch of the different conceptions of the ideal man which had animated the ancient world. He reviews in turn the Jewish, Platonic, Greek, and Roman ideals, and he finds that one and all of them come short of the Christ of history. He has no difficulty in showing that the natural mind, as represented in the searchings of the ancient world after the highest type of manhood, has come woefully short of the Christ of the Gospels, and he is driven to the conclusion that the explanation can be sought in one direction only, in the fresh revelation which was imparted to the world in the Incarnate Word. "If," he concludes,

we find Judea reaping where she has not sown, and gathering where she has not strawed; if we see her the birthplace of an idea which surpassed her power of origination, and when originated surpassed her power of comprehension; if in her contact with the Gentile nations we fail to discover any germs from which that idea could have naturally sprung; if we find it in essence and in portraiture directly at variance with all heathen aspirations, reversing the world's ideal of physical strength, transforming its estimate of mental power, casting into the shade its conception of æsthetic culture, and placing on a contrary basis its hope of a theocratic power; if we find it introducing a new standard of heroism which caused every valley to be exalted, and every mountain to be made low; and if, above all, we perceive that when that standard of heroism rose upon the world, it rose upon a foreign soil which received it as an alien and an adversary, are we not driven to ask if, even on the lowest computation, we have not reached the evidence of a new life in humanity, the outpouring of a fresh vitality and the manifestation of a higher power?

In his article on "Science and the Christian Idea of Prayer," he tries to find a place for the believing heart in the new world of inviolable forces which the modern world was fast girding round it. Science contended that nature is immutable, that its laws are unknown, and the idea of Christian prayer that was current at the time seemed to contradict both these positions. Matheson, on the other hand, declares that Christianity really admits them, and that thus far both it and science are at one. There is a common ground on which both can meet, and that is the belief that the veil may be lifted, that the Creator and creation are in communion, or, as he puts it: "According to the modern doctrine of forces there is one inscrutable and ultimate Force which is everywhere present and everywhere persistent, and in which all other forms and forces live and move and have their being. The universe is but its manifestation, the laws of the universe are but its expression. Christianity employs a different terminology, but it asks no more. It only desires the possibility of some communication from the infinite to the finite. Like science it perceives an immutable nature, like science it recognises its ignorance of that nature, and like science it forecasts the hope that the law which is unknown will in some way manifest its presence." Here, then, is a sphere in which Christian prayer can exercise itself. Its great desire is that the will of God should be revealed so that the heart of the petitioner may know and be in sympathy with it, and that the life of the believer may be in conformity with its behests. It is this which differentiates the Christian from the Pagan idea of prayer. The Pagan knows of nothing save individual desires, the Christian of nothing save the desires of God, and so he concludes :

Paganism had questioned what it should eat and what it should drink, and wherewithal it should be clothed; Christianity perceived that none of these things constituted the essence of human need. Paganism desired the gratification of the individual life; Christianity started with the definite assumption that the only ultimate gratification which that life could find was to cease from its own self-seeking, and desire the universal good. Christian prayer has become the antithesis of heathen supplication; and it has reached this antithesis by entering into union with that scientific life of Nature where the interest of the one is the interest of the many, and where the liberty of the individual is the service of the highest law.

If there was one subject more than another in which Matheson was deeply interested it was Immortality. It is the theme of his earliest and of his latest writings. There is hardly a book or an article written by him in which there is not some reference to it. It was with him a subject of perennial interest. Nor was there any question to which he had given a more definite answer. He had no doubt concerning it. He believed as strongly in the immortality of the soul as he did in his own personality. Some may think that the reason of his absorbing interest in this subject was the fact of his being blind. It was natural that he should look forward to another world in which the film would be taken from his eyes and he could see the " King in His beauty." Matheson had formed to himself a very vivid conception of what the Hereafter was to be like. He had created a "new heaven and a new earth," and in moments of frank communication he gave his friends a glimpse of what he himself saw; but his hope of immortality arose from another cause. As a spiritually minded man, as a Christian theologian, as one who had pondered the problems which face all serious men, he felt that there could be no escape from a belief in this great doctrine. The very idea of God made it necessary to his thinking, and the Christian religion would fall to pieces were the doctrine of immortality to be blotted out.

In two articles which he wrote at this time, the one in *The Expositor* and the other in *The Princeton Review*, he deals with both sides of the subject: the future life of the soul, and the future condition of the body. It is in the light of Christ's life, death, and resurrection that he views it; and he contends that the believer who is mystically united to Christ, who is a member of His Divine body, is bound to be a sharer in that life which Christ brought to light. The power of Christ in the believing soul will make it eternal, and the glorified body of Christ will also be shared in by the Christian. Apart from Christ, Matheson does not discuss the question. What immortality there may be for those outside the pale of Christianity he does not in these two articles pretend to consider. As a Christian theologian he confines himself to the subject which his vocation naturally called him to ponder. To most minds the question of the soul's "transition garment," as Matheson calls the resurrection body, will be of more interest than the question of the soul's future life; for the latter is tacitly accepted, while with regard to the former not a few are in doubt.

Matheson's views on this subject then are worth considering. He says :

> We believe the pervading thought of the New Testament to be that the resurrection body of Christ forms the germ or nucleus out of which is to spring the transition garment of the believing soul. Let the student of the Gospels and the Pauline epistles approach their study with such a thought in his mind, and he will be struck with the marvellous concentration of all other points around it. He will find a new significance in that grain of mustard-seed which, though buried, rises up into a mighty tree and branches forth into the dwellings of the homeless. He will see a fresh meaning in those elements of communion which are professedly the symbols of Christ's earthly body—the body broken in death, but distributed in resurrection. He will read in another light those narratives in which the Messiah conquers death, and measure by a new standard the "power of His resurrection." He will ask, not without intelligence, if when Christ spoke of the Father's house with many mansions— the house which His own resurrection was to prepare—He meant anything less than that human body which had been the scene of the Incarnation? He will ask yet again, and with still deepening conviction, if when Paul spoke of "the building of God, the house not made with hands, eternal in the heavens," he meant anything less than that same Father's house which the evangelist had beheld in the form of Jesus? He will inquire if Paul had any meaning when he said that Christians were "members of Christ's body," that they were crucified together with Christ, that they were "buried with Him by baptism into His death," that they were already "risen with Him," and "made to sit together with Him in heavenly places," that the Christian dead "slept in Him," and that He at His coming would "bring them with Him"; above all, that their rising was so bound up in His resurrection, that if there were no resurrection of the dead, then Christ Himself was not risen; but that, if He were risen, they had already their "conversation in heaven." These are startling

statements, but they are marvellously consistent with one fundamental thought ; they point, in our view, unmistakably to the belief that when the soul is clothed upon with the house which is from heaven, it is clothed upon with the resurrection body of the Son of Man. The effect of such a belief was to abolish death. The soul no longer needed to linger in an impersonal sleep, awaiting the consummation of all things. " He that believeth on Me shall never die," was the last word on the subject of immortality.

The most striking thought in his article on the " Christian Idea of God " is one which he elaborates more fully in his Baird Lecture. It is his view of revelation. " Revelation," he says, " signifies the drawing back of a veil. Supernaturalism worships the veil and would perish by its withdrawal. Rationalism has no veil to withdraw. Revelation is the middle form between supernaturalism and rationalism." Matheson held that revelation was impossible except on the belief that there is something in common between the Divine and the human, between God and man. Unless man had in him something akin to God he would be unable to understand God's manifestation of Himself; and unless there was in God something akin to man, God would be unable to hold communion with the creature. Hence in the Incarnation, God manifest in the flesh, Matheson finds the Christian idea both of God and of man. In the article on the " Basis of Religious Belief," he enters on a very fine discussion of the different grounds for this belief as held by various schools of thought, both without and within the Christian Church. As is customary with him, he treats the subject historically, he shows how each basis when it proved untenable gave birth to a new one, until at last the theory of Schleiermacher is reached, which is only the Christian conception of Faith in another form ; that "the sense of absolute dependence" is the real basis of religious belief. To feel our limitation is to take the first step towards a conception of the infinite. "Faith," he remarks, "is essentially a Christian term. It differs from religious belief in general, as the species differs from the genus. Belief is the recognition of a Divine principle, faith is the recognition of a Divine principle which bears to us a moral relation. The peculiarity of faith as a religious phenomenon, in other words the peculiarity of Christianity as a system of belief, consists in this, that it imports into the idea of God an element of moral rectitude with which we as worshippers have specially to do. Nevertheless the basis of Christian faith is, by its own admission, precisely the same as the basis of religious belief in general, the sense of absolute dependence."

These articles, dealing with some of the most important subjects in theology, and handled by Dr. Matheson in an earnest and scholarly manner, however valuable in themselves, were but a preparation for his next book, published in 1881, under the title of the *Natural Elements of Revealed Theology*. This was the Baird Lecture for that year. It was a distinct honour to be appointed to this Foundation, especially at so early a period in

11

life. He was only in his thirty-ninth year, and
with a single exception this lectureship has all
along been given to men who at the time of their
appointment were, to say the least, beyond the
meridian of life. It has always been regarded
partly as a reward for lengthened services to the
Church and to theological literature, and partly as
an opportunity for men of ripe scholarship to give
their matured views to the world. The other
exception referred to was Professor Flint. He, like
Matheson, was Baird Lecturer at a comparatively
early age, and it is remarkable that the lectures of
these two are regarded on all hands as among the
best that have been delivered on this Foundation.
Some may see in this an argument for the appointment of young men, but it ought to be remembered
that every youthful theologian is not a Flint or a
Matheson.

The lecturer's design was to ascertain to what
extent the doctrines of revealed religion have a
basis in the natural instincts of the human mind.
In the introductory chapter he discusses at length
the main thought of his article on the "Christian
Idea of God," namely, the nature and possibility of
revelation. Elaborating the idea which we have
already seen to lie at the basis of his views on the
subject, that revelation simply means the " drawing
back of a veil," he remarks : " The act of drawing
back the veil is the supernatural part of the process.
It is too high to be touched by the human hand,
and therefore its removal demands the agency of

another Hand. Yet no sooner is the veil withdrawn than the mystery vanishes. The human spirit recognises the vision not as a new vision, but as that for which unconsciously it has been waiting all along. It bounds to meet it as the normal fulfilment of its destiny."

This conception of revelation will be generally accepted as sound and satisfactory, and the attitude taken up towards natural religion, just keeps the mean between too sombre and too flattering a view of the latter. Christianity is not a mere collection of mysteries standing in no relation to human reason or experience, and incapable of commending itself to the human heart as the solution of its problems and the satisfaction of its needs and desires. It is the complement of human nature, it gives to nature the very thing she needed, it satisfies the instincts manifested in ethnic or natural religion.

In setting himself to prove this thesis, Dr. Matheson first of all endeavours to ascertain what the instincts and aspirations of natural religion are. He seeks for these in the religions which prevailed before the advent of Christ, and in them he discovers three great problems, namely, What is God? What is His relation to humanity? Is His Glory consistent with the existence of moral evil? The solution of the first he finds in the Christian doctrine of the Trinity; of the second in the tenet of the Incarnation; and of the third in the faith in the Atonement. Dr. Matheson works out these ideas with great originality, eloquence, and skill. The book was welcomed by the public as a glad surprise. It was felt to be a new departure in Scottish theology, and was hailed as significant of a broadening of religious thought. Dr. Robertson Nicoll, in the discriminating and sympathetic appreciation which he gave in *The British Weekly* of Dr. Matheson after the latter's death, referring to this course of lectures, remarks: "The first time we saw Dr. Matheson must have been somewhere about 1881. He was delivering the second of the Baird Lectures on a Sunday evening in St. George's, Edinburgh. The great building was but scantily filled, but the address, alike in matter, in form, and in utterance, was worthy of any audience. It seemed," he continues,

as if we had in Dr. Matheson the coming prophet of the time. His face was turned with eager welcome towards the new light, and his strong brain was busy in the work of reconstruction and reconciliation. When the lecture was over we went to the Synod Hall and heard the latter part of an oration by Principal Cairns. This was a grand defence of the old apologetical positions, delivered with overwhelming passion and uncompromising in its orthodoxy. That evening was indeed spent well and nobly. We had heard the fittest representatives of the old school and of the new.

The late Professor Bruce, in an able review of Dr. Matheson's book in *The British and Foreign Evangelical Review*, was impressed much in the same way as Dr. Nicoll. He says: "With this publication the Baird Lectureship passes into a new phase. The book before us, while distinctly and

decidedly evangelic, is modern, liberal, and original.
It may not be the ablest of the Baird series,—that
honour probably belongs to Dr. Flint's two series
of lectures on Theism and Antitheism,—but it is
certainly the most genial. Dr. Matheson has
poetry and genius in him, and it comes out in all he
writes, and very markedly in this work on the
Natural Elements of Revealed Theology, in which
there is hardly a dull or a prosaic sentence," and he
concludes as follows :

The book is an earnest and eloquent endeavour to
utilise the results of the science of comparative religion
for the defence and commendation of Christianity as a
revealed religion. Specially worthy of note is the mode
in which the doctrine of Atonement is handled, the theory
advocated being what may be called the organic, in which
the idea of Headship plays a prominent part. Again, we
heartily commend this work to the attention of all interested in such questions, and especially to those who hail
the appearance in the field of apologetics of a theologian
of Dr. Matheson's type—orthodox, yet catholic in sympathy; a sincere believer in the revelation of grace, yet
broad and genial in tendency.

Reviews of the book appeared in many of the
leading journals, and while for the most part discriminating in their criticism, they were all, without
exception, hearty in their appreciation, and regarded
the author's position as thoroughly established, and
of the first rank.

CHAPTER VII

DEVOTION AND POETRY

It was about this time that Dr. Matheson began to publish the long series of devotional books upon which, in the opinion of some, his fame will rest. He began at an early period of his ministry, as already pointed out, to substitute for the reading of the Scripture Lesson a meditation on some text or short passage of Holy Writ. He went through in this way, for instance, the whole of the Book of Psalms, and his thoughts, carefully conceived and written out, are contained in a manuscript volume. The majority of his hearers were greatly struck by these meditations. They preferred them to the ordinary reading of the Word, and they proved more helpful to some than the sermon which followed. As far back as 1872 he was urged, as we have seen, by Dr. Sime, who only expressed the desire of others, to publish a selection of these meditations in book-form. It was not, however, till ten years afterwards, in 1882, that he acceded to this request, and gave to the world the first of his devotional books, *My Aspirations.* It was published by Cassell and Company, as one of their "Heart Chords Series." Its popularity was instantaneous. It has been frequently published since, the last edition coming out a few months after his death. It is not, I think, indulging in any exaggeration to say that no modern book of devotion has had so wide a circulation or has been more deeply prized. Soon after its publication it was translated into German, and it has formed the faithful companion of devout souls in many lands. A writer in *The Examiner* of November 10, 1904, in a review of the author's book, *Leaves for Quiet Hours*, remarks that on one occasion "he stayed at the house of a busy literary man, through whose study there was constantly streaming a flood of current literature for review. He was attracted by the deeply spiritual view-point of his host, and wondered how this attitude of mind was maintained in the critical atmosphere of such a life. A hint of an explanation was accorded, when the professional reviewer asked, 'Do you know George Matheson?' and when he brought a shabby little book from his bedroom (was it *My Aspirations*?) and added, 'I read this every day.'"

The cordial reception given to this booklet encouraged him to repeat, and with even greater success, his venture in *Moments on the Mount*, which appeared in 1884. This was followed by *Voices of the Spirit* in 1888, *Searchings in the Silence* in 1895, *Words by the Wayside*, also translated into German, in 1896, *Times of Re-*

tirement in 1901, *Leaves for Quiet Hours* in 1904, and *Rests by the River*, the last book published by him, in 1906, a few months before his death. This list would make a good record for any ordinary man, but with Matheson these books were the production of his leisure hours, of those moments when he snatched himself from the strenuous labour of congregational work or sustained literary effort, and gave up his spirit to meditation on God, man, and immortality. They were in very truth the fruit of his times of retirement. In them he breathed forth his aspirations, they were leaves plucked in the byways of life to be fondly gazed at in quiet hours. In them he soared on the wings of the spirit, and they tell us what he saw when he stood on the Mount. In them more than in any other of his writings will the reader find the real George Matheson, the seer who saw because he had felt, and who quickened the emotions of his fellows because he had thought deeply on human life and destiny.

Matheson must have known in publishing these volumes that he was entering on a field which had been in unbroken possession of some of the greatest names in Christian literature, and that he would be put into competition with the half-dozen authors whose devotional works had for generations been regarded as classics. It is indeed by the highest standard that he must be judged, and if the opinion of his contemporaries be of any value, he will rank for all time coming as one of the

select band of devotional writers whose names the
world will not readily let die. Matheson's great
popularity may in the opinion of some be largely
owing to the fact that he possesses the note of
modernity, that his writings appeal to the day
and the hour in a way that cannot be expected
of meditations written centuries ago. But the
human heart, with all its hopes and fears, has
remained the same, and a book that has the true
ring of devotion in it is as permanent as the spirit
of man to which it appeals, and will comfort and
inspire in every age and under every clime.
True genius bridges the gulf of time; it destroys
space; and this note of survival marks, in the
opinion of many, the devotional writings of Dr.
Matheson.

Matheson in writing his meditations contented
himself with being an interpreter of the devotional
writings of the Jewish people. In other words, he
invariably took his suggestions from some passage
of Holy Writ. He did not pretend to create a
new religious literature; he did not presume to be
independent of the source of all inspiration; he
contented himself with expounding and applying
to the heart of the modern world the thoughts
which found expression at the hands of the various
writers of the Bible. In this we see a true instinct.
Granted the gift of spiritual insight, deep personal
experience, a knowledge of human life, and literary
expression, a man so guided could not fail to be an
interpreter of the devout life. Matheson possessed

all these qualities in a supreme degree, and his books could not fail to win the popularity which they so quickly achieved. Having put himself in communion with the Spirit of truth, he was able to put himself in touch with the heart of humanity. Matheson was saturated with that book of devotion which is the pattern and precursor of that mass of literature, embodying the experience of the spiritual life, which has grown up during Christian centuries. I mean the Psalms. "They," as Dean Church remarks, "are the records of the purest and loftiest joy of which the human soul is capable, its joy in God; are also the records of its dreariest and bitterest anguish, of the days when all seems dark between itself and God, of its doubts, of its despair. Their music ranges from the richest notes of triumphant rapture to the saddest minor key." Like the Psalms, Matheson's devotional writings "vary widely in their scale and tone. They reflect the many sides, the countless moods, of the soul in its passage through time, confronted with eternity and its overpowering possibilities. They tell of quietness and confidence, of strength and victory and peace. They tell, too, of the storm, of the struggle, of the dividing asunder of soul and spirit; of perplexities which can be relieved only by the certainties of death; of hope wrestling, indeed undismayed, unwavering, but wrestling in the dark, and when beheld for the last time on this side the grave still obstinate, but still unsolaced. Christian life may be upon the heights and in the sunlight;

the lines fall to it in pleasant places, and 'the voices of joy and gladness are in its dwellings.' But its lot may be also 'in the deeps,' where 'all God's waves and storms have gone over it'; where the voices are those of 'deep calling unto deep amid the roar of the water-spouts,' voices of anxiety and distress, of 'majestic pains,' of mysterious sorrow."

Matheson had formed a definite conception of devotional writing as a whole. He was familiar with Augustine's *Manual,* and its wonderful spiritual intensity; with the lyrical outpourings of the immortal *Imitation,* with the beautiful mysticism of Francis of Sales, with holy George Herbert, with plain-spoken and melancholy Jeremy Taylor, and with the saintly Keble. It cannot be said that his meditations bear any deep trace of their influence. The man who, in one sense at least, impressed him most was Pascal. At all events he was at one with the writer of the famous *Pensées* in believing that "devotion to be kept pure needs ideas as well as feelings." This is the point that he touches on in the Prefaces to three of his devotional volumes. In his *Times of Retirement* he refers thus to the subject :

It is often said that devotion is a thing of the heart. I do not think it is either merely or mainly so. I hold that all devotion is based upon intellectual conviction. Even your sense of natural beauty is so based. Whence comes that joy with which you gaze on a bit of landscape you call a "picture-scene"? Precisely from your intellectual conviction that it is *not* a picture; if you believed it to be a painting your emotion would die altogether. A man may have *faith* in what he does not understand, but he cannot have *emotion* in what he does not understand. The heart must have a theory for its own music. Therefore the devotional writer must have a message as much as the expositor. Devotion must be the child of reflection; it may rise on wings, but they must be the wings of thought. The meditations of this little book will appeal to the instinct of prayer just in proportion as they appeal to the teaching of experience; therefore before all things I have endeavoured to base the feeling of the heart on the conclusions of the mind.

In his next devotional volume, *Leaves for Quiet Hours*, he reverts to the same subject. It would seem as if he were anxious to guard his readers against the two dangers to which devotion is exposed. "The danger of becoming formal and uninterested, a sleepy routine; and the danger of becoming artificial, fanciful, petty, of wasting itself in the unchastened flow of feelings and words; of sinking into effeminacies and subtleties and delicate affectations of sentiment and language." So he remarks:

Each devotional piece consists of two parts. The first is a suggestion of a thought, the second is the expression of a feeling—either in the form of a prayer or of an invocation. But I hope that these two parts will never be divided in holy wedlock — that every fresh thought will be tinged with the heart's emotion, and that every emotion of the heart will be winged by the inspiration of a thought. A devotional book is believed to be a very simple thing. It ought to be the most difficult composition in the world, for it should aim at the marriage of qualities which are commonly supposed to be antagonistic—the insight of the thinker and the fervour of the worshipper. My own conviction has increasingly been that the hours of our deepest devotion are precisely in those moments when we catch fresh glimpses of hidden things.

In the last Preface which he ever wrote, the one to *Rests by the River*, he harps upon the same thing. He says these meditations are

intended for devotional moments, but by devotional moments I do not mean moments of vacuity. It is not in its season of intellectual barrenness that the soul yields its spiritual fruit. Religious sentiment if it is worth anything must be preceded by religious perception. Accordingly I have divided these pieces into two parts, —the first containing a thought and the second either an invocation or a prayer. The appeals are to various moods of mind; if some of them should find their way into hearts that have been unconsciously waiting for their message, the aim of this book will have been abundantly achieved.

In an interesting interview, which he gave about two years before his death, he discusses at length the subject of devotional literature. "There is an idea abroad," he said,

that devotional literature is altogether on a wrong basis. Well, while there is much to be remedied, I must say that I consider that is going rather too far. I think that literature of this kind is, as a rule, characterised by great honesty of purpose and thought. But we want more than that nowadays. It appears to me to be wanting in originality of thought and treatment; indeed, I know certain good people who consider that the less originality it possesses the more it is adapted for devotional purposes, but my view is the very opposite. Devotion requires stimulation, exactly as it does any other human attribute;

the soul must be taught to think just as much as the mind
is taught to think.   I believe that our moments of devotion are just those when we have great ideas.   Well, are
those ideas not to be fed and encouraged?   It is on the
wings of the intellect that the heart rises.   Now it is on
that basis that I have endeavoured to write all my
devotional books.   My remedy for the weakness of which
we have been speaking would be to write books of a
different nature; to write *Thomas à Kempis* on the side,
not of asceticism, but of the appropriateness of the world.
I hold the deepest self-surrender, the noblest sacrifice to
God, lies mainly in going into the world, not in running
away from it.   It is there that your devotion displays
itself at its highest and best.

As a devotional writer Dr. Matheson has many
rare characteristics.   One cannot take up the
smallest of his volumes without being struck by its
wide range of subjects.   He sounded the heights
and depths, the lengths and breadths of man's
spiritual experience.   The variety of his themes
secured him a multitude of readers.   The most
indifferent cannot turn the leaves of any of his
books of devotion without lighting upon one
meditation, at least, which appeals to his heart.
His moods, too, are as varied as his themes.   A
page that you would pass by to-day will rivet your
attention to-morrow.   Another striking feature is
his catholicity.   It would be impossible to tell the
Church to which he belonged, or the school of
thought which he favoured.   He struck a note
which found a response in the hearts of men whatever might be their creed.   His universality, too, is
a marked quality.   He appeals to the few and to

the many, to the inner and the outer circle of discipleship, to the learned and to the unlearned, to the king and to the peasant.

His devotional writings are characterised by certain qualities which single them out from the general mass of contemporary literature of the same class, and give them a foremost place among all the books of devotion which have been the offspring of Christian thought and experience. They are marked by profound thought. Matheson could not write a line unless his intellect were satisfied. He was not one of those who believed in dividing human nature into so many compartments, of which mind was one and soul another. Man, in all his complexity, he believed to be of a piece; and for him to have written what some might regard as religious, because it was void of thought, was impossible. His thought, besides, is always original. He could not help being original, and, as he remarks, "devotion requires stimulation." It is perhaps in his possession of this quality, more than in any other, that his excellence chiefly consists. Each meditation is based on a text of Scripture. How many have gazed at this same text without ever having received from it any inspiration or consolation. In Matheson's hands it shines with a new face, speaks with a divine voice, and utters the very word that the soul needed.

Dr. Matheson is not a writer for the sickroom merely; he steadily keeps in view those whose

duty lies in the "dusty lane and wrangling mart."
He has a special message for the man of the world.
Religion in common life is the ideal he ever kept
before him. He was thus a practical mystic, and
in this is to be found the secret of his success and
the power of his teaching. The last of the qualities
which characterise his devotional writings is his
rare gift of style. There is a charm about it, a
music in it, which appeals at once to the artistic
and spiritual senses. The beauty of form may be
but the natural expression of the beauty of thought,
but it is the crown, and would of itself give his
meditations a high place in devotional literature.
Let me select two examples, one from his earliest
and another from his all but latest book of devo-
tions, in which these qualities are illustrated. In
My Aspirations there is a meditation on "Christian
Liberty." It is suggested by the text John x. 9:
"I am the door: by Me if any man enter in, he
shall be saved, and shall go in and out, and find
pasture."

To go in and out of a house at will is the mark of
perfect liberty. It is the mark, not of a servant nor even
of a guest, but of a son; he who at will goes out and in is
conscious that he is a member of the family. Our Lord
says that the saved man is the free man—the man who
goes in and out at the door. I had always thought it to
be the contrary. I had come to persuade myself that to
be saved was to be narrow, to be curtailed in the path of
freedom. I never doubted that the saved man went *in* at
the door; it seemed to me that to be in the temple of God
was to be about his Father's business. But that this man
of all men should have a right to come out again at the

same door by which he entered; should have a right to go back into the pursuits of that world from which he came; this was a thought which it did not enter into my heart to conceive. Yet this, and nothing less than this, is the teaching of our Lord. He says that the saved man had alone the right to be called the man of the world, alone the right to come out into the secular pleasures of men. He says that such a man will not only get no harm from the world; he will get positive good from it, "he will find pasture." He will get from the things around him what he has brought to those things—a pure heart. He will see God in everything, because he has seen Him in his own soul. He will find good in everything, because he himself is good. He will recognise in the world green pastures where the world itself recognises only a desert. He will hear the song of birds where the natural ear catches only the silence of the wilderness; he will behold the myrtle where the eye of sense gazes only on the briar.

My soul, art thou afraid of the Son of Man? Art thou afraid to enter in at the heavenly door? Art thou afraid that in becoming a Christian thoushalt lose thy power to act as a citizen? *Thou shalt for the first time gain that power!* Christ shall intensify thy natural gifts; the rest *He* gives is the ability to do better that earthly work which has been given thee to do. Dost thou fear that the pleasures of God's right hand will blunt thee to the joys of human affection? They will quicken them. God's love helps all other love as surely as the vision of the sun helps all other vision. God's love is something to love with, just as the sun's light is something to see with; it teaches the loveless how to love. He who has been in at the Door is distinguished not only among angels but amongst *men*. He is marked out by the intensity of his human nature. Thou shalt know him from other men by his superior zeal in all earthly causes. He shall hope more for the world, he shall work more for the world, he shall suffer more for the world; for it is in the world that he seeks for the pasture which has been provided by the Shepherd-King. He that enters by this Door goes in and out at will!

12

The second example is from his *Leaves for Quiet Hours*. It is on " In the Light of Eternity." There is a personal note in it which is not without its pathos; it is at the same time a triumphant note. This son of affliction has a word of cheer, not only for the man of the world, but also for the child of sorrow. The meditation is suggested by two passages, the one from Psalm xxxvi. 9 : " In thy light shall we see light"; and the other from Revelation xxi. 23 : "The Lamb is the light thereof."

Nothing is seen in its own light—not even a visible thing. A landscape is not seen in its own light; it is perceived very much in the light of yesterday. How little of what you see is mere perception ! Every sight of nature is tinged with the light of memory. The poet looks from the bridge at midnight upon the rushing waters; but what he sees is not the flowing tide, it is a tide of *memory* which fills his eyes with tears. You listen to the babbling of the brook; but what you hear is not the babbling, it is the utterance of a dear name. You visit Rome, you visit Jerusalem, you visit Greece ; do you see any of these by its own light? No; they are all beheld by the light of yesterday; *there* is their glory, there lies their gold ! " Even so," cries the Psalmist, "it is with this world; if you want *to* see it, you must look at it by the light of another world—God's *coming* world. He does not mean that when we quit the scenes of earth we shall have a bright light in heaven. It is more than that. It is for the scenes of earth he wants the heavenly light. He says you cannot interpret your own skies without it. We often say that in the light of eternity earthly objects will fade from our sight. But the Psalmist says that until we get the light of eternity earthly objects will not be *in* our sight. It is by the light of the Celestial City—the City which has no need of the sun—that alone we can tell what here is large and what here is small.

Thou Lamb, slain from the foundation of the world, Thou art the Light thereof! When God said, "Let us make man!" He meant not Adam, but Thee. Thou art the plan of the great building; to Thee all things move. By no other light can I understand the struggles of this earth. Not by nature's light can I understand them; I have seen the physical sunshine sparkle on my pain, and I thought it a cruel thing. Not by philosophy's light can I understand them; I have seen the great thinker impeded by poverty and I thought it an unseemly thing. Not in beauty's light can I understand them; I have seen the artist lose his eyesight and I thought it an unrighteous thing. But if the world is being woven for *Thee*, I understand. If Thy type of sacrifice is the plan of the Architect, I understand. If Thy cross is Creation's crown, I understand. If the Celestial City is a home for hospital training, I understand. If Thine angels are all ministering spirits, I understand. If the purest robe is not the white robe but the robe *washed* white, if the goal of man is not Eden but Gethsemane, if the glory of Thy Father is the sacrificial blood of love, then have I found the golden key, in Thy Light I have seen Light!

As might be expected, Dr. Matheson received from almost every part of the world letters of the deepest gratitude for the comfort which his meditations afforded to weary and despondent souls. It may be sufficient to give one letter as an example of the many that he received expressing the gratitude of those who found in his books the consolation that their souls needed. The letter is from a clergyman in Belfast, and is dated 14th October 1904:

I have just got your *Leaves for Quiet Hours*. I feel that I ought to put on paper what has been in my mind and heart since I first began to read your helpful messages.

Ten years ago, when a probationary minister in our

Nottingham circuit, I visited a poor woman, who for thirteen years had been afflicted with a lingering form of cancer which had affected her head. Night and day she was in pain. She told me she could not remember much nor think out anything, but said she, "I have a little book and it does help me." It was a well-worn copy of *My Aspirations*. "Which was the one she liked best," I asked? "Ah!" said she, and I shall never forget her bright look, although her head was as though there were coals of fire upon it, "And God saw everything that He had made, and behold it was very good." In fragments she almost gave me the whole of it. Said she, "My Sabbath is coming; it seems as though sometimes I hear the morning bells." I remember, not long before she passed away, I called late one night, and I found her suffering acutely. Her devoted daughter had dressed her terrible wounds—a task from which the trained visiting nurses would turn away, almost overpowered. I noticed the laudanum bottle almost empty, and then it flashed upon me, in spite of their comfortable home, they were feeling the pinch of poverty. The daughter, with tears in her eyes, told me that laudanum cost so much. When someone went out to get what alone could allay the burning pain, I saw in the hand of the sufferer, as she lay apparently asleep, the little book, *My Aspirations*. She once said the doctor wondered how she could bear the burning of her wound with so little outward relief, but, added the frail woman, "I know." I have often wished to tell you what service your book was to that poor afflicted woman. It was through her I was introduced to your unspoken ministry, and I venture to take this opportunity of respectfully expressing my great indebtedness to you for your inspiring and sustaining writings.

I have sometimes thought that if a few of your valued meditations were printed on little slips, or cards, with a view to their circulation in hospitals and amongst the sick at home, I believe your messages would be words in season for the weary and more than welcome to the afflicted. I have put *My Aspirations* in more than one chamber of sorrow. It has brought heaven a little nearer and their lives have been blessed, while others have been helped to quietly wait until they entered into rest.

The year that saw the publication of his first volume of *Meditations* also witnessed the composition of his famous hymn, "O Love that wilt not let me go." The circumstances under which it was written are well-known. He himself has furnished the following interesting account of its genesis: "My hymn was composed in the manse of Innellan on the evening of 6th June 1882. I was at that time alone. It was the day of my sister's marriage, and the rest of the family were staying over night in Glasgow. Something had happened to me, which was known only to myself, and which caused me the most severe mental suffering. The hymn was the fruit of that suffering. It was the quickest bit of work I ever did in my life. I had the impression rather of having it dictated to me by some inward voice than of working it out myself. I am quite sure that the whole work was completed in five minutes, and equally sure that it never received at my hands any retouching or correction. The Hymnal Committee of the Church of Scotland desired the change of one word. I had written originally 'I climbed the rainbow in the rain.' They objected to the word 'climb' and I put 'trace.'"

Matheson at the time at which this hymn was written was no novice in the art of poetical composition. This form of literary expression was, as we have seen, the earliest practised by him. He wrote, when quite a youth, long poems, but, apart from the two referred to in a previous chapter, nearly all his writings in this form were on sacred subjects. He had the lyrical note strongly developed in his nature. Much of his writing, particularly his meditations, was couched in a poetic strain ; he delighted in song and music, and his soul demanded at times to utter itself in verse. There still remains a very considerable collection of unpublished poems by him, all in the strain with which readers of his *Sacred Songs* are familiar. They were written at different periods, and were collected at intervals into forms that suggest the intention of publication, but he delayed this purpose until 1889, when, after a final revision, he gave a selection of them to the world.

In a scrap-book, carefully preserved, it is interesting to find a number of sacred songs by him, cut out from some magazine or periodical in which they first appeared. They are framed in coloured flowers, and evidently show the tender guardianship of his sister's hand. There is no guide as to the journals in which they were published, but so early as 1875 one of his best-known hymns, " My voice shalt Thou hear in the morning," appeared in the *Sunday Magazine*. This he thought worthy of reproduction in his volume of *Sacred Songs*. Again, in 1878, under the heading of " God with us," there appeared in the same magazine the hymn which he afterwards published under the title of "Jacob at Bethel." Two more hymns, "Strength for the Day" and "Jesus, Fountain of my Days," also found a place in the *Sunday Magazine*; the former with the heading, "Times of Need," in 1881; and the latter with the title, "Above every Name," in 1884. Other poems by him were sent, as the occasion arose, to various magazines, which gave them a ready welcome.

Matheson never took himself very seriously as a hymn-writer, but the public has largely reversed his judgment, for his volume of *Sacred Songs* ran within a few years into a third edition. In his Preface to the issue which appeared in 1904, he says: "I was originally much exercised as to what title I ought to give these verses collectively. The difficulty arose from the desire to avoid pretentiousness, by seeming to claim for them more than they aspired to be. I decided that, in point of form, their distinctive feature was a varied rhythmicalness, and therefore I called them *Sacred Songs*. The subject-matter was suggested by Scriptural texts, but there was no attempt to classify or systematise: I simply followed the impression of the moment and endeavoured to express the sentiment in its appropriate cadence. These pieces were never intended as a volume of hymns; but, contrary to my expectations, many of them have been so adapted."

It is but right in estimating Matheson's poetic

effusions to keep what he thus says clearly in mind.
There are few kinds of composition about which
there has been so much controversy as hymns.
The lines on which lyric, epic, and dramatic poetry
are composed are well marked, and generally recognised and followed; but some of the most popular
hymns, according to experts, violate every canon,
and captivate the heart in spite of their rebellion
against the laws which ought to govern them.
Matheson accordingly was perfectly justified in
guarding himself against the criticism that might
be brought to bear upon his productions in verse.
He declared that they were Sacred Songs, and not
Hymns. Looking at them in this light, one is
impressed, not only by their variety of rhythmicalness, but also of theme. Like his *Meditations*, they
touch religious thought and experience at almost
every point, and open windows of feeling and
emotion through which divine light and comfort
pour in. The themes may be varied, but they
have one subject: the Divine Love. "And now
abideth Faith, Hope, Charity, these three, but
the greatest of these is Charity," might be taken
as their motto; and right through them there
breathes that spirit of Christian optimism which
characterised his preaching, his writing, and his
life. The darkest day does not dismay him; the
sorest disappointment does not crush him; the
bitterest anguish or the cruellest pain does not
daunt him; the waves and the billows of life
may pass over his soul without quenching its

ardour or drowning its hope. The Divine Love he sees in all; the Cross of Christ assures him of victory.

Matheson had very clear notions of what a hymn should be. At all events, he subjected to sharp criticism modern hymnology in one respect at least, its lack of human sentiment. Being asked on one occasion what he thought of our hymns generally, he shook his head strongly as he replied :

To my mind they have one great defect; they lack humanitarianism. There is any amount of doctrine in the Trinity, Baptism, Atonement, or the Christian life as such, but what of the secular life—the infirmary, the hospital, the home of refuge? When I was asked to preach a charity sermon some time ago, I searched through the hymnal in vain for any hymn that would suit my subject, but there was no incentive to charity as such. I don't think our hymns will ever be what they ought to be, until we get them inspired by a sense of the enthusiasm of, and for, humanity. It is rather a theological point, perhaps, but the hymnists speak of the surrender to Christ. They forget that Christ is not simply an individual. He is Head of a body, the body of humanity; and it no longer expresses the idea correctly to join yourself to Christ only, you must give yourself to the whole brotherhood of man to fulfil the idea. I like "Lead, kindly Light"; it is universal, though not practical, perhaps; it is vague, and applies to any religion. Another good hymn is "Trust in God and do the Right," written by Dr. Norman Macleod, a good and practical hymn. "We give Thee but Thine Own" sounds the real humanitarian note to the fatherless and widows. Hymnology is feeble and ineffective when it ignores the humanitarian side of religion.

There is a strong note of modernity in this criticism. Matheson lived in the age of practical

Christianity, and he appreciated its significance
to the full.   It may be true that he was a mystic.
He was constantly brooding upon divine things;
his spirit was frequently in other lands than this.
He was convinced that the ideal is the real, and
that the life which is perceptible to the eye of
faith encircled all life, that it was the beginning
and the end, the Alpha and the Omega, of human
experience.   Such a belief, however, did not trans-
form him into a mere dreamer of dreams.   He felt
it to be his vocation to interpret man's varied
life in the light of the divine, and to see the law
which is behind all facts revealing itself in human
vicissitudes.   It was this that made his preaching
so inspiring to the vast majority of his hearers,
and caused his *Meditations* to be welcomed, as
glad tidings, all over the world.   It is this also
which will preserve his *Sacred Songs* from
falling readily into oblivion; they will continue
to have a message for the day and the hour;
their humanitarian note will preserve them from
growing out of date, as writings which have no
relation to man's troubles, man's needs, and man's
aspirations.

The criticisms on his volume, *Sacred Songs*,
refer with a unanimity which must have good
ground, in fact, to a feature which is common
indeed to nearly the whole of Matheson's writings.
They emphasise the note of catholicity that
pervades the book.   But Matheson's catholicity
did not arise from indifference.   He did not

simply assume a theological standpoint of his
own and quietly ignore all others. It was his
aim to stand on a platform so broad that he
could find room on it for every one, whether
Pagan or Christian, who was struggling towards
the light. In such a position is to be found
the true spirit of reconciliation, which sees the
unifying element in each, seizes it and links all
together in a bond which they interpret, and
which at the same time interprets them. They
find their meaning in it, and it finds its meaning
in them. Such a method does not lop off what
may seem incongruous, or irreconcilable, in the
different forms of faith which it unifies. If it did,
it would be a destructive, and not a constructive,
method. It, on the contrary, gathers them together
as they are ; and the central truth of each, being at
bottom an eternal truth, linked to Him who is the
Truth, of its own accord sheds what is defective,
and receives new strength and life from Him to
whom it is joined. In a poem of sterling excellence
Matheson clothes his teaching on this subject in a
form which is certain to live. He entitles it "One
in Christ," and bases it on Ephesians i. 10: "That
in the dispensation of the fulness of times He might
gather together in one all things in Christ."

 1 Gather us in, Thou Love that fillest all !
   Gather our rival faiths within Thy fold !
   Rend each man's temple veil and bid it fall,
     That we may know that Thou hast been of old ;
       Gather us in !

2 Gather us in! we worship only Thee;
   In varied names we stretch a common hand;
In diverse forms a common soul we see;
   In many ships we seek one spirit-land;
      Gather us in!

3 Each sees one colour of Thy rainbow light,
   Each looks upon one tint and calls it heaven;
Thou art the fulness of our partial sight;
   We are not perfect till we find the seven;
      Gather us in!

4 Thine is the mystic light great India craves,
   Thine is the Parsee's sin-destroying beam,
Thine is the Buddhist's rest from tossing waves,
   Thine is the empire of vast China's dream;
      Gather us in!

5 Thine is the Roman's strength without his pride,
   Thine is the Greek's glad world without its graves,
Thine is Judea's law with love beside,
   The truth that centres and the grace that saves;
      Gather us in!

6 Some seek a Father in the heavens above,
   Some ask a human image to adore,
Some crave a spirit vast as life and love:
   Within Thy mansions we have all and more;
      Gather us in!

In the third edition of his *Sacred Songs* he included his hymn "O Love that wilt not let me go," which first appeared in *Life and Work.* Whatever may be the future of his other writings, this hymn, we may confidently hope, will be sung by congregations of the Christian Church so long as the Cross and the Divine love of which it is the symbol will continue to lift up the head of

fallen humanity. He himself always regarded
this hymn as his *pièce de résistance.* He in a
way took no credit for it; it was given to him
in a moment of divine afflatus, and he simply
transcribed what was communicated. This is the
orthodox view of inspiration, and so far it may be
sound enough; but it should not be forgotten that
poets are cradled into poetry by wrong, and learn
in suffering what they teach in song. In other
words, like the prophets of old their moments of
inspiration are preceded by years of earnest
thought and spiritual communion. The subjects
on which they have long brooded may, in the
twinkling of an eye, and without conscious effort
on their part, be seen in a new light; the mystery
is unveiled by an unseen hand, and the soul gazes
upon the land delectable. One should not, accordingly, be surprised to find critics of this hymn
pointing to the fact that Matheson had in previous
publications expressed its thoughts almost in
similar words. They quote passages from his
Meditations in which the very phrases of the hymn
are anticipated. But I can do more : there is in
manuscript a poem by him on the rainbow, of
which the first line is " Jesus, Rainbow of my
Sorrow." Here we have a forecast of the line so
much admired, " I trace the rainbow through the
rain." Indeed, such anticipations, in place of
detracting from ought to enhance the value of this
hymn, for in it we see the fugitive, the scattered
experiences, the chance phrases of the poet gathered

together, and under the pressure of a deep spiritual experience fused by his genius into a perfect whole.

Dr. Matheson always modestly insisted that his hymn was greatly indebted to the music written for it by Dr. Peace; indeed, there may be some excuse for those who declare that, but for Dr. Peace's tune, it would not have attained its great popularity. When somebody once complimented Cardinal Newman on the great vogue of his " Lead, kindly Light," he replied, " Ah, yes; but, you see, the tune is by Dr. Dykes." What " Lux Benigna " did for Newman's hymn, " St. Margaret " did for Dr. Matheson's. The latter tune was composed with as little deliberation as Dr. Matheson wrote the hymn. As . musical editor of the *Scottish Hymnal*, which at the time was passing through the hands of the Committee of the Church of Scotland, Dr. Peace was in the habit of always carrying in his pocket a copy of the words for careful study. Sitting one day on the sands at Arran, he was reading " O Love that wilt not let me go " when the tune came upon him like a flash, and, taking out his pencil, he dashed it off in a few minutes.

Dr. Matheson was in the habit of receiving constant communications regarding his hymn. The most frequent of these was asking his liberty to use it for one church or congregational book of praise or another. But he also received letters from different parts of the country, and indeed of the world, expressing the gratitude of some soul

to whom its teaching and its music had proved a
source of unfading comfort. Of such a character
is the following :—

OAKFIELD, GLASLYN ROAD,
CROUCH END, LONDON, N.
February 26, 1904.

MY DEAR SIR,—You have before very kindly permitted
me to use some of your hymns and poems, and I am
again coming to you as a beggar. It happens that I
have just completed a new *Hymnal for Boys*, to be used
in Public Schools, Boys' Brigades, Clubs, etc., and Young
Men's Meetings. I have also just completed arrangements
for a revised edition of the *Christian Endeavour Hymnal*,
and in both of these books desire to include " O Love that
wilt not let me go." I trust that you will be able to
accord me the desired permission, and presume that for
the tune I must apply to Dr. Peace.

It will interest you if I refer to an incident that has
touched me greatly within the last few days. In the
church where I was pastor in Southampton there was a
young girl, a very beautiful character, the daughter of an
artist. She was stricken with a terrible illness, and
suffered intensely, but recovered in a wonderful manner,
remaining apparently well for a year. Then, suddenly,
the old disease reasserted itself, and she again passed
through a fiery furnace of pain. The fires were those of
purifying, for a wonderful change was wrought in her
character and in her very face. Your hymn was learnt
in our choir, of which she was a member, and from the
first it became a ministrant influence in her life, and
became for her the expression of deepest desire. She
was a girl exceptionally gifted, and clung to the very
last to the hope that she might continue her studies ; and
when the doctor told her that she must give these up,
after a long struggle she found the haven of trust and
rest through the hymn, and relinquished her ambition,
resting in the Divine love. When the end came, and
when her own voice had gone, the mother saw that she
wished to speak—and, bending over her, heard her whisper,
" Mother, sing me ' O Love that wilt not let me go ' " ; and

the music of this song ushered her into the presence of the Father. She was laid to rest a few days ago, and her comrades of the choir gathered round the grave and again sung the hymn.

How great a privilege and joy are yours in this marvellous ministry?—Believe me, most truly yours,

CAREY BONNER.

The world-wide reputation of the hymn receives emphatic proof from the following communication. It relates· to the Sunday-School Convention held at Jerusalem in the spring of 1904, when the representatives of fifty - five different Christian communions, gathered from twenty-six different nations of the world, united together to the number of 1800 in singing Matheson's famous hymn on the brows of Calvary :

GLASGOW,
Sunday Evening, February 18, 1906.

DEAR DR. MATHESON,—I have just been reading in the last issue of *Saint Andrew* an interesting paper on your noble hymn "O Love that wilt not let me go." It brought back to memory an incident connected with your hymn, of which I wish to tell you.

I was one of the pilgrim band in the Fourth World's S.S. Convention which assembled in Jerusalem in the spring-time of 1904. It was possibly the most cosmopolitan assembly that ever met in the name of Christ. Convened in the interests of the Sabbath-school cause, it seemed to realise a strange fulfilment of the promise, "A little child shall lead them." Representatives from the ends of the earth were present. It would be difficult to name a country that was *not* represented. Fifty-five different sects or faiths were there, gathered from twenty-six different nations. Our meeting-place was a huge tent seated for 1800, pitched on Calvary—close by Gordon's Calvary. On the Sunday morning of our mission the vast tent was crowded with worshippers. Archdeacon Sinclair, of

London, preached a noble sermon from Matthew xxi. 15, 16. The closing hymn was your own noble song, " O Love——" I have joined in the singing of it times without number, but never did I hear it sung with such fervour. In that strange assembly of divers nations nearly all seemed to know it and to love it, and a mighty flood of melody swept through the vast tent, as if all hearts knew only one common brotherhood in Christ. I was so deeply moved that ere the last verse came round I could only read in a convulsive sob.

Two thoughts gave birth to this emotion.

Here, in distant Syria, was I, a Glasgow man, sharing in this song from the pen of a fellow-citizen, and the melody also written by one closely associated with the Service of Praise in the Cathedral of Glasgow. I thought of the " ocean depths" of that wondrous Love that is fashioning one great family of all the nations on the face of the earth.

The other thought was, that we were standing, possibly within a few paces of the veritable spot where was planted that Cross that lifted up our heads, the actual ground where was shed the sacrificial blood whence blossoms red life that shall endless be. It was in my mind, when I came back from Palestine, to write telling you this little story; but alas! how often purposes are allowed to slip unfulfilled. The reading of the sketch in *Saint Andrew* revived the memory and rekindled the desire.

Suffer an aged friend and warm admirer of your writings, one who has passed the extreme limit of the life's journey assigned by the Psalmist, to express the earnest hope that God may spare you for many years to continue to enrich the Christian world with your noble, inspiring thought.—Believe me, etc.

J. INGRAM.

The last contribution which I shall give in this connection was sent to me by a missionary in India. It testifies to the overwhelming power of

13

Matheson's hymn when played and sung by a musician of the first rank :

It was in March 1904, and the sunshiny scene still lives in my memory. I had left my hotel and made my way through the picturesque crowds in the streets of A——. The Sabbath was essentially a French one. By force of habit I had turned aside that day from globe-trotting pursuits, and taken my place in the Church of the United Frees among some threescore of God's people, whose mother-tongue was English.

On my right and left were missionaries of the North African Mission. They found it refreshing to assemble for worship, in the midst of their labours among a fanatical Mahomedan people ; they from Africa and I from India. It seemed to me a meeting of the oceans, that we should stand for worship in the same pew, and sing out of the same hymnal. I could not, of course, turn round to see who sat behind, but worshippers in front looked like those who might be residing in this watering-place for purposes of health or trade,—some were certainly, like myself, of the tourist type. Immediately in front of me was the English Consul, a man well over six feet, with shoulders like Sandow's. On his left was his wife—also tall and well built.

The church was not built for show, but for use. By this I do not mean that it was common. There was an aisle on each side, and the seats ran right across the width of the structure. A platform was placed in front, on the side of which the organ stood. The pulpit was at the rear of this platform, and suitably raised for its purpose. Thus minister and organist were in our full view.

The organ was in keeping with the building: a plain instrument of the American type. The organist was a lady.

What the minister preached about I really forget. Perhaps that was not the preacher's fault. He was a pastor there for his health, and displayed no special vigour. I have no objection to a written sermon, but that morning the read sermon seemed, though an able treatise,

to fall flat. The order of service was what I had been
used to in Wellesley Square United Free Church,
Calcutta. To me it was all lifeless, formal, uneventful,
messageless, comfortless. Even the words and music of
the hymns had failed to stir the deeps of my nature that
day. I blame no one. Perhaps I was not in a receptive
spirit. I cannot tell—but so it was. On went the
minutes, and I was not sorry.

The hour had at last fled. Invocations, lessons, prayers,
sermon, collection, announcements were all over. What
had been a most uneventful service to me was now to
be punctuated by a hymn and a benediction. The
minister announced George Matheson's "O Love that wilt
not let me go." When a much loved hymn is announced
in Wales, the land I know best, the people stir with joy,
and cast meaning glances at each other. The worshippers
stand as if to pour out their hearts, and one gets thrilled
before a chord is struck. That morning it was all
contrary. "Listless" could have been written over the
whole service. The announcement of even that hymn
seemed to stir no one.

While the minister was reading the first verse I
noticed a man of, perhaps, fifty change seats with the lady
organist.

It was nothing to mark. "He is the local organist,"
I thought, "and the lady is a visitor." Suddenly the
notes were touched and the little American organ seemed
to have been "born again." Bar followed bar. We all
brightened up. There was a master at the keys. We
stood and sang:

> "O Love that wilt not let me go,
> I rest my weary soul in Thee:
> I give Thee back the life I owe,
> That in Thine ocean depths its flow
> May richer, fuller be."

Was the change in me or in my environment? I
cannot tell. The lost chord seemed to have been found.
If a seraph had come to wake me with a song of Zion,
the surprise would not have been greater. The organist

seemed in the third heaven. Here and there he made pauses not in the book. He sang and played and carried us on irresistibly. Then we plunged into the second verse:

> " O Light that followest all my way,
>   I yield my flickering torch to Thee:
> My heart restores its borrowed ray,
> That in Thy sunshine's blaze its day
>   May brighter, fairer be."

I could not fail to notice the deep emotion of the Consul's wife, for she stood in the next pew in front. She had ceased to sing, her trembling was manifest. The music was like the sound of many waters. The volume of it increased. The third verse was reached:

> " O Joy that seekest me through pain,
>   I cannot close my heart to Thee:
> I trace the rainbow through the rain,
> And feel the promise is not vain,
>   That morn shall tearless be."

With a strange suddenness the Consul's wife fell on her knees and was convulsed with emotion. With her hands she covered her face, while the majestic music swept on. The husband knew not what to do, for all eyes were turned towards his wife. With inborn calmness and strong sympathy he then bowed in prayer at his wife's side. The sight was beautiful, and there were many wet eyes near where I stood. But what of the organist? He was in rhapsody. Down his furrowed face tears made their way. His head of curls added impressiveness to the scene. Bending over the keys, he poured out his very soul. Of time and space he seemed ignorant. The emphasis was that of intense feeling, born of rare experience, controlled by musical ability—both instrumental and vocal.

When we reached the last verse I, for one, wished blind Matheson had provided us with more. And yet we might not have been able to bear it.

"O Cross that liftest up my head,
    I dare not ask to fly from Thee:
I lay in dust life's glory dead,
    And from the ground there blossoms red
        Life that shall endless be."

The scene continued the same to the end, only with deeper feeling. Great was the relief when the last note died away, and the minister, as awed as the rest of us, pronounced the benediction. So great was the solemnity of the occasion that no one wanted to disturb the silence by rising from their knees.

When the congregation did rise to disperse, several went forward to thank the organist. I was one of them. In the group were several Americans, and one said to the organist, still bathed in tear-marks, "We knew your wife." The one answer was a quiet smile, followed by a quick retirement from the church. This man did not feast on plaudits or compliments. He was gone before we could say a tithe of what we felt.

In the aisles and at the church door I learned that the man who had waked up everybody's soul was a distinguished Christian singer of England and Scotland. Two years before his wife lay a-dying—and she was an American, equal to him in musical talent. She had asked him to sing to her, as she entered the valley of the shadow of death, "O Love that wilt not let me go." He did so, but had not ventured to sing it again until that memorable morning. Ah, that was a sufficient explanation. Sorrow had wrought the power.

I wended my way hotel-wards, but my thoughts were on the wings of the music—"blossoming red." *Such* music (that lost chord), set to *such* words, I can never hope to hear again until I stand within the gates of the New Jerusalem.

CHAPTER VIII

LAST YEARS AT INNELLAN

DR. MATHESON'S congregation at Innellan now
felt that it was time they should give some expression to their feelings of admiration for him
as their minister. He had been with them for
fifteen years, and he had endeared himself to them
in many ways. As a preacher and a writer he
had won recognition from a wider public. His
reputation had gained for him academic honours,
and theological experts had cordially accepted his
claims as an author of undoubted ability. The
people of Innellan, who had from the very first
responded to his eloquence in the pulpit and
who had all along appreciated his pastoral care,
resolved to give expression to their gratitude.
By the visitors to the seaside village, and by a
growing circle of readers of his books, one side
of his character and one aspect of his work were
known; but by his parishioners he was also
admired for his interest in them, for his concern and sympathy in cases of moral failure,
of bodily sickness, or of spiritual distress. Dr.

Sime, speaking of his work in this connection, says :

As our professional lives in the place intermingled everywhere, it was not only in the library of the manse that we met, and seldom have I seen a clergyman so near the heart of parishioners, not merely in prosperity and success—that is easy and hardly wanted—but in sorrow and distress, in health and disease, in work and worship. His cheerful, uniformly unclouded optimism was every-where welcomed, alike in joy and unhappiness, in disap-pointment and failure. He was the instigator of the public lectures during winter and the centre of every good movement of the place, and his humour on the platform was as excellent as it was in the library or in private, being of the genuine thistly Celtic character, with much imagination, an imagination appealing to the brain quite as much as the heart. But he could be found manly with all his cheerfulness and unwavering optimism. An intelligent farmer, a favourite of his, who read and studied much beyond agriculture, but who at one time was un-fortunately addicted to occasional fits of bad excess, once, for example, told me, that he was established in his quiet, manly restraint by one or two observations of the blind young clergyman. His failing, the minister said to him, was no doubt due to a hereditary weakness, but there was no use blaming for it one's forebears; that was not manly, it was cowardly. The giving way to the failing was a return to the brute, a still older forebear; all sensuality and selfish appetite and ungovernable greed being a return, a reversion, to the beast in man. The weakness was there, in even a good, noble man, for him to conquer, and to make a good, clever man the best of men. Renunciation, he said, was the essential to the primary condition, for a brave worthy man to show his sterling worth.

Again, to reveal the condition of mind of my friend as he even departed from, not entered, the house of genuine tribulation. On another occasion I remember to have suddenly met him with his private secretary, which I often did, as they were just coming out of the garden of a patient. This patient had been long ill of a mortal disease, and was at that time near death. The resignation of this lady and her saintly suffering had been long noted, and spoken of, by Dr. Matheson. As I passed into the garden walk, my friend, laying his hand on my shoulders, assured me in a word that the serenity of the summer sky was now in the lady's talk, for possibly, he added, there was in her vision the rosy gates of some Paradise.

It was on the last Saturday of August 1883, just before the crowd of summer visitors had begun to leave Innellan, that Dr. Matheson was invited to meet the congregation in the Parish Church, to receive at their hands a token of their esteem and admiration of him personally, and of gratitude for the help his books and sermons had given them.

Mr William Stevenson, Colinwood House, a lifelong friend and admirer of Dr. Matheson, presided, and, in making the presentation, said :

Dr. Matheson has now been fully fifteen years in Innellan, having been ordained on 28th May 1868. Those present know how the church had grown. I remember a few years ago, when their minister was plain Mr. Matheson, saying to him : Well, Mr. Matheson, I'll live to see the day when the people will fill the passages. Dr. Matheson laughed at me, but I leave those present to judge whether or not I was a true prophet. I had taken a leading part in getting the little church endowed and Innellan erected into a parish. That was in 1873. Looking over old books and papers, I find that at that time the ordinary collection was very modest, and when it ascended to the munificent sum of a few shillings we were all surprised, and rejoiced with an exceeding great joy. That was not long ago. Now the ordinary collections average over six

pounds. To what was this due? To what and to whom
but to the work and person of him in whose honour we
have met to-night. I do not need to speak to you of the
good works and words of Dr. Matheson. Dr. Matheson
is known over the length and breadth of the land, and our
Innellan is known and renowned as the place where lives
and works Dr. George Matheson, the Preacher, Theologian,
and Poet.

Dr. Matheson, replying on behalf of his sister,
who was associated with him in the gift, and himself, said :

It is with feelings of deep emotion that I rise this night
to thank you. I have to thank you, Mr. Stevenson, for
that energetic kindness which, after having been one of
my main supports since the inauguration of this parish,
has crowned itself in the initiation of a movement so
friendly and so disinterested ; and I have to thank you,
ladies and gentlemen, for the warm and generous co-
operation with which the movement has been seconded
and sustained. There are times in a man's life in which
he seems to stand on the summit of a Nebo, not to behold
a promised land in the future, but to survey the trodden
country of the past. Such a moment have you brought
to me. You have caused me to hear a rush of old
memories—the spiritual refrain of a ministry of fifteen
years. The costly and munificent gift which this night
you have presented to me is no mere piece of mechanism ;
it is a piece of mechanism with a heart in it—the united
hearts of a congregation. What you have really given me
is yourselves. You have given me your affection, your
sympathy, your interest, your responsive greeting, and I
feel that the labour of life is cheered, and that the work of
life is rewarded, in receiving the communion and fellowship
of so many kindred souls.

To me, in more senses than one, your gift measures
time. It takes me back to the days when I stood amongst
you an untried, inexperienced youth, not perhaps illiterate
as to what is called the lore of universities, but altogether

unread in that noblest of all studies—the book of human
nature. To you, ladies and gentlemen, am I indebted for
this crowning knowledge; it is I, this night, that should
be the donor and you who should be the receivers. It was
in union with your joys and sorrows, it was in sympathy
with your summer and winter hours, that I first learned
that greatest lesson of humanity—the need of man for
man. It was in the dawning of that new interest which
made your cares my responsibilities, that life itself woke
into reality, into solemnity, into joy. Need I say that the
chain you have woven round me is one that can never be
severed. No change of locality could sever it; it no longer
belongs to any locality, it is a fact of the spirit. The
associations of our youth are like Tennyson's brook—Men
may come and men may go, but they keep on for ever.
Youth fades, times change, prophecies fail, forms of knowledge vanish away; but the loves of our early years, the
friendships of our morning's glow, are photographed in our
hearts in beams that cannot die, and keep their fadeless
bloom when suns have set: such a remembrance will I
have of you.

Matheson's intellectual interests began about
this time to take a new direction, or, more correctly
speaking, to flow in a fresh channel. He had for
the time being exhausted all he had to say on the
great questions of speculative theology. He had
discussed religion from the point of view of
philosophy, and he now felt called upon to treat
it in relation to science. In his three important
works up to this date—*Aids to the Study of
German Theology*, *Growth of the Spirit of
Christianity*, and *Natural Elements of Revealed
Theology*—he had endeavoured to expound the
development of religion in its threefold aspects as
a necessary process in the mind of man, in its

visible manifestation in the Christian Church, and as it had revealed itself on the larger plane of universal experience.   The recent trend of scientific thought put a stop for the moment to his buoyant flight, and brought him to the earth by the startling question, What if the religious instinct itself be but a mere dream, and human belief and man's speculation on divine things be but empty shadows? The doctrine of evolution, which had now received a twofold exposition, first by Darwin on its scientific, and secondly by Herbert Spencer on its philosophical side, appeared to hold the field, and to confine man within the bonds of nature, and to control him by inviolable laws.

Matheson, even previous to this date, showed keen interest in scientific pursuits and discoveries. His friend Dr. Sime, who had also a lively interest in such matters, used to discuss them frequently with him.   He says:

He was deeply interested in scientific study. Archæology, anthropology, and prehistoric humanity constituted a very frequent subject of thought and talk. The worship of a mere boulder, or block of stone, so characteristic of savages to this day, was of deep significance to him, and an indication of the intrinsic difference between man and beast. When man came, wonder and worship came. "The prehistoric man," he used to say, "did not bow down to worship the block of stone any more than does the modern savage.   That is a weak, even an absurd, deduction of the good, well-meaning missionaries. He knew that as a lonely, weird boulder it stood on the moor or headland in his father's, his grandfather's, and his great-grandfather's time; he knew that it would stand there in his children's and his great-

grandchildren's time. Everything else passed away; the
clouds, the leaves, the flowers, the beasts, men, everyone,
but the boulder remained. As a rugged symbol of the
permanent in the passing—for even to him there was
something enduring in the universe—it was his nearest
conception of God, it was the one permanent thing he
could see." Again, the revelations of Pasteur in respect
of micro-organisms and their influence on disease, his
opening up the new great field of bacteriology, like a new
avenue into the most secret arcana of nature, and likewise
Lister's godlike creation of the antiseptic treatment, filled
him with enthusiasm. Lord Kelvin's works and Huxley's,
Tyndall's, and Max Müller's, were also often in his mind.
His interest in the greatest scientific questions was so
profound, and so materially did they influence him, that
in after years he was elected a Fellow of the Royal Society
of Edinburgh.

Referring to the conversation that took place
between the late James Sime and Matheson,
on the evening already spoken of, the doctor
continues :

How much these two had to say to each other.
Agnosticism was discussed, and a good idea of Dr.
Matheson's talk on the subject may be had in the fine
article on "Agnosticism," which years afterwards he
wrote to *The Scottish Review*. My brother's account of
Lessing's *Education of the Human Race* thrilled the young
poet-preacher, for although the work was not unknown to
him, its significance in the thought of our own times came
upon him as a great revelation. Not that he was not
familiar with some of the works of Lessing, especially
with *Laokoon* and *Nathan the Wise*, the latter of
which he greatly esteemed as the radiant picture of a
calm, radiant soul.

"Why, this essay of Lessing you speak of," I remember
him saying, "I shall get it at once. It is grand, a poet's
precursor, the very dawn in purest, sweetest light of
Hegel's growth, and of Darwin's sublime evolution of life.

After all, education does not create any new faculty or power, it only educes, brings to light and into action what powers are there; so perhaps it is with evolution." It was suggested that for every new type of being in the living kingdoms, that for every family or class in the vegetable and the animal worlds, that for every rising in the scale of life there was a new access of deity, and that certainly there was this on the arrival of man in the animal kingdom, and on the appearance of every man of genius since. My brother liked the suggestion that evolution began and still continues from above, not from below, like spring from on high awakening the lilies of the valley. "My dear fellow," said my friend, turning to me, "the highest and most perfect access of deity, and which can never be transcended—it is unique—is the Christ of Galilee. You are right, evolution begins from above, and the Christ is the transcendent beginning and end of evolution."

The incident thus recorded must have taken place in the early seventies, for it was before Matheson had published anything. For the next decade the ideas which began at that time to germinate in his mind steadily grew and developed. The balance of the serious thought of his day towards evolution, and its relation to, and effects upon, religious belief, naturally deepened his interest in the subject. He had written no book of a scientific nature in theology or philosophy since his Baird Lecture, and during the five years that had elapsed between it and his next important book, *Can the Old Faith Live with the New?* he made a profound study of the doctrine of evolution and its bearings on religious belief. The first-fruits of this study was the fine article on " Agnosticism," referred to by Dr. Sime, which was published in

The Scottish Review in 1883. But more striking and significant was the address delivered by him at the Pan-Presbyterian Council, which met at Belfast in the beginning of June 1884. The subject chosen by him for his address was the " Religious Bearings of the Doctrine of Evolution." In it we have the leading thought of all he ever afterwards wrote on the subject. His delivery of the address made a deep impression. As a token of its power and eloquence certain of the Scottish newspapers did it the honour of publishing it almost in full. No similar tribute was paid to any of the other speakers, though among them were Drs. Hodge and Schaff, and other leading lights of the Presbyterian Church. A correspondent thus describes the occasion :

" The most interesting appearance yet made by any member of Council has been that of Dr. Matheson of Innellan. Unable, from his affliction of total blindness, to read the paper on Evolution which stood in his name, Dr. Matheson asked and obtained leave to expound the gist of it verbally ; and for much more than the usually allotted time— twenty minutes for each paper—he held the Council in delighted attention to one of the most lucid and eloquent philosophical expositions we ever heard. Dr. Matheson sat down amidst a tempest of applause, again and again renewed." The late Professor Lee of Glasgow, who was present, declared : " None of us will ever forget the intellectual treat experienced in that admirable, and, in many respects, wonderful address on Evolution, delivered by a neighbour of my own, Dr. Matheson of Innellan." And the late Professor Calderwood expressed the unanimous feeling of the audience when he said : " The Council all feel that God has closed your eyes only to open other eyes, which have made you one of the guides of men. Your speech to-day was a perfect guide to the Council."

Dr. Robertson Nicoll, who was present at the meetings of the Council, and who was also a fellow-guest with Matheson, gives the following impressions :—

My first meeting with Dr. Matheson will always be memorable to me. It was at the Pan-Presbyterian Council in Belfast, held, I think, in the year 1884. We were the guests of the late Rev. Dr. William Johnston and Mrs. Johnston, and we had as fellow-guests the late Rev. Dr. William Wright of the Bible Society and his wife. Our host and hostess made a very notable couple. They had no children, and they were at the head of the magnificent orphan scheme carried on by the Presbyterian Church of Ireland. By this every Presbyterian orphan child in necessity is taken care of. Dr. Johnston had also a very large congregation, mostly of the working class, and was particularly active as an ecclesiastical and philanthropic leader. His wife, a lady of very marked ability, was his right hand in everything. Never have I seen such days of strenuous work, beginning when the post arrived with a huge number of letters, and never closing till midnight. It was an education to live with them. Dr. Matheson came with a great reputation, and amply sustained it at the Council. In the house he immediately became a favourite with everyone. I shall never forget his hearty interest in all that went on within and without. He strenuously attended the meetings, and brought back the most vivid impressions of them. What struck me most was his keen sense of humour, and his delicate perception. You were always forgetting that he was blind. He seemed to know who were in the room and where they were sitting. Mrs. Johnston was in delicate health, and unable to attend the meetings of the Council, and Dr. Matheson very thoughtfully and sedulously set himself to tell her everything that had happened. We who were privileged to listen saw how he had learned to compose mentally. Every sentence he uttered might have been printed. His criticism was often keen, but it was always kindly. I had the privilege of accompanying him to several of the meetings, and was amazed by the acuteness with which he summarised and criticised the speeches. One speech he disliked. It was made by an American professor, and was a defence of verbal inspiration. Dr. Matheson took exception to the confident tone of the professor, and thought his arguments inadequate. The great day of the Council was one on which an American, the late Dr. G. P. Hays of Denver, was chairman. At first his pronounced Americanism seemed to bode ill for a peaceful day, but very soon he established an extraordinary dominion over the audience, and poured out such a wealth of wisdom and wit as to surprise and delight everyone. Dr. Matheson was sitting next me, and at first expressed his discomfort and dissatisfaction, but he was soon subdued, and then he became radiant. I went home with him, and for Mrs. Johnston's benefit he went through the story of the day. His memory was truly marvellous, and his power of imagination. I shall never forget the helpless laughter to which we were all reduced by his reproductions of Dr. Hays' racy anecdotes. Dr. Matheson himself laughed more heartily than any of the rest. It was truly a good evening. On another night he was intensely pleased with a speech by Dr. Stalker in favour of a more ornate and elaborate ritual in Presbyterian churches. It was a bold thing to make the speech, for at that time the Presbyterian Church of Ireland was discussing with some keenness the use of organs in public worship. Dr. Matheson was heartily in sympathy with Dr. Stalker, and said that the arrangement and expression of his speech could not have been improved. He searched for an adjective to describe the speech, and found rest at last in the word Aristotelian.

I had an opportunity of some private conversation on theological questions with Dr. Matheson. He said that he had been a strong Evangelical, and was so still, but that he was now very decidedly in sympathy with Broad Churchism. I do not think he went so far in that direction as he supposed, for he spoke in warm praise of Dr. Liddon's lectures, entitled *Some Elements of Religion*. In particular he praised the lecture on Prayer. He left the impression on my mind of a singularly noble, beautiful, and unselfish personality. He did everything he could to keep his blindness out of sight so that it might not weigh on anyone's spirits, and he succeeded so well that it was only on occasion that one became aware of how much he was missing. His was a truly valiant and indeed heroic spirit. I will only add that I had many occasions to remark Dr. Matheson's great gratitude for trifling kindnesses—a gratitude which often seemed much in excess of the occasion. He was able to do his work without praise, but the friendship and recognition of his fellow-workers was precious to him, and, staunchly attached as he was to the principles of his own Church, his spirit was most catholic and wise.

The address, which was afterwards published in the *Transactions of the Council*, blunts the edge of the evolutionist's attack, by declaring in its opening sentences that the doctrine of evolution originated in the Christian Church itself. The speaker points in proof of this to the controversy that arose in the first centuries between Creationists and Traducianists; the former holding that the soul of man came into the world at birth by a separate act of creation, the latter holding that the soul of each man was derived at birth from the essence of the soul of his parents, and that therefore all souls were originally

14

included in a single life—the primeval Adam.   The
traducianist's view was clearly the very principle of
the modern doctrine of evolution, the reduction of
the many to the one, a view which the Church
maintained to be on the whole more orthodox than
the other.   Having thus shown that the new idea
which the doctrine of evolution had introduced into
the thought of the day was in reality an old doctrine
of the Christian Church, he proceeds to discuss the
conception of force and its relation to matter, and

in a lucid piece of argumentation shows how the
belief in the Divine Spirit, which was of the essence
of the Christian faith, was a more intelligible view
of the genesis and development of nature and of life
than the inscrutable Force of the evolutionists.   In
any case, that there was nothing in modern scientific
belief which could be regarded as contradictory to
the fundamental principles of the Christian religion ;
in fact, that these principles, worked out on evolu-
tionary lines, give a more rational view of the world
than the Spencerian philosophy.   Matheson accordingly, while neither accepting nor rejecting
evolution as a fact scientifically proved, welcomed
the ideas which it embodied as aids to the study
and better understanding of the Christian religion.

In the following year, the spring of 1885,
Matheson published the most important of his
books hitherto, *Can the Old Faith Live with the
New? or, the Problem of Evolution and Revelation.*
I remember meeting him a month or two before
its appearance.   He was in the most cheerful of

moods, and told me about his new book, which had
just been accepted by Blackwood. This was the
first occasion on which he had been brought into
business relations with the famous Edinburgh
house, and he felt not a little pleased at his work
being so readily accepted by it. He was full of the
subject, and I was deeply impressed by his attitude.
He struck me as a man who had achieved a
triumph, who had overcome some great difficulty,
and felt the increased power which his victory
gave.

Matheson's position in relation to the doctrine
of evolution as discussed in his book is very
characteristic. He does not commit himself to
it; he expresses no opinion as to the validity
of the doctrine; his sole object is to inquire, If
the doctrine be true, what then? He differs in
this respect from two important books which he
declares stimulated his attempt; that of Mr. Joseph
John Murphy on the *Scientific Bases of Faith*, and
that of Professor H. Drummond on *Natural Law
in the Spiritual World.* "Both of these books," as
he remarks, "are in their nature constructive; their
aim is to build a faith on the acceptance of the
modern doctrine of evolution." He, on the other
hand, pronounces no opinion on the validity of the
doctrine; his purpose is purely analytic. He places
evolution side by side with those doctrines of
revelation which seem to come into contact with it,
and seeks impartially to consider the question, How
the adoption of the former would affect our accept-

ance of the latter? In the opening chapters he
considers the scientific value of the religious sentiment in general. He felt compelled to do this,
seeing that natural evolution is supposed to involve
religious agnosticism. He accordingly discusses
the place for faith in the system of nature, whether
the object of faith is knowable, and the conditions
requisite to Divine knowledge. In the subsequent
chapters he treats of the special doctrines with
which evolution comes directly into touch, and
considers how, if at all, it affects them. These are
"Creation," "Special Creation," the "Divine Origin
of Life," "Primitive Man," "Providence," "The
Second Adam," the "Work of the Spirit," "Divine
Communion," and "Immortality."

Matheson's book was opportune. It fell upon
a public ready to welcome it. The subject had
been gradually assuming large proportions, and the
faith of many was distressed. Darwin was being
out-Darwined, and many scientific men, without
the caution of the author of *The Origin of
Species*, were driving his ideas to extremes that
seemed dangerous to religious belief. Apologists
of Christianity were taking their place in the field;
and the press, the pulpit, and the platform rang
with the war-cries of the opposing schools of
thought. It was freely admitted at the time, and
it has never been denied since, that Matheson's
book was the most important contribution made to
the controversy up to the date of its publication.
And this was the opinion of both sides. Its

breadth of view, its freedom from dogmatism, its
cordial recognition of the position of the evolutionist as well as of the religionist, its grasp of
fundamental principles, its intimate knowledge of
the points in dispute, its keen logic and its urbane
spirit, caused it to be welcomed by every party and
to secure a hearing in every quarter. Its value as
a contribution to the subject in dispute consisted in
the simple, yet far-reaching, fact, that even though
evolution, as rationalised in the philosophy of
Herbert Spencer, were accepted, it would not in
the slightest degree invalidate the doctrines of the
Christian religion, which it was supposed to
destroy. On the contrary, that these doctrines
shone more luminous in the light of the ideas
which the new age introduced, and became more
pregnant of Divine meaning because of them.

Matheson in this book, as in most of his other
writings, was true to his own spirit. His work in
the world was that of a great reconciler. He had
already in the sphere of theology done his part in
bringing into intelligible relationship the conflicting
creeds of mankind. He had now started on a new
enterprise, and aimed at bringing under one great
idea religious thought and scientific discovery.
Here we have the true Christian Theist; and
Professor Flint in his article on " Theism," in
the *Encyclopædia Britannica*, elaborates and con-
firms this position. The Christian idea of God is
flexible and comprehensive enough to find room
for truth, from whatever quarter it may come.

Every new fact is unintelligible until it is related to this idea; this idea itself is imperfect until its content is enriched by every new fact. If evolution, then, has made discoveries, why should the scientist be arrogant or the Christian be afraid? Matheson's book was an answer to this question, and it contributed not a little to that mutual understanding between science and religion, the first-fruits of which Matheson saw before he died.

The reception given to the book was hearty in the extreme. Long reviews of it appeared in the more important literary organs of opinion. Objections here and there were taken to details, but the book as a whole was accepted as of the first rank. Matheson's position was now thoroughly established. He was only in his forty-third year, and although he might attain fresh triumphs, these could only add to a reputation already great.

His name now began to be a familiar one in the highest quarters. Among his admirers was Lord Tennyson. He appreciated in his writings profound thought set forth in picturesqueness of phrase, and imaginative beauty balanced withal by intense practicality. This union of qualities, usually severed, commended his writings to the poet. An interesting letter from the late Duke of Argyll to the Rev. Dr. MacGregor of St Cuthbert's, Edinburgh, bears on this point. It was written a year or two after the publication of his book, *Can the Old Faith Live with the New?* but it is more than likely

that it is the volume referred to in the letter. One
may feel some surprise at the Duke being ignorant
of so near and so distinguished a neighbour of his
own, and one who had just.written on a subject
with which he himself was so familiar. But even
so universal a man as the Duke could not be expected to know everyone and everything :

ARGYLL LODGE, KENSINGTON,
August 3, 1888.

I have been to see old Tennyson—soon to enter his
eightieth year—yet writing as beautifully as of yore. I found
that the Bishop of Ripon had lately been on a visit, and as
the poet is an omnivorous reader, he had recommended,
among other books, some by Dr. Matheson of Innellan, of
whom I had never heard before. I saw one of his books
on Tennyson's table, and his son told me it seemed a
strong book. Tell me all you know of Matheson, who I
hear is a friend of yours.

The final crown to his reputation was still to
come. It was the ambition of ministers of the
Established Church of Scotland, during the reign
of the late Queen Victoria, to be invited to Balmoral
to preach before Her Majesty. Ever since the day
when Dr. Norman Macleod and Principal Tulloch
won her confidence and esteem by their large-
heartedness and simple presentation of Christian
truth, Queen Victoria had a liking for the Church
of Scotland and its ministers. It was her custom
to summon to Balmoral during her residence
there the more noted of the clergy of the Established Church, in order that they might conduct
the service in the Parish Church of Crathie on

the Sunday, or, should Her Majesty prefer it, in the Castle itself. In most cases names were submitted to the Queen for her approval, and by her command the clergyman selected was invited to appear. In rarer instances she suggested the name herself, and this was the case with Dr. Matheson. It was by her unsolicited royal command that he preached before her at Balmoral. No one of her subjects had passed through so many sorrows. She bore the burden of a great Empire, she also carried the weight of her own personal griefs. Without the consolation of our Holy Faith she would have been unable to bear up as bravely as she did under the many trials that she was called upon to endure, and it was with unfeigned gratitude to the author that she welcomed those meditations of Dr. Matheson's which had been placed in her hand by the Bishop of Ripon, and in which she found the consolation that her soul needed. It was in October of 1885 that Dr. Matheson was summoned to Balmoral, and in a letter to his friend Mr. Stevenson he gives an interesting account of the occasion :

MANSE, INNELLAN,
October 31, 1885.

MY DEAR STEVENSON,—My visit to Crathie has been a tremendous success, though I write with considerable reserve as I should much prefer to have stated the facts orally. The Queen sent word after the sermon that she was immensely delighted with the preaching and the prayers, the word "immensely" being underlined. She stated through Lady Ely, who gives her orders, that she desired me to be presented to her and to the Royal Family at a quarter-past ten in the evening, and that as I was unable to see her with the eye she and the Royal Family would shake hands with me. She has presented me with a little bust of herself, and she has requested that the sermon should be printed for private circulation and sent to her that she may have the thought beside her. She says that she never understood the subject before. She requested that I would send her a letter in my own hand; this, however, I have declined to do. When I came into the room she came forward, took my hand, saying, How I admired your sermon, most beautiful and most interesting. She asked all manner of questions regarding Innellan, its situation, population, etc. I afterwards conversed in turn with the Duke of Connaught, the Duchess of Connaught, and the Princess Beatrice. These are all the facts which I can put on paper, but they will serve to show you that I have received an almost unprecedented distinction. I may say that among the Royal Household there are many applications for a copy of the sermon, which is now being printed.—Believe me, yours very sincerely,

G. MATHESON.

The sermon which he preached on the occasion was on "The Patience of Job," from the well-known text James v. 2. It is a most beautiful sermon, and one on reading it can well understand how it appealed so strongly to his Royal hearers. The point of the discourse is the thought, fresh and original, that the patience of Job consisted in his endurance of the repeated and overwhelming calamities that befell him, without asking, Why? It was only when his would-be friends endeavoured to trace the dealings of Providence, and to find the motive of God's anger in Job's transgressions, that he cried out. But the Patriarch's outburst, the preacher declared, in place of being a denial was only an additional proof of his patience, for it was an outburst, not against his calamities or against Him under whose hand they befell him, but against those who set themselves as judges over man and his Maker. This standing with an uncovered head before the mystery of life and saying nothing, this acceptance of suffering which could not be explained without a murmur, this undying faith in God in the midst of troubles whose source and whose meaning were a mystery, was an exhibition of patience which was once paralleled only in the history of the world—in the death of the Son of Man on Calvary. The Patriarch's cry of "Though He slay me yet will I trust in Him" was an anticipation of the Saviour's prayer, "If it be Thy will let this cup pass from Me, yet not My will but Thine be done." "Stand, then, where Job stood," concluded the preacher,

under the shadow of Gethsemane, side by side with the Son of Man. Keep green thy love with His love. For remember that, after all, the patience of Job is the patience of hope. Wherever love is, there is no despair. There is a withered peace, a stoic peace, a peace of autumn leaves ; a peace where rustling ceases, not because the winds have lost their power but because the life has lost its sap. That is not the patience of hope ; it is the patience of despair. But if love be there,—His love that under the shadow could keep the heart undimmed, that under the wintry sky could preserve the summer foliage green,—then come what may, though cloud rise on cloud, and night come down without a star, already above the heights of Calvary there shall gleam the sunlit peaks of Olivet, and beyond the vale of death shall shine the glory

Life losing its sap

of the resurrection day. Love is the prophecy that the night is not eternal, and he that listens to love amid the cold hears already the song of the swallow that tells that summer is nigh, for the patience of Job is the patience of hope.

CHAPTER IX

THE EDINBURGH MINISTRY

A DEVOTED member of the Parish Church of
Innellan expressed the fear, when in 1883 Dr.
Matheson received a presentation from his congregation, that it was fated he should not remain
long among them. As anticipations often arise
from contradictories, she said that this fear was
caused by Dr. Matheson's own words, when he
declared that he would continue for the remainder
of his life as their minister. He no doubt at the
time believed this. He had never sought a
change. He was contented and happy in his
work. He felt that the sphere in which Providence had placed him was perhaps the one above
all others specially suited for him. He might have
been in an equally easy charge in some country
district, but he would have been without the
stimulus which came from the inroad of summer
visitors, who latterly were drawn from every part
of the United Kingdom. He was within easy
access of the social life and literary opportunities
of Glasgow, with its University and libraries.

Besides, he belonged to the West of Scotland, and he felt thoroughly at home among its people. In a true sense he was prophet, priest, and king of his parish, and he ruled by the spirit of sacrifice, which formed the special note of his preaching and his life. He toiled incessantly in the interests of his congregation and of the larger public who enjoyed his writings, and as he never went beyond his province, so no one dreamed of invading his. His life indeed at Innellan was one of pleasantness and peace.

It cannot be said, however, that he had no visions of a larger field on which he might play his part. He had become conscious of his power and his influence, and, having a message, he naturally longed to have it delivered to those who, in their turn, might spread it far and near. Had he been an author only, he might have contented himself with the platform which Innellan supplied. But he was a man of action as well. He rejoiced in coming into contact with other minds, in exchanging ideas, in discussing questions of far-reaching interest, in seeing his views carried out into practice; above all, he was a born preacher, whose chief joy was in communicating his thoughts by the power of his eloquence to the minds of men, and moving their hearts by his fervid appeals. No one was more susceptible to the influence of numbers. He could *feel* a crowd, and a large congregation drew from him his very best. His childlike nature revelled in the play of thoughts and words which were rendered possible by mingling with masses of people; and it was only in some great centre of population where the whole man could find fit expression.

Those who knew him, therefore, were not altogether surprised when they heard that he was not unlikely to accept the call which was to be presented to him from a large Edinburgh congregation. The movement was in some respects a surprise. It came upon all who were concerned in it as a thief in the night. Even those from whom it issued had never meditated calling Dr. Matheson, until by accident almost it was told them that he might not altogether refuse their overtures. The reason, probably, why so many congregations, to whom Dr. Matheson would have made a most acceptable minister, never thought of inviting him, was simply because it never dawned upon them that he would be willing to accept a call. They had the impression that he was so contented at Innellan that no inducement whatever could tempt him to leave it. There was probably another reason. They felt that his blindness would be a hindrance to him in the discharge of the pastoral duties of a large congregation. There can be no doubt, however, that if he had been a minister in the Church of England he would have found his proper sphere long before. In the Church of Scotland, which is Presbyterian, there are no posts for preachers. The minister of a charge must undertake all its duties, of which preaching is only one ; and though he should have the eloquence of Chrysostom, if he fails in the minor tasks he, in the opinion of some, has failed altogether. In the Church of England Dr. Matheson would have been appointed a Canon in St. Paul's Cathedral, and at Lent or at Easter he would have attracted great congregations. When his term of service there had expired, he would have retired to his country living, where he would have written his books and prepared himself in quietness for his next term of office.

There is one kind of congregation in the Church of Scotland which, it seems to me, would have suited Dr. Matheson. A suburban charge in connection with which there would have been a minimum of congregational and parochial work, and centrally enough situated to command a large body of hearers every Sunday, would have been a fit sphere for him. I remember on one occasion asking a leading member of such a church why it was when a vacancy had occurred, the members did not think of giving a call to Dr. Matheson. He said, "Would he have come?" I replied that I thought he would. "Well," he exclaimed, "if that had occurred to us we would only have been too proud to have had him as our minister." But it was ordered that his translation from Innellan should be to a large congregation, in which the demands upon him as a pastor were greater than as a preacher. The sequel will show the wisdom of the step which he was now meditating. It was a difficult choice. No one, however, should regret that he made it. If it was put in his way by a Higher Hand for the purpose of testing to the very fullest his Christian heroism, George Matheson did not fail. His spirit was ever willing. The victory which he achieved over the circumstances of his new lot can only be paralleled by his triumph over the catastrophe of his early youth. His indomitable courage enabled him to prevail in both instances, and he only yielded when his physical frame was unable any longer to endure the strain.

There is a touch of romance about his call to St. Bernard's, Edinburgh. The members of that church had failed to elect a minister within the period of six months, which the law of the Church allowed. The right of appointment had fallen into the hands of the Presbytery, but, as is usual in such cases, the Presbytery was willing to receive suggestions from the congregation as to whom they would like to be elected to the charge. The convener of the congregational committee was Dr. Currie, the Rector of the Normal School in connection with the Church of Scotland. It chanced that some seven or eight years previously he had been on a visit to Innellan, and on the Sunday he went to hear Dr. Matheson. It was a winter's day, and fierce gusts of wind were driving the rain against the windows of the little kirk. Dr. Matheson preached to a handful of worshippers. He was disappointed at the meagre attendance, for the sermon which he had prepared was a specially good one. There

was, however, one stranger in the congregation; that
stranger was Dr. Currie, and the eloquent words of
the preacher made a deep impression upon him.
When, therefore, St. Bernard's people found themselves in their difficulty, the name of Dr. Matheson
at once occurred to the convener's mind. He
remembered his ability in the pulpit, he knew his
power as an author, and he felt that he was the
man of all others who should be appointed to
the charge. The following letter from Dr. Currie
to a member of the congregation tells how the
matter came about :—

SHANDON HYDROPATHIC,
January 26, 1886.

You may be interested to hear the sequel of our
proceedings, and the help you gave us in our earlier stages
fairly entitles you to know. I must say I have found the
business not a little anxious and engrossing. At the time
that I wrote you, we were making special inquiry about
three men, but a meteor came across our sky in the
person of a minister whom you will know very well by
name and reputation at any rate. I mean Dr. George
Matheson of Innellan. It came upon us as a sort of
revelation that he would be willing to change, and from
the moment that idea was seriously borne in upon us it
has carried us captive. Of course there were great
difficulties to be considered in respect to how a blind
clergyman could carry on our parish work. We have
faced these, and, with the information we have been able
to get of him, we resolved at our committee meeting that
night to recommend him to the congregation. He
preached among us on Sunday last, forenoon and afternoon, and created an enthusiasm which will probably carry
him through the ordeal of a congregational election.
Personally, I go for him heart and soul, for the sake of
the young people of the church mainly, who cannot resist
his manly eloquence. I think he will be a power in an

15

Edinburgh pulpit; one of those men who appear at intervals to shake up our dulness, and to compel the attention of the listless and the cynic. It is no disparagement to our other candidates, and I trust it will not appear to them to be any, that the claims of such a man should be preferred. Of course there is sometimes a slip between the cup and the lip, but from what passed at our long interview with him in Glasgow last week, and also on Sunday last, I expect that our courtship will end in a union.

The meeting of the congregation of St. Bernard's, held for the purpose of hearing the committee's report, took place on the evening of February 9, 1886, and resulted in a unanimous call to Dr. Matheson. The convener, in moving the adoption of the report, expressed the belief that Dr. Matheson if appointed would keep St. Bernard's as one of the high places of spiritual teaching in the city; and he moved that the Presbytery be petitioned to appoint him to be their minister. The die had now been cast, and the usual formalities took place for the translation of Dr. Matheson to his new charge. One of these was the severing of the ties that bound him to his church and congregation at Innellan. It was not an easy matter for pastor and people to part with each other; they both felt the wrench deeply. It was only three years since they had in a sense renewed their union and exchanged gifts—tangible tokens of affection on their part, words of the profoundest gratitude on his. But the unexpected had happened, and the hour had approached when they must part. The congregation, however, were determined to give a final proof of their admiration, so one evening, the 13th of April, they gathered in full numbers in the Parish Church, and presented Dr. Matheson and his sister with handsome gifts. Dr. Matheson, in acknowledging the presentation, said:

This has been for me one of the most trying—I should say the most trying—day in my life. I have had this day to undergo the terrible process of being loosened from my charge. I have been loosened from my charge this day by the Presbytery of Dunoon, and now I am reminded this night that I am being loosened from my church. I told the Presbytery of Dunoon to-day that I had experienced both their binding and loosening power. I had experienced their power of binding nearly twenty years ago, when they ordained me to this ministry; and I experienced their loosening power to-day, when they gave me permission to go to Edinburgh. I told the Presbytery, and I repeat it now, that the power of loosening was the more terrible of the two. On my ordination to this parish I felt great trepidation and fear, but I feel infinitely more now at the time of my being loosened from it; and you have revived in all its force this sad feeling by giving us—my sister and myself—this double presentation. You have reminded me by a tangible token that no loosening power can ever unbind those ties—those indelible ties—of affection that subsist between us. I have to return you my most sincere thanks for this handsome present. The timepiece will be much prized by me, and it will always remind me of those eighteen years I have spent among you.

Eighteen years ago I came to you as an old man, but now I am leaving you as a young man. This may seem a wondrous paradox, but I speak to you in the language of the Spirit, not of the flesh. I came to you in those days very much afraid, rankled in mind, perturbed, and disturbed, for I knew not the way before me. I was ignorant then how the duties of this parish ought to be performed; you have taught me. I have renewed my youth; I cannot express myself better than to say I have grown younger. Do you know, I think the ultimate glory of us all is to grow young. I owe to you a debt of gratitude which I can never repay. On behalf of my sister, I ask to be allowed to say that the work that she has done for this place has been, from beginning to end, a labour of love. I feel sure that the lessons which, during these years, she has learned, must have rekindled her youth and made her stronger to continue the same work in the new sphere to which she is going. In her name I thank you deeply and abundantly for this warm token of your appreciation and your regard, and I may say—what she would have said had she been permitted to speak—that she will always cherish this gift as a memorial of days which have been to her days of pleasantness and of peace.

Dr. Matheson was inducted to his new charge on May 12, 1886, and on the following Sunday he began his ministry of thirteen years in St. Bernard's Parish Church, Edinburgh; one of the richest and most brilliant ministries of which the Church of Scotland bears record. He had now found his true position, it might be thought, for was he not the minister of one of the largest congregations in the capital of Scotland? Edinburgh has always been regarded as the city of light and leading in the northern half of the United Kingdom. It was the home of the Scottish kings; in it sat the Parliament, and it still glories in its Law Courts. Its historic memories are romantic; it witnessed some of the most stirring events in the national history; and from it issued the commands that turned the course of affairs. Its very situation is inspiring, and its picturesque beauty draws to it visitors from every part of the world. Its ecclesiastical and literary associations, especially from the Reformation downwards, are notable. It was the city of John Knox, of Principal Robertson, and of Thomas Chalmers; and also of David Hume, Walter Scott, and Thomas Carlyle. Hundreds of other names of lesser lustre illuminate its history, and if there was one place more than another in which a man of Matheson's genius should find a fit sphere it ought surely to have been Edinburgh.

There is no doubt but what he felt the stimulating influences of his new surroundings. He began his ministry in St. Bernard's in the full vigour of a strong manhood. His bodily strength was unimpaired, his natural force was unabated. He was on the crest of his fame, and he felt himself possessed of inexhaustible resources. He was master of ancient and modern thought; he had breasted the waves of speculation; he had met and turned the edge of the most recent attacks on what was fundamental in the Christian Faith. His daily reading and profound study of the Bible had given him a knowledge of its meaning and spirit which enabled him to interpret it in the light of the day, and to apply its riches to the needs of the hour. His acquaintance with science and with literature, ancient and modern, native and foreign, made him a man of the broadest culture; and his supreme intellectual ability, lit up by flashes of genius, gave him a commanding position among the most capable and the most learned. Add to these his rare oratorical gifts, his charm of style, and above all his sincere, warm-hearted nature, and we have surely a preacher the like of whom it is not the fortune of every generation or of every country to possess.

Edinburgh responded to the unique personality that it now found in its midst. St. Bernard's Church became full to overflowing, and Sunday after Sunday Dr. Matheson poured forth a stream of eloquence that delighted, charmed, and inspired the large audiences that came to hear him. "Dr. Matheson's fame as a preacher," writes one who had the closest personal and official connection with him in St. Bernard's, "was so great, that every seat was occupied at the morning service, and many found only standing room; in fact, even seat-holders had to attend punctually or run the risk of being temporarily dispossessed of their pews." But the most striking compliment to his popularity and power was the character of his hearers. "His audience," continues the same friend, "was a mixed one, drawn from all ranks and classes of society : clergymen, leading members of the Bar, University professors, scholars and scientists, artisans and workmen; and whilst he himself never despised those occupying good social positions, his democratic spirit seemed intensely gratified by the fact that the common people heard him gladly. Possessed of a well-modulated and powerful voice, he readily gained a favourable hearing from every audience; and if some of his propositions were startling on their first statement, no one with an open mind left without being convinced that every word was proved."

His preaching had developed since the old Innellan days. His own character had grown and his nature had become enriched. In particular his sense of humour and frank outspokenness had become a leading trait both of his conversation and of his preaching. He restrained himself in writing, but when, on the spur of the moment, he had, in the pulpit, to express his present thoughts, and being so engrossed in his subject as to be altogether unconcerned about what was held to be proper, or respected as conventional, he frequently gave utterance to what surprised many and startled not a few. There were two classes of hearers who found in Dr. Matheson's preaching the word that their souls needed. These were the students of Edinburgh, who attended his church in large numbers, and those whose faith was distressed— men who had given up attending church, and who perchance had ceased to believe in God. It was surely a Divine blessing to Edinburgh that it had in its midst a preacher who could lay his restraining hand on both these classes, who could lead the wayward thought of ingenuous youth into the path of true knowledge, and guide the wandering mind of the doubter into the way everlasting. I have received two contributions, one from each of these classes. Let the student speak first. The Rev. Sydney Smith, Parish Minister of Keith, who attended the classes in Edinburgh University during Matheson's ministry in St. Bernard's, writes as follows :

To write of Dr. Matheson as a preacher is for me to relive some almost ecstatic moments of my life. Again and again as I heard him, it is but little exaggeration to say that I seemed as it were caught up into the seventh heaven, whether in the body or out of the body I could hardly tell. It was often in a kind of bewilderment that I left the church. The value of every ordinary sensation was lowered, and I was alone with the great thoughts and profound emotions which the preacher had stirred.

Sometimes the effect of the whole was pathetically modified. One recalls little incidents, half touching, half amusing, but to me more touching than amusing, drawing one into tenderer sympathy with the preacher, heightening the impression made in so far as they reminded one forcibly of the victory which he had won in his own life.

For youth, and especially youth as represented at the universities, the preaching of Dr. Matheson had peculiar charm. It was no uncommon thing, I remember, for a student of any denomination on a Sunday morning or afternoon to look up another student and suggest a visit to St. Bernard's. Nor is it very hard to understand wherein for the student-mind the attractiveness of Dr. Matheson's sermons lay. His boldness of interpretation would not be without appeal to the young man's sense of the heroic. The student as a rule is little of a traditionalist, and the way in which Dr. Matheson was wont to set aside time-honoured exegesis harmonised with the radical or revolutionary strain in the student's nature. "I have been through all the commentators", was a sentence with which he regularly introduced his own exposition. Then Dr. Matheson showed respect, even though it might be only the respect of recognition, to certain great names in the scientific and philosophic world. "Herbert Spencer would call it the vibration of the ether; I would call it the heaving breast of God," is an interjection which comes back to me. Sometimes he went further. It was the annual sermon, if I remember aright, of the Primitive Methodist Conference, which was being held that year in Edinburgh. The place of meeting was what is now the United Free Church Assembly Hall. The preacher's text was, "Who are these that are arrayed in white robes?" He portrayed heaven as a vast concert hall, and asked his audience to take a sweeping glance over it. "Who are these in the centre, '*before* the throne'?" For answer he quoted part of the text— "These are they," etc. "Who are these, and these, and these?" He replied by mentioning different classes of Christians. Then he asked, "Who is that man at the very back of the hall, the man with the pale thoughtful face? That is Spinoza. He has only got an angle of the truth, but he is working his way to the front, to the centre." And from all parts of the hall there came cries of "Hallelujah!" and "Help him, Lord; help him, Lord."

Then Dr. Matheson delighted in the use of biological terms to express facts of the spiritual world. Just as Professor Drummond in his addresses to students used to speak of sin as a microbe, so Dr. Matheson would describe Peter's words, "Be it far from Thee, Lord," or the wish of the multitude to make our Lord an earthly king, as "attempts to arrest His development." Characteristic too of the preacher, and attractive to the student because of the contrast suggested to his daily fare, were the bold metaphors, the illustrations drawn from present-day fiction, the apparent spontaneity of much of the thinking, the wealth and effortlessness of language, the delight of the preacher in his self-expression, the constant element of surprise, and the magnetic glow which pervaded the whole. One of his daring and unusual figures comes back to me as I write. The context I have forgotten, and I cannot well explain the impression made, but I can remember the emotion which quietly surged through the

audience, causing them literally to sway from side to side
as they heard the words. The preacher was speaking of
Robert Burns. " They brought the bard up to Edinburgh,"
he said, "and he wouldn't sing, and they had to take him
back again."

There is an impression abroad that Dr. Matheson's
preaching was to some extent deficient in qualities which
are supreme conditions of appeal—lucidity and ethical
force. So far from this being the case, almost every
sermon I heard was a branching system of thought, and
the preacher's emphasis on the sacrificial love of the
Cross and the glory of humanitarian service was felt by
many of us to be a strong moral influence in our lives.
Yet it is not difficult to understand how numbers of
people have thought otherwise. When one recalls how
often the unity of the sermon was more imaginative than
logical, how sometimes the discourse was formally little
more than the elaboration of a single figure, one can understand how for many the sense of all objective truth or relation to the real world might be lost, the cord of interest
snapped, and the impression of the whole destroyed.
George Meredith has said somewhere that the English
mind does not take kindly to metaphor. It is even more
true one would think of the Scottish mind.

For the rest, while it may be maintained that Dr.
Matheson's analyses of Bible characters, for example, were
highly speculative, and the range within which many of
the truths he discovered appeared true was very limited,
yet if, as Professor Flint once said, the essence of the
Gospel is God's love to man, and if the supreme dynamic
is the answering love of the soul, there were few of Dr.
Matheson's sermons without an element of evangelical
and practical power.

The other, who had wandered from church to
church, as he himself records, in search of an abiding place for his soul, chanced to alight at last on
St. Bernard's. He there found what he needed.
Matheson's voice appeased his fears, and his

presentation of Divine truth won the doubting disciple for the Kingdom. The writer, the Rev. T. R. Barnett, is now an honoured minister of the Christian Church—

It must have been some time in the year 1890 that I first began to attend the morning service at St. Bernard's in Edinburgh. I was a most diligent and at the same time a most unorthodox church-goer, and during these years I must have visited most of the better known churches in Edinburgh—Presbyterians of all denominations, Episcopalians High and Low, Roman Catholics and Jesuits; seeking sound doctrine in the first, music and æsthetics in the second, and information at first hand with a variety of sensations in the third.

But St. Bernard's saw me oftener than any other church in the city. For here there was something which drew me irresistibly back again and again. I now know that it was the inspiration of the preacher's personality. How well I remember the long walk from Merchiston to St. Bernard's on the clear, sharp winter mornings, or on dismal, drippy days when even the rain did not deter me! And the expectations were never disappointed. If the day was bright, the preacher used the very sunshine to illustrate the Eternal Light; if the day was depressing, he used the gloom to illustrate the clouds and darkness of experience, on which he always managed, somehow, to pour a radiance of Divine Mercy.

Dr. Matheson's first prayer was often the finest part of the service. And what a prayer it was! A lifting up of the heart and upraising of the spirit, a reaching out after God, an outpouring of the soul, like the rapturous song of the lark, mounting higher and higher into the blue, to find in the limitless skies the satisfaction of its whole nature. I confess that it was this first prayer that often lifted us up into the Mystic Presence more than any other part of the service. How difficult it was to keep the eyes closed! There, upon the high pulpit, was the blind poet, with uplifted hand, always reaching out and up into his own illumined darkness, as if trying to catch something of the mystery of God and draw it down to man. He carried us all up into the heights along with him; and he drew down, for the most commonplace of us, something of the transfiguring blessing; so that, often before the rapture of aspiration was over, the eyes that watched the blind, praying man in the pulpit had to view him through a mist of unconscious tears. How many of our preachers draw tears from the eyes of the worshippers as they pray? Through this man's aspirations, God laid His hand on the heart of us all. In other churches we could get more sustained eloquence, more elaborate theology, more orthodox statements of Christian doctrine; but in this poet-preacher there was the illuminating flash of a Divine imagination which revealed the beauties of many a hidden truth; there was an aspiration and an inspiration and a spiritual glamour which created an atmosphere of worship that infected us all with a sense of God's very self. There were three great facts of Christian experience which, I can personally testify, Dr. Matheson restated for us all.

The first was the great truth of *Reconciliation*. In those anxious days the doctrine of Reconciliation seemed often a very difficult and a very departmental doctrine to accept. But Dr. Matheson changed all that for us. He lifted a truth out of its provincial connection and showed it in its universal bearing. He showed us life in the light of the Eternal mercy, until God and man, man and man, pain and joy, sorrow and mirth, light and gloom, were all made one in the great mystic unity of God's Love. And then he taught us to have the patience of faith to believe in the Great End of God, when man would see, as by a vision in retrospect, that all things had been working together for good.

Then another great foundation fact of his preaching was *the perfection of man through suffering*. He shed many a ray of light on the mystery of pain. He taught us that God meant us to overcome the pains of life, not by avoiding them, but by taking them to our hearts and passing them through our souls. We were to conquer all enemies by conquering all our *enmity* to them. We were to look upon pain as a friend (disguised), to be received, not as an enemy to be shunned. Man was made by God to become perfect *through* sufferings, not to be made perfectly free from sufferings.

And most of all, I think, he showed us *a new way of Faith.* I well remember that it was a blind man who made me see, most vividly, that there is no contradiction to Faith in Reason. Reason and Faith were twin-sisters, only Faith was ever one step in advance of Reason, whom she nevertheless held firmly by the hand. It is with a distinct sigh of relief that the seeker after truth finds, for the first time, that Faith has nothing to fear from Reason. And this was a very favourite subject with Dr. Matheson. Faith, to him, was that sense of the soul which transcends Reason. It was the sense in man which made him fly to God, as the lark flies to the morning.

All this was Dr. Matheson's best gift to the distressed in faith who came to hear him preach. He had been in the depths himself; yet this man, who had fought his doubt and conquered it, infected men with his magnificent faith. He lifted them up to God. He taught them to look upon the world as one vast unity in God's sight.

And yet it was not the least compliment which we paid to him that we sometimes did not agree with him. He was an erratic as well as an inspired preacher. Sometimes we smiled at his irresistible thrusts of humour, at his extravagant flights of imagination, at his wayward interpretation of Holy Scripture. But no one who possessed in the very slightest degree the imaginative sense, would ever have dreamed of misunderstanding him. He was, above all things, suggestive. In those past days he was to me a blessed star of guidance, and but for him many of the deep truths of life, which it is now my duty to preach to others, would have had less meaning to me, and to them, if it had not been for those student days when I sat in a pew at St. Bernard's.

On the eve of leaving Edinburgh for my first assistant-ship in Glasgow, I sat down and wrote him a letter of thanks, from my own heart to his. And while it is a deep privilege to be able to set down this small testimony to one who opened the eyes of many an inquiring soul, it is also with pleasure I add the letter which he wrote in reply to mine—a letter which, at the time, sent me on my way rejoicing, and which I have ever since kept as a precious memento of one who was to me a light in the darkness:

19 St. BERNARD'S CRESCENT, EDINBURGH,
January 10, 1893.

MY DEAR SIR,—You do not ask an answer and I know you desire none, but I cannot forbear just dropping a single line to tell you how deeply I am touched by your singularly beautiful and manly letter. It is such a letter as would atone to any minister for years of obloquy and seasons of neglect, and any man who received it might go to his grave with the proud and grateful consciousness that his work had not been in vain. To light one torch which itself is destined to be a torch to others, is as much as any minister can desire.—With all the sympathy of a kindred nature,

Believe me, my dear sir, yours very sincerely,
GEORGE MATHESON.

Strangers on a visit to Edinburgh flocked in large numbers to hear Dr. Matheson. American tourists in particular made a point of attending St. Bernard's. His books had been carried across the Atlantic, and several of his devotional volumes were greatly prized in the sister continent. Many of these tourists were clergymen of distinction, and several of them contributed a sketch of the poet-preacher to one or other of their magazines. The following, by the Rev. Charles Parkhurst, gives the best account I have seen of Dr. Matheson's appearance and manner of preaching at this time. "Spending a Sunday in Edinburgh, our first inquiry," he remarks, "was for Dr. George Matheson.

This was occasioned by the fact that his book, *Moments on the Mount*, had fallen into our hands a year ago. We were greatly charmed and helped by the book; it was so devout, original and fresh, in its exegesis. To our inquiry, Who is Dr. Matheson? we could get no answer. We could only learn that he preached at Edinburgh. Great was our surprise to learn that he was totally blind, and had been all his ministry. This excited our curiosity and desire to hear him. At an early hour, therefore, with unwonted curiosity and expectation, we are in his church. Of the intelligent usher we make many inquiries, which are cordially answered. Dr. Matheson has been with them one year. The church had taken on new life and activity in his pastorate. It was with difficulty now that seats could be secured on the Sabbath for those who pressed to hear him. He was a most excellent pastor, spending the greater part of each afternoon calling throughout his parish.

We are anxiously awaiting the coming of the preacher. What a quaint church is this! It is the old box-pew, very poorly cushioned, and if the architect had planned to make the seats as uncomfortable as possible, he could not have succeeded better. There must be some unusual attraction to bring people to such seats as these. We should never come but once, unless the pulpit had so much of intellectual and spiritual vitality as to make us forget where we were. A high gallery runs clear round the church. The bell has ceased to toll, but the people are still coming, and we are compelled to sit closer together to make room for those who desire seats. On a greatly elevated position in front is a small pulpit, not larger than a flour-barrel, with only room for one person. Above it is a sounding-board, the like of which we have once seen in America. Behold! a rear door opens, and in comes our long-looked-for preacher. Have we been a long time in introducing him? Well, it seemed a long time before he came; perhaps because we were so anxious

to see him. We have desired that you should be thus
anxious; but he does not look as we had fancied. We
thought at first it could not be he, but an unfortunate
exchange; but we are assured by the stranger at our side
that it is indeed Dr. Matheson. We confess to strong
likes and dislikes. We rather enjoy having our favourites
in the pulpit. We had created Dr. Matheson into such
a one. That he? Why, we had cast his face into that of
the typical Scotch student, a Dr. M'Cosh in earlier years,
but he is not that at all. I should not look for him in the
pulpit, but on the farm. Forty-five years of age? He looks
ten years older. He has the face and form of General
Grant when the hero of Vicksburg was most stout. Taller,
however, rather more muscular, yet he makes you think
most of the man the American people loved so much.
With full beard and natural open eye, you would have
not thought that he was blind had you not been so
informed.

He has a remarkable congregation in numbers, in an
indication of intelligence and spiritual sympathy and
anticipation; but he does not know it. Can a blind man
preach with enthusiasm when he must lack the responsive
help and inspiration which the seeing eye could get from
such an unusual audience? Are we to be disappointed?
Have we expected too much? We do not believe it.
The man who can write such a book must have it in him
to preach. Now he rises, his body swaying a little until
he gets his equilibrium. Announcing a psalm for alternate
reading, he takes his verses without the mistake of a word,
and throughout the whole service, calling for several hymns
and Scripture references with chapter and verse, he never
made an error. Of course it was all memorised. Then
he prays; and such a prayer! It seems profane to write
about it. Two things are evident, however: though his
visual sight is entirely eclipsed he does " see God," and he
does see into the souls of his hearers. Like a skilled
harper, he has touched every string of the human soul and
made it chime into the ear of God. In that prayer we
have been to the mount of worship, and we could go away
content even if we heard no more. It was wonderful the

way in which that blind preacher talked with God and uttered the aspirations of the people.

In the afternoon of the same day we heard one of the most scholarly of the faculty of the Presbyterian College preach and pray, but it was all cold, inapt, unresponsive. The thoroughness with which Dr. Matheson apprehended the life of his people, their struggles, sorrows, defeats, victories, and his almost superhuman sympathy with such actual life, was the most remarkable characteristic of the man. For forty minutes he preached on the text, " Holy men of God spake as they were moved by the Holy Ghost." Though we undertook to make a full abstract of the sermon, and it lies before us, yet so *faint* and imperfect is our *negative* of that discourse that we will not do this great man, so little known as yet in America, the injustice here to produce it. Such a sermon is never forgotten. Much that we had often vaguely felt he expressed. It was not metaphysical nor controversial. He never said anything about different theories of inspiration. He just showed how natural it was for God to reveal Himself in His word, just as He has done, and how each personality through which it came, like David, John, James, Paul, retained his identity and his peculiarity. The whole range of illustration in art, science, history, and in practical life, was touched with the familiarity of the master in each department. We were instructed, refreshed, inspired. God has given that faithful man, with his studious habits, his pastoral nurture and sympathy, an immense equivalent for the loss of physical vision. Dr. Matheson is to become a special favourite to tourists, who long to have the Sabbaths come that they may hear instructive and inspiring preaching.

Hearers of Dr. Matheson, as can be seen from the impressions of his preaching just quoted, were always struck by the originality, fervour, and devoutness of his prayers. Most of his life, indeed, was spent in close fellowship with the Father of Spirits. His hours of solitude were seasons of

16

communion. He never felt himself to be alone, and though he could not see the outward world he peopled a world of his own with the spirits of just men made perfect. All his meditations end with a prayer, and so does each chapter of his *Portrait of Christ*, and of his *Representative Men and Women of the Bible*. Even his sermons were not infrequently caught up by this spirit of adoration into the seventh heavens, and it seemed to be the most natural thing in the world, when he was carried away on the wings of some Divine thought, to find his eloquence culminating in a prayer. It was in this form, indeed, that he made his most effective appeals. In place of bringing the truth home to his hearers, as is the practice of most preachers, he brought his hearers home to the truth; carried them up into a region of Divine communion, and lifted their souls above the things of time and of sense to those which are unseen and eternal. Under the spell of his eloquence they seemed to see their souls transfigured before their very eyes. Like the disciples of old, on the Mount of Transfiguration, the prayer of many was, "It is good for us to be here; let us make tabernacles."

Several of his members, who thought that the strain under which he was put, not only of preaching but of giving out the psalms and hymns, of reading and commenting upon the lessons, and offering up the prayers as well, suggested to him that he ought to relieve himself of a part of the

service and to ask his assistant to take the prayers.
They were not aware of the dangerous ground on
which they were treading. He would much rather
have given up the sermon than the prayers, for it
was in those moments of ecstatic communion that
he carried his hearers to the throne of grace. So
his reply to the well-meaning petitioners was both
pointed and characteristic. " Prayer," he said,
" never causes me an effort. When I pray I know
I am addressing the Deity, but, when I preach, the
devil may be among the congregation."

Another feature of his preaching, upon which
the majority of those who were in the habit of
hearing him are agreed, was his power of fusing
all theological dogmas into the glow of a spiritual
and moral presentation of Christian teaching and
truth. Indeed I would find in this the very
essence of Dr. Matheson's preaching. He taught
religion, and not any formal or scholastic aspect
of it. The Christ of history was to him the
Christ of experience. He was the Lamb slain
from the foundation of the world; in Him was
realised the Divine ideal, and that ideal was the
goal towards which the human race was striving.
It was not an ideal of doctrine merely, nor of
history, nor of tradition, nor of churches, nor
of priests, nor of creeds, nor of confessions:
it was an ideal of thought, an ideal of life, an
ideal which was beneath, and above, and beyond
any possibility of the mind of man to determine
by mere symbols. We have, it may be said, in

this conception of Christianity the views of a poet rather than a theologian. So be it. Religion is not theology. There is far more poetry than dogmatics in the teaching of Christ ; and poets, as we know, are our greatest teachers. Matheson had been in the depths. He had found how unsatisfactory all purely formal teaching is. He had fought his way to the surface, and he held the truth as he had found it, through spiritual storm and stress, with a tenacity which no power could break, and he presented it with an intellectual conviction, and under an imaginative glow which carried his hearers captive. Under such preaching all differences of creeds and churches, of faith and reason, of the natural and supernatural, of the Here and the Hereafter, of the Divine and human, of earth and heaven, vanished ; and listeners were lifted into a sphere of Divine fellowship, and their souls were wafted into regions of ineffable bliss.

It may be interesting to hear how he impressed one who was in close official connection with him. The Rev. Marshall B. Lang, minister of Old Meldrum, at one time an assistant to Dr. Matheson, writes as follows :

In the pulpit Dr. Matheson was at his fullest and best. Sunday after Sunday new treasures were presented to his spell-bound hearers. Old texts shone out with fresh meaning, and the common experiences of life became glorified under the preacher's poetic imagination. The best testimony to his preaching power that I ever received, was from an old woman who once lived in a dungeon of a house in Stockbridge, but who informed me that Dr. Matheson's sermons had made it impossible for her to live in such sordid surroundings. She was thereafter to be found in one of the brightest top attics in a new street, not far off. One effect of Dr. Matheson's preaching was an increased sense of self-respect. He seldom dwelt on the humiliation of sin, but frequently on the exalting power of righteousness, and the magnetic influence of the person of Christ on the human character. Not unfrequently did he allow humour to lighten and brighten his discourses. Describing on one occasion the visit of people in different perplexities to St. Paul, who was represented as sitting in the study, ready to hear their grievances and to answer questions, and after giving imaginary conversations between Paul and members of the Corinthian, Ephesian, and Galatian Churches, the preacher suddenly stopped, and represented on the pulpit what purported to be a low knock at the door of the study. "Come in," was twice called out before the door was timidly opened, and there entered one who was described to the life, a man tall, thin, nervous, and anxious in expression. "Oh, it is teetotal Timothy," exclaimed the preacher, "come to ask St. Paul if it would be right to take a little wine for his stomach's sake." Such vivid imaginative delineations of character were listened to with breathless interest, and in these graphic portraitures lay much of the preacher's power.

Often he commenced his sermon by telling his people that he had had a new revelation on the text chosen. Indeed, he told me on one occasion that he never got a text without reasoning himself into the belief that it was a distinct revelation and contained a message hitherto undelivered. Whilst at the beginning of the sermon the startling novelty of his interpretation was often apparent, sometimes towards the close the listener would find himself gradually led into the old and accustomed way of thought, and be surprised or disappointed according to temperament. At other times the preacher's method—and it was an artful method—was to throw as much doubt and darkness upon the text as he could, evolving all the possible difficulties in its reception as truth, and then suddenly to lift the text out of its darkness by proclaiming the transparent truth contained therein. It seemed often as if he inverted the natural way of approach, and led us through a back door—with its dark passages, until we were suddenly shown out at the front door in the full light of day. No one who was a constant hearer can ever forget the wholly characteristic habit he had of lifting his arms when he "scored a point," or when a sudden flash of humour surprised him in speech. On these occasions the very eyes that were blind seemed full of expression. As when he solved the riddle of the name and number of the "Beast" in the Book of the Revelation by declaring that its name was "Selfishness" and its number "No. 1," and when he defended preachers who were "high" or "low" by affirming that there was a worse than either, namely, the preacher who was "thin."

Once when preaching in St. Bernard's he was graphically describing the approach of the Philistine army over a distant hill. "What is that I see?" he exclaimed, and then depicted the appearance of the army as the sun flashed upon their armaments. "What is that I hear?" he further exclaimed, and to this question there came a most unexpected response. The congregation had been absolutely still in their contemplation of the beautiful word-picture, but just as this question was asked one of the audience in a far-off gallery gave a most unseemly and surprisingly loud sneeze. Whilst his audience could hardly refrain from audible laughter, the preacher was seen to be as keenly alive as any to the humour of the incident, and for a while he withheld the answer until the effect of the surprise had gone.

Mr. Lang's reference to Dr. Matheson's description of St. Paul in his study, solving the difficulties of young inquirers like Timothy, was illustrated in the preacher's experience. Many, especially young, men came to him with their religious doubts. He thoroughly appreciated their position. His attitude towards them was most encouraging and sympathetic, for had he not passed through a similar mental and spiritual trial himself? The Rev. Mr. Drummond, now at Jedburgh, who, from being at one time a member of Dr. Matheson's Bible-class, came to be his colleague, bears witness to the service rendered by Dr. Matheson in this connection. He says :

The minister of St. Bernard's was much more than a popular preacher—he was a teacher of religion. Inquiring young men, puzzled by the problems of modern thought, came asking difficult questions in Christology, or about the relation between science and religion, or some particular book in the Bible, or some difficult doctrine of Christianity. Dr. Matheson always answered at once, clearly and fully, as if he were giving a previously considered opinion, or as if he had just risen from a fresh study of the subject.

Let me now give a specimen of the way in which Dr. Matheson prepared the skeletons from which he preached his sermons. Here is one that seems to have been a favourite with him. It is headed "The Length and the Breadth," and might have as a sub-title "Proportion of Character." The text is taken from Rev. xxi. 16 :

The secret of all beauty is proportion. A feature may be perfect in itself and yet incongruous; hence Hawthorne makes Donatello not quite Grecian. Distinguish contrast from incongruity. Quote the lines, "Now upon Syria's land of roses," etc. The union in these lines of summer and winter is all right, but it would be all wrong if they were transposed in geographical position. A child playing on a grave is all right; but not a man. The most hard thing is to get proportion of character. There are littlenesses in great men—for example, Elijah; and there are greatnesses in little men, *e.g.*, the miser at Innellan who bore so well the fall of the City Bank. Three types of irregularity. First, Men of isolated height, *e.g.*, John. They soar aloft and seek a higher world; but they are apt to ignore the claims of length—the walking along the prosaic plain of practice, *e.g.*, Samaria. Second, Men of isolated length, or the walk along the plain, *e.g.*, James. It comprehends the young men who spend their whole life in a routine of work, and never raise their eyes to justification by faith. Third, Men of isolated breadth, *e.g.*, the nameless young man in the Gospel who always refused to do what he was desired to do. This type rejoices in breadth for its own sake—because it is doing a forbidden thing, *e.g.*, skating on Sunday, or promenading in Waverley Market. But there is no beauty in breadth for its own sake; it must be breadth for the sake of height, *i.e.*, not the desire to break a fence, but to carry something across the field.

The city of God has these three elements of proportion. Human life leads through each in turn. Its progress is marked by the three words, "aloft," "along," "across." We begin by seeking the height—a fairer world than ours. Youth is the most dissatisfied period. By and by we are stopped by some practical weakness in ourselves, and we give up trying. Whatever the weakness is that stops us becomes to us the only thing in the world to be conquered. If it is drink, our gospel becomes teetotalism; if pride, we insist that everyone shall feel himself a poor creature. We move along a narrow plank, and admit no breadth beyond it. At last there comes a new revelation, that our brother and we have not been impeded by the same weakness, and we grow broad; we move across, to meet in sympathy his way of salvation. Christ's training of the Twelve is directed to bring out one of the three elements. Peter is too materialistic. He presses along the road of practical action so keenly that he has length without height or ideality. Christ takes him up to the mount. Apply to those who are withdrawn from the world by illness. John has height or ideality, but he wants practice or length of road. Christ sends him to cast out devils; God often interrupts our dreams by sending us the need for hard work. Paul has both height and practice, but at first he wants breadth, *e.g.*, his attitude towards circumcision. God sends him the thorn—a difficulty in his own sphere of labour. Nothing broadens us like trial in our strong-point. Christ includes all three—heights of prayer, day of walking, work; and sympathy with aims distinct from His own, *e.g.*, the man who would not follow Him. Hence Christ unites the guild of humanity.

CHAPTER X

PASTORAL AND LITERARY

"Dr. Matheson has now completed his visitation of the congregation. Some no doubt have been omitted, although the list has been made up as carefully as possible. Dr. Matheson would be very sorry to pass over any of his congregation, and he would be obliged by any in the parish on whom he has not called letting him know of the omission." Such is the announcement on the first page of the Parish Magazine of St. Bernard's for December 1886. Dr. Matheson was inducted to his charge on the 12th May of that year, so that within the brief period of six months he had visited every family in connection with his church.

To the layman, the fatigue and mental strain involved in such an ordeal are quite unknown. The congregation of St. Bernard's at this time numbered close upon 1500 members. There were in addition many seat-holders who were not in communion with the congregation; outsiders, who identified themselves with the church solely on account of Dr. Matheson's preaching. They also were visited; so that, altogether, the new minister must have paid within the short period mentioned not fewer than between five and six hundred calls. And all this, be it remembered, in addition to visits paid to the sick, to the aged, to the infirm, and to the dying. Dr. Matheson at the same time was preparing and preaching sermons of the rarest quality, attending assiduously to the various associations in connection with his church, and discharging the numerous demands of a public nature that were being made upon him. In addition he was busy at work on important literary ventures, writing articles for magazines, and keeping himself fully abreast of the literature of the day. No layman, I have remarked, can fully appreciate what is meant by a minister of Dr. Matheson's temperament paying so many visits within so limited a space of time. He was so warm-hearted and full of sympathy that every new person whom he met in his ministerial capacity drew, so to speak, virtue out of him; made a demand upon his spiritual nature which was bound to be exhausting. Indeed, I know as a fact that the visits that he paid at this time made a lasting impression upon his congregation. The very expressions which he used were remembered by them. He put himself so closely in touch, not only with their particular circumstances, but even with their special idiosyncrasies, that his words were ever cherished. And he was blind. This son of genius, whose true sphere, in the opinion of

many, was the study on the week day and the
pulpit on the Sunday, divested himself, with the
utmost cheerfulness, of his favourite robe and
clothed himself with the garment of humility.   He
descended to the depths of Stockbridge, visited
poor widows in sunken areas or climbed to highest
attics, and with his hearty, sympathetic words
cheered them in their loneliness and comforted them
in their sorrow.

No one ever heard of a minister with his full
power of vision and with the sturdy limbs of a
Goliath ever accomplishing a feat like this.   The
vast majority of the clergy make no pretence to
genius.   If they possessed it they might very
well say, "Such laborious, physical toil can be
performed by men of lesser mark ; let us confine
ourselves to our God-appointed task of ministering
to the intellectual wants of our people on Sundays."
Matheson, at the time the one minister of genius
in the Church, thought otherwise.   He did not
even make his blindness an excuse.   He visited
the fatherless, and widows in their affliction, and
kept himself unspotted from the world.   Some may
have thought that his teaching failed in practicality.
No one with a spark of his spirit ever believed that.
His teaching, especially during his St. Bernard's
ministry, was full of reality.   Every sermon almost,
was an application of Christianity to common life ;
but, should there be any doubt, his labours during
his first six months at St. Bernard's ought to be a
sufficient answer.

"He was," writes the Session Clerk of St. Bernard's, "an indefatigable visitor"; nor did this feature of his ministry belong to his first year in St. Bernard's only, it marked his ministry on to the time he applied to the Presbytery for a colleague. Dr. Matheson perhaps felt himself put on his mettle. The great fear on the part of some of the St. Bernard's people, with regard to his appointment, was that he would be unable to discharge the ordinary duties of a parish minister. In the case of St. Bernard's these duties were not ordinary but extraordinary. The church was situated in the north-western part of Edinburgh; the parish included a large working-class element, and in it was Stockbridge, a district bordering on slumdom. The congregation was thus a mixed one. There were a number of well-to-do-families, representing the professional and mercantile classes; but the vast majority of the congregation were of the artisan order, and under recent ministries the church was worked on the "modern" system. Organisations were multiplied, agencies were increased, schemes were set on foot; in fact, St. Bernard's, when Dr. Matheson came to it, was a very bee-hive of associations. What such a church really required was a manager and not a minister, a man of business faculty who could keep the concern running, rather than a man of genius who could supply ideas for the illumination of conduct and of life. The spirit of the church was mechanical rather than dynamical, and at the first blush Dr. Matheson was the last man in the world who ought to have been appointed its minister.

Here is the calendar of the various meetings of the different Associations in St. Bernard's for a single week :

Forenoon and Afternoon Services, Children's Church, Sunday Schools, and Class for Women and Girls on Sunday; Evening Work Party, Boys' Carving Class, Girls' Club, and Literary Society on Monday; Mothers' Meeting and Sewing Class on Tuesday; Boys' Brigade on Wednesday; Choir Practising on Thursday; Savings Bank and Boys' Brigade Reading Club on Saturday. In addition to these there must not be omitted the Young Men's Fellowship Meeting in the Session House on Sunday; the Forenoon Work Party and the Bible Class in the Session House on Wednesday; and the Minister's Class for Children in the church after Forenoon Service on Sunday; as well as the Parochial Coal Fund and the Flower Mission. The services of the Lady Collectors are well known.

Dr. Matheson achieved many triumphs in his day, but the one which he obtained over the difficulties that faced him in St. Bernard's seems to me to have been his greatest. There are few ministers in the Church who would lightly enter on such a sphere. The chances of failure would, in the vast majority of cases, far outweigh those of success; and yet Matheson succeeded. During the first five years of his ministry his communion roll steadily increased. In 1886 it was 1494; in 1887, 1530; in 1888, 1591; in 1889, 1676; and in 1890, 1703. The revenue of the church increased in similar proportions. I have before me, as I write, notebook after notebook filled

with addresses, most carefully prepared, which
Dr. Matheson delivered to the different agencies
and organisations of the church.   These include
lectures to the Sunday-School teachers ; addresses
to District Visitors, to the Young Men's Guild, to
the Young Women's Association, to the Boys'
Brigade, to the Literary Society, to the Prayer
Meeting, Mothers' Meeting, etc. etc.   An ordinary
minister would have excused himself from making
any preparation for such gatherings.   He would
have trusted to the spur of the moment.   Not so
Dr. Matheson.   Every address was as thoughtful
and as appropriate to the occasion as his greatest
sermons.   A selection from them would make a
fascinating chapter in Homiletics, and would be
invaluable to the pastor whose chosen sphere was
the cure of souls.

There was one body in particular that received
the very best which he could give them ; that was
his Bible Class.   It consisted of two divisions :
young men and young women, who met on
alternate weeks.   There were two books which he
selected for his addresses, the Book of Genesis
and the Acts of the Apostles ; and he so prepared
himself for his work that his remarks upon each
chapter and verse might be published as most
luminous commentaries on these two portions of
the Bible.   His method combined criticism with
exposition.   The text was elucidated, side lights
were thrown upon it from history and archæology.
The customs of the times were brought in to shed

further light upon it. Then followed his own fresh interpretation, and its practical application to the lives of the young men and young women who were listening to him. These lectures formed an epoch in the lives of many who heard them.

A specimen of his Notes on Genesis and the Acts of the Apostles may not be unwelcome. Let me give his opening remarks, first on Genesis, and then on the Acts:

Chap. i. ver. 1.—Explain in what senses Genesis records the beginning of things. " In the beginning"; one book goes farther back still (John i. 1). Exhibit how each of the Gospels progressively antedates Christ's genealogy. Give the two different views regarding the words, " In the beginning"—those of Hugh Miller and Chalmers. " In the beginning God created"; His existence is assumed. State the four words in which this chapter expresses creation—(1) "Created," Gen. i. 1, 21, 27; (2) " Made," Gen. i. 7; (3) " Formed," Gen. ii. 7; (4) " Build," Gen. ii. 22. Catechism makes it creation out of nothing, but nothing means no *thing*. Compare Heb. xi. 3. Defend the emanation view, illustrating by a candle lighted at a fire. This is proved by the fact that everything is referred to the breath or Spirit of God. " The heavens and the earth"; the heavens before the earth, true to science. *P.S.*—Explain the different words for God.

The Acts of the Apostles, Chap. i. ver. 1.—" The former treatise." Analyse the preface of Luke's Gospel, taking up the origin of the Gospels from oral tradition and showing how the different parties in the Church would each emphasise the facts bearing on their own tendency. Show how the four Gospels are coloured by the parties of James, Peter, Paul, and Apollos respectively, and describe the evangelists by the figures in Ezekiel's vision—man, lion, ox, and eagle. "O Theophilus"; the "most excellent" in Luke is dropped through greater familiarity. " Began to do and to teach." This, Luke's peculiar formula;

he goes to the sources; it means, "Did and taught from the beginning." "To do and to teach." Matthew deals chiefly in his teaching, Mark in his deeds, Luke in both.

This is how Dr. Matheson prepared himself for his Addresses to Teachers. The following, one of forty or so that I have counted, is based on Psalm lxxxi. vers. 11, 12, "But My people would not hearken to My voice; and Israel would none of Me. So I gave them up unto their own hearts' lust: and they walked in their own counsels."

Child's greatest danger is self-will or love of independence. Its origin is not love of self, for self-willed people are generally discontented. It comes from an intellectual error — the belief that independence is manly. This again comes from a false notion, that all the grand things in nature are self-acting. Teacher should counteract that, should teach the child that there is no such thing in nature as a thing hanging upon nothing. When we come to man we do find cases of laudable independence, i.e., people refusing to be a burden to anyone. But teachers should point out that even in these cases we only reach independence of one thing, by leaning on another thing, e.g., independence of praise comes from sense of duty; fearlessness of man from fear of God. Hence if a child should become independent of the bands of conscience, verse 12 says it can only be by getting entangled in other bands, "I gave them up unto their own hearts' lust." Every paltering with conscience does indeed loosen the bond, and teacher should scrupulously watch the initial attempts to get this false freedom.

One of his most characteristic and thoughtful addresses bears the following title :—

ADDRESS TO "CAT AND DOG" HOME

Begin by Goethe's two stages: Christianity first taught the reverence for inferior things—the reverence

17

for man as man, irrespective even of brotherhood. In later times the reverence has gone down beneath even humanity—to the animal world. Darwinism has preached the gospel of a ground of sympathy between man and beast. They have a perfect community of nature in the possession of one thing—pain. All creation is sympathetically united in the sense of want, and whatever creates my sympathy becomes thereby my creditor.

Here is a little sketch of the way in which he moved among his parishioners. It relates to the year 1893 or 1894, after he had been seven or eight years in St. Bernard's. It throws some light also on his labours in other relations, upon the calls made upon him in connection with baptismal, marriage, and funeral services. These, in so large a congregation, were numerous indeed. It does not refer to his work in connection with his young communicants' classes. No minister ever undertook that duty with a more serious consideration of its importance than Dr. Matheson, and his many addresses, also carefully and thoughtfully prepared for these classes, are models of their kind. Speaking of his parochial and congregational work, the Rev. Mr. Lang, already quoted, says :

Dr. Matheson, while I was assistant to him in St. Bernard's, certainly did not neglect these duties. Baptisms were conducted in the church once a month, and frequently in his own dining-room. He always used the same form of service in baptism, a form of his own, but always the same. In my day he also conducted the service at a great many of the funerals. His prayer on such occasions was most beautiful, and I only wish I could remember it correctly. I recollect on one occasion, at the funeral of a child, he used some such expressions as the following :—

"Sometimes Thou sendest Thine angel when the sun is setting and the leaf is ready to fall. At other times, when the sun is in its meridian and the flower is in fullest bloom. But here Thine angel has plucked a tender bud, ere even the sun had opened its petals, and we murmur not, for in the sun of Thy love it has opened to the perfect day." Such, but very imperfectly recorded, was part of the prayer. In the visitation of the sick he was always assiduous. One woman told me she always felt better when she heard his footstep. His cheerful, but wholly sympathetic, manner at the bedside was sure to be a tonic. In his interesting prayer he used to pray that to the sad and sick there might be given that grandly irrational and wholly incomprehensible peace which the world cannot give, much less take away. His relation to children and his sermons to them were not the least striking traits in his rich and many-sided character.

Matheson had not been long in St Bernard's until a movement was set on foot for renovating the church. He was to do for his new charge a work somewhat similar to what he had done for his old one. He was to raise a large sum of money. At Innellan his object was to build a manse and to endow and erect the church into a parish; at St. Bernard's his purpose was to bring his church structurally up to date, to provide some necessary accommodation, and to make the whole building, with its appurtenances, suitable for the service of God and the work of the congregation and parish. A sum of two thousand pounds was required, and within a year the money was raised, the work done, and the church reopened. This was in October 1888, after he had been minister of St. Bernard's for a little more than two years. This effort, so quick and so successful, is a further proof of Matheson's capacity as a man of business, and his keen interest in the practical side of church life.

Many who are familiar with him solely through his *Meditations* may regard him as a recluse and a dreamer, a student of the devout life, given to introspection. Others who have read his more ambitious books, dealing with theological and philosophical subjects, may hold him to have been a man of rare speculative power, and some who chanced to hear him preach once or twice in their lifetime, may look up to him as a prophet, who could read the soul of things and inspire his hearers with lofty and beautiful ideals. But very few of them perhaps ever believe him to have been the rarest of all men—a practical Christian; one who carried out in the daily routine of duty the thoughts that he breathed, the beliefs that he cherished, and the emotions which filled his soul. It was only those who came into personal contact with him, who were aware of his multitudinous labours on behalf of his congregation and parish, of his indefatigable zeal in ministering to the wants of all ages and classes, and inspiring the different associations and agencies in connection with his church with a true conception of their vocation and duty. True, he was a mystic, but he was a practical mystic, of all men the most irresistible; a dreamer of dreams that he realised in fact; a seer of visions which he transformed into reality. Preaching at the reopening of his church, he paid a generous tribute to his predecessors in office, and proclaimed the Gospel of humanitarianism, of practical Christianity, of religion in common life, which was to those who knew him the main note of his preaching and the foundation of his work and life. "We have this day," he said,

reopened our "holy and beautiful house." It has not been unclothed, but clothed upon. I am glad that it has not been unclothed, glad the old memories still surround the ancient walls. Sixty-and-five years has this church been in existence, and its life has been a progress from the streamlet to the sea. With that progress I myself had little to do; other men have laboured, and I have entered into their labours. I have been indebted to a long line of illustrious predecessors—to the evangelical fervour of Martin, the genuine ability of M'Farlane, the energetic power of Cæsar, the intellectual vigour of Brown, the popular eloquence of Robertson, the literary fame of Boyd, the profound spirituality and unblemished piety of my immediate pre-runner, Mr. M'Murtrie.

But looking back on the labours of others, and speaking purely from the standpoint of a spectator, I may be allowed to feel proud. I may be allowed to congratulate myself that I have been privileged to be the minister of the congregation which has done so much for the cause of humanitarian interests. No one can say that, originally, the lines were cast to you in pleasant places. Around you was the city, with its sins and sorrows—its sins of deepest colour, its sorrows of darkest dye. Before you were poverty, squalor, vice, personal failure, social corruption, human degeneracy. Over this trackless region you have made a path, through which already the flowers begin to peep. Your vast Sabbath Schools, your flourishing Fellowships, your extensive classes for males and females, your Clothing Club in which self-help has been made to blend with benevolent help, your munificent donations to church schemes; above all, your power of personal visitation, have contributed to purify the air and have left to the germs room to grow.

And now what should be our guerdon of this extended building?   More sacrifice, more work to do; that is what you expect—you and I.   We have opened wide our doors that more of humanity may enter in.   But if in the language of the hymn we look for " many a labour, many a sorrow, many a tear," we look also for that which shall wipe away all tears from the eyes.   We look for an increase of that humanitarian love which is itself the love of Christianity's divine Head, and in whose light and leading we believe that the weight of the burden shall disappear. It is this conviction which to-day emboldens us to con-secrate our building to the Highest, and to say to the Chief Corner-Stone of all its architecture—" Establish Thou the work of our hands."

The amount and character of the work which we have thus seen Dr. Matheson accomplished on behalf of his congregation and parish, would be sufficient to tax the energies of most men ; but when we follow him into his study, and consider his labours there for the wider public who knew him mainly as an author, we are filled with genuine astonishment.   His literary output during the thirteen years of his ministry in St. Bernard's was equal in quantity to what he produced at Innellan. It may not, however, have taxed him quite to the same extent, for the subjects on which he wrote demanded less research and less profound thinking. It may be said, of course, that his choice in this respect was natural because he had less leisure, but this was not the whole reason, and it will be afterwards shown that his departure from the themes that attracted him in his Innellan days was

the result of a natural development. His mental
and spiritual growth drew him into new paths and
attracted him to fresh subjects.

One important change is noticeable : his contributions to periodical literature during this time
are fewer in number, and they are on more
biblical themes. They are of a lighter vein, more
expository in character, and better adapted for the
general religious public. They are found, consequently, in the pages of those magazines that are
meant for Sunday reading. We find him accordingly writing for *Good Words*, *The Homiletic
Magazine*, *The Quiver*, *The Expository Times*, *The
Christian World*, and *The Children's Guide*. His
fame had now crossed the Atlantic, and contributions by him are solicited by such magazines as *The
Biblical World* published in Chicago, and by *The
Sunday School Times* of Philadelphia. All his
articles in these magazines are characterised by his
usual freshness of thought and finish of style, and
one of them on the " Feminine Ideal of Christianity,"
which appeared in *The Biblical World*, is of exceptional ability and interest.

The very year after his induction to St. Bernard's
he published a new volume, *The Psalmist and the
Scientist, or the Modern Value of the Religious
Sentiment*. This was the aftermath of his important work, *Can the Old Faith Live with the New?*
It was a selection, so to speak, from the chips that
had collected in his workshop while he was engaged
on that striking volume. The subject continued to

interest him during the remainder of his life, and
ten years afterwards he reverted to it in a volume
which he wrote, but never published, on Natural
Religion. The special subject of *The Psalmist and
the Scientist* he had already anticipated in a long
and thoughtful article which he wrote on "Modern
Science and the Religious Instinct." The question
which he asked in that article was: "Is the modern
doctrine of evolution unfavourable to the development of the religious sentiment? Does it tend
naturally to dwarf the growth of the primitive
instinct or to exert a chilling influence on the
warmth of early days?" Conceding that there is
no incompatibility between the spirit of early faith
and the spirit of modern science, his article is an
attempt to answer these questions; and, beginning
with the statement that the three elements which
constitute the natural basis of religion are a sense
of wonder, a sense of fear, and a sense of dependence, he shows that on the principle of evolution
these three elements not only remain but are intensi-
fied and purified, broadened out and strengthened to
such a degree, as to make them surer foundations of
religion. In another article, which he wrote about
the same time, on "Evolution in relation to
Miracles," which appeared in *The Homiletic
Magazine*, he touches on the same question, and
defining miracle in the Christian sense to be the
"initial stage of that process by which a lower law
is transcended by a higher law," he finds nothing in
evolution that would contradict it. It was thus his

habit to prepare himself for his more important books by a series of articles or addresses; he threshed out the subject first of all in his own mind, and looked at it from every standpoint. This largely accounts for the clearness of thought and sureness of step which characterised all his writing. In his preface to *The Psalmist and the Scientist*, he states the purpose of the book. He says: "I design to inquire whether the religious sentiment of the past has been superannuated or rendered obsolete by the modern conception of nature? I have expressed respectively these seemingly opposite standpoints by the title, *The Psalmist and the Scientist*. Science is confessedly the author of the modern conception of nature; the Book of Psalms is admittedly the repository of the religious sentiment in its largest and most comprehensive form."

This may not be one of Dr. Matheson's greatest books, but it has proved itself to have been one of his most useful. It popularised the subject of his former volume, illustrated its arguments in various ways, and put material into the hands of preachers which they were not slow to use. The ordinary reader may not have been able to follow the reasoning of *Can the Old Faith Live with the New?* but in the newer volume the subject is brought down to the level of every man who possesses a religious sentiment, and the Book of Psalms, with which every Christian is more or less familiar, is made the starting-point and ground of the argument. The mind of the ordinary worshipper was, at the time of the appearance of Dr. Matheson's book, sorely distressed by the fear that the modern conception of nature had made religion impossible. This was the man that Dr. Matheson appealed to. In his earlier book he deliberately chose for his audience the thoughtful and the learned. In his later volume he selected the wider public for his hearers. His appeal to both was successful in the extreme. No man of his day did more on behalf of true religion, in relation to the danger that threatened it, than Dr. Matheson. He enabled the religious public to breathe freely once more, and he did this not by stemming the new tide of thought, but by allowing it to spread over the religious sentiment which absorbed it. The writer, in this volume, discusses such subjects as the "Psalmist's Argument for God"; his "View of the Origin of Life" and of "Human Insignificance"; his "Ground of Religious Confidence"; his "Principle of Survival and Conservation." He shows how, when the sentiments of the religious consciousness come into contact with the views of evolution on the same subjects, there is no real conflict; the older truth is simply widened and deepened by the impartation of the new. The success of the volume was immediate and deserved.

In 1888 he published two new volumes, *Landmarks of New Testament Morality*, and *Voices of the Spirit*; the latter, a devotional volume, has already been referred to. Shortly after he came to

Edinburgh, Dr. Matheson had been asked to deliver a lecture to the Church of Scotland Young Men's Guild; the first of a series by distinguished preachers. He chose as his subject, "The Relation of Christian to pre-Christian Morality," and this forms the title of the first chapter of his new book. In his preface he declares his aim to have been to compress into a few connected chapters what seemed to him to be the distinctive and salient principles of New Testament morality. The book formed one of *Nisbet's Theological Library*, and in it such subjects as the "Motives of Christian Morality," the "Christian View of Sin," the "Moral Place of Faith," the "Moral Place of Prayer" are discussed. The volume is full of vigorous thought, and contains some of Dr. Matheson's most characteristic teaching. As a chapter in the important subject of Christian Ethics, treating it in its fundamental aspects, it was timely in its appearance, and is still of value.

Two years afterwards Dr. Matheson gathered together and published in volume form a selection from the hymns that he had been writing at irregular intervals from his early manhood, and published them under the title of *Sacred Songs*; and about the same time, in 1890, there appeared what many regard as his most important book, *The Spiritual Development of St. Paul.* If one can judge of its value from its popularity it was certainly the most successful of all his serious efforts. It has had a larger sale than any of his other books, with the exception of his devotional volumes and his later publications, such as *Studies of the Portrait of Christ*, and *The Representative Men of the Bible*. The Apostle Paul would seem to have had a wonderful fascination for Dr. Matheson. Some of his earliest articles in *The Expositor* have him as their subject. In twelve successive issues of that magazine there appeared from his pen contributions on the " Historical Christ of St. Paul," and subsequently, at frequent intervals, he wrote on various themes suggested by the writings of the great apostle. Wherein, one may ask, consisted the charm of Paul for Dr. Matheson? An answer might be found in the fact that between the two there must have been a close intellectual and spiritual sympathy. They were both eager spirits, full of enthusiasm for the highest things, and carried along by a passion of thought which nothing could stay. They had both a tender and chivalrous love for their Master, and they had penetrated to the secret of His life as few have done in ancient or modern times. Each was dissatisfied until he made clear to himself the ground of his belief, and had made that belief a living reality in his own soul and in the souls of others. Even in their style of writing, or at all events of thinking, there is a strong similarity. The Apostle to the Gentiles certainly did not aim at that finish of style which characterised his modern admirer, but in their love of paradox they are both alike. They saw at a glance, they photographed in their minds an idea or a truth, and they cast it forth in what seemed to be an inverted form, which at once caught the eye and riveted the attention, and only on reflection could the beholder perceive its meaning and appreciate its true significance. In dealing with the characters of the Old and New Testaments, even with those which had caught most of the spirit of Christ, Dr. Matheson shows no hesitation in pointing out their limitations. They are at best but broken lights of the great Sun that they reflected; but in dealing with Paul he manifests a whole-hearted admiration, and if he points out defects or failures it is only because the great apostle had not as yet attained to his full development. These defects or failures simply mark stages in his spiritual growth, steps in his religious advancement. The life at the close is full, rounded, and completed, the brightest and most precious gem in the crown of Christian discipleship.

Now, it seems to me that there is one feature common to the Apostle Paul and to Dr. Matheson in which the latter found a special bond of union : each had a thorn in the flesh, and in both cases the thorn was the same. According to certain critics, of whom Dr. Matheson was one, Paul was a martyr to defective eyesight; and the chronicler of his spiritual development was blind. On no occasion does Dr. Matheson refer to this bond of union. Of all men he was the most reticent with regard to his own afflictions, and so far as his great affliction was concerned he was, for the most part, absolutely silent. He never bemoaned his fate; he made no

parade of his calamity, nor did he even show any
natural pride in the triumph which he won over
it. Paul was almost as reticent, but now and again
he had to speak out, because in his case the thorn
in the flesh was made a cause of reproach, and this
reproach he in the end was able to turn to the
glory of God and his own spiritual advancement.
It is well for us that he did give indications of what
he suffered, and of the experiences which he passed
through, before he attained his final victory; and
the great and permanent value of Dr. Matheson's
book lies in the fact that he makes this thorn in
the flesh the guiding element in tracing Paul's
spiritual development. The outward affliction and
the inward experience, the physical defect and the
spiritual sufferings, would seem to go hand in hand.
The one reacts upon the other, and together they
account for the development of Paul's inner life
and of his religious views.

A book that has taken so strong a hold on
the public mind, and one possessing so many
exceptional qualities, ought to receive a fuller
notice than I intend, in this connection, to give
it. My reason is that in an article which Dr.
Matheson wrote, seven years afterwards, to a
volume issued by Dr. Lyman Abbott, of New
York, on *The Prophets of the Christian Faith*,
he gives a résumé of his book on St. Paul which
for fulness and brilliance of treatment far exceeds
what any other might accomplish. In that sketch,
extending to twelve pages only, he gives the gist

of the larger volume, and anyone who wishes to know, at a glance, his mind on the subject will find it there.   But one thing he does not do ; he does not trace the close resemblance between Paul's spiritual development and his own.   It is quite possible, of course, that in writing his book he was altogether unconscious of that resemblance ; but the very fact that, according to his own confession, he lingered over the composition of the volume, spending two years on its writing and many more on its thinking, that of all his books it bears the most traces of loving care, patient treatment, and sympathetic handling, show that the subject had a fascination for him which cannot be explained on literary or theological grounds merely ; it can only be accounted for on reasons that were personal.

Dr. Matheson points out, to begin with, that Paul's first conception of Christianity was absolutely different from that of the other apostles.   His first vision of Christ was in the air ; theirs on the earth. He knew Him, at the start, in His resurrection glory ; they as the Man of Galilee.   His first glimpse was of His divinity ; theirs of His humanity. The writer then goes on, in a series of chapters bristling with suggestive thoughts and full of the subtlest yet conclusive reasoning, to show how the development of Paul's spiritual life was a descent, a coming down from heaven to earth, from the divine to the human, from the conception of a glorified Christ to a Saviour of the world.   In

pursuance of his argument Dr. Matheson shows
how, according to Paul, Christ is the Head of the
universe, of the state, of society, and of the family;
not only coming into touch with, but sanctifying,
the commonest duties and things of life. His flight
is towards the gospel of humanitarianism, of saving
the world by being its servant, of redeeming man
by ministering to him, of gaining the crown by
bearing the cross. The resurrection Christ of
Paul's completed journey is the Christ of sight
who has passed into that of faith, who again has
passed from that of faith to that of love, and from
that of love to that of hope. Hope for the individual, hope for the family, hope for society, hope
for the state, hope for the world, hope for the
universe. Christ is the Head of all. "In Him
all are gathered together," and this gathering in
has taken place through Christ's emptying of
Himself, through taking upon Himself the form
of a servant, and becoming obedient unto death,
even the death on the Cross.

Now, a close follower of Dr. Matheson's career
as a preacher and a writer is bound to find in it
the counterpart of the development which he traces
in the life of the Apostle Paul. He too began with
the worship of a glorified Christ. Reflecting on
the sermons which, during his early ministry, he
preached at Innellan, and those which crown his
later life, one is conscious of a progress which,
in its own sphere and on its own lines, is similar
to that through which the great Apostle of the

Gentiles passed. Early hearers of Dr. Matheson were carried up into the seventh heaven by his flashes of thought, by his spiritual aspirations, by his imaginative flights. But not infrequently they were left there. In his sermons there may have been that lack of reality, of food for common life, which characterised the early preaching of the Apostle Paul. But, as the years advanced, the thought, without losing its strength or buoyancy, became more sober. It grew more into touch with the experiences of men. The preacher descended to the earth and took up its common sights and sounds, put himself into sympathy with the ordinary lot of human existence; nay, he did more, he showed a tender concern for the sorrows and sufferings of men, and brought the gospel of Divine love to bear, with its redeeming grace, upon the calamities of existence, and showed how the love of the Father as revealed in the death of the Son transformed the experiences of His children and made them the means of spiritual advancement and religious growth. In other words, the Gospel of Dr. Matheson became more humanitarian, and showed how the Cross of Christ sanctified and glorified human existence. A similar development can be seen in Dr. Matheson as an author. His earliest books and articles deal with subjects which are purely theological and philosophical. They are themes that are, so to speak, in the air; they interest the mind of man, and at first sight they do not seem to have much

18

relation to or influence on his life. But as the
years advanced new subjects present themselves.
They are in a sense more real, more human,
more personal. "The Growth of the Spirit of
Christianity" gives place to "The Spiritual Development of St. Paul," "The Natural Elements of
Revealed Theology" to "The Portrait of Christ"
and "The Men and Women of the Bible,"
religion to theology, and religion as a spiritual
development to its practical expression in the
life of man.

But what I regard as the personal note in the
book is by far the most interesting and suggestive.
The opening chapters deal at considerable length
with Paul's special affliction, which he indirectly
refers to as a "thorn in the flesh." Dr. Matheson
is at particular pains to show, by a process of very
careful and thorough exegesis, what this particular
affliction may have been, and he comes to the
conclusion that it was defective eyesight. In this
is to be found Paul's thorn in the flesh. A number
of the reviewers disputed this conclusion, but none of
them did so in more than a doubting way. For us,
however, the suggestive point is that Dr. Matheson
held this opinion. For us the luminous fact is not
the conclusion which Dr. Matheson came to, but
the manner in which he uses it to interpret the
spiritual development of the apostle. Taking his
stand on the apostle's confession that he "besought
the Lord thrice" to deliver him from his calamity,
the author searches for the occasions in the life of

Paul when this prayer was uttered. Each, he believes, marks a crisis in the spiritual growth of the apostle, and if one can lay his hand on the particular moment when the cry for relief was uttered, he can also discover the stage in his development which Paul had reached. The theological views of the apostle, his interpretation of Christianity, and his own relation to it as an individual, will be found to synchronise with each particular cry.

The first step, accordingly, in Paul's spiritual struggle Dr. Matheson would see in the apostle's glorification of the flesh, in his belief, inherited from his Jewish training, that the servant of the Divine must be flawless, not only in spirit but also in body. Paul had been taught to believe that a physical defect was a mark of the Divine anger, and how could he, with his impaired organ of vision, hope to be an accredited missionary to the Gentiles. Paul's solution of this difficulty Dr. Matheson would find in the note which he struck in his earliest preaching. The apostle at this stage shared the belief that the Lord was at hand. The troubles of the present time would soon be over; the millennium was near, and by the glory which was about to be revealed to waiting souls the sufferings of life would be obliterated. The soul of the believer would be caught up into the heavens, and the bodily sufferings of earth would give place to transports of eternal joy.

The second stage in the struggle Dr. Matheson

would see in Paul's hatred of the flesh, in the warfare which he waged against it during the period of his Galatian ministry. If his Epistles to the Thessalonians afford a key to his attitude in the first, his Epistle to the Galatians reveals the stage which he had reached in his second struggle. The vision of the resurrection Christ was beginning to fade; the speedy deliverance which he had hoped for was not to be his; the battle of life must be fought to a finish; his thorn in the flesh must still be endured. Well then, said the apostle, let me endure. If the flesh lusteth against the Spirit, and the Spirit against the flesh, let me trample the flesh under foot; let me keep my body under; let me " beat it black and blue." My prayer is not to be answered as I expected; my defective eyesight is not to be improved; well then, let my prayer be answered in another way. I shall endeavour to forget my thorn; I shall do my work in spite of it; the mission of my life shall not fail because of physical suffering. I shall fulfil my God - appointed task in the face of every hardship and of every pain.

The third stage of the struggle has still to be noted. The apostle's cry was heard at last; and his prayer, like all prayers, was answered, not in the imperfect way in which he had at first desired, but in a manner far beyond his thinking or his asking. In this third stage, which is marked by the Epistles to the Corinthians and the Pastoral Epistles, which close the apostle's career on earth,

Dr. Matheson sees Paul's final triumph. His first solution was in being lifted up from the earth; his second in despising the earth; and his third in loving it. In other words, he had now come to see that the crosses of life, and his special cross, could only be understood, only be borne, in the light of the Cross of Christ. The Man of Sorrows bore with patience not only a thorn, but a crown of thorns; He conquered by submitting; He proved victorious by yielding; nay, He found in the afflictions of the present time the means for His spiritual growth. His attitude accordingly towards the trials of life was one of love, a love which in the end was crowned by a hope that those who had learned of Him would, through patient endurance, also conquer and be awarded the palm of victory. Hence, in the last stage of Paul's life Dr. Matheson sees the apostle's true solution of his difficulty, an answer to his prayer; for his attitude towards the homely things of life, the troubles and trials of man's lot in the world, had changed, and the note of his teaching became that of the gospel of his Master: "Perfect through suffering."

I have dwelt at some length on these points, for the reason already stated, because in them there is a personal note. The author in thus interpreting Paul's spiritual experiences was also tracing his own. He may have done so quite unconsciously, but all the same the result of his analysis throws a flood of light on his own life.

At an earlier stage I endeavoured to account for Dr. Matheson's Christian optimism, and I did so in much the same way as he accounts for Paul's. One was dimly conscious of the struggle through which he passed, and of the battle which he fought. On a priori grounds it was found that he could have conquered only as a Christian; but here, so to speak, he gives us a bit of his autobiography; he shows us, in tracing the spiritual experiences of Paul, what his own were. Indeed, I believe that, having passed through them first, having reached the goal before he came to the study of the apostle's life, he was able to understand that life through a sympathy born of a common trial and a common victory. It was the Cross of Christ undoubtedly which interpreted for Dr. Matheson the meaning of his thorn in the flesh. In the light of the Cross it became plain. This explains his Christian optimism, his enthusiasm, his cheerful outlook upon life and upon the world. This also accounts for his message of comfort and consolation to the weary and to the heavy laden. By his lips and by his pen he spoke the word of hopeful submission to the sufferer on the bed of pain, and of steadfast courage to the soldier engaged in the Christian warfare. To the man of sorrows and to the man of the world his message was the same: "Fight the good fight of faith, lay hold on eternal life"; accept your thorn in the flesh; the troubles and trials of the present time, not as messengers of Satan sent to buffet you, but as angels of mercy leading you in triumph to your home on high.

In his next work Dr. Matheson reverted to a subject which had been of much interest to him from his early days at Innellan. Some of his first contributions to periodical literature and his third important work, *Natural Elements of Revealed Theology*, show that the old religions had a special attraction for him. He manifested in his Baird Lecture a familiarity with certain of the pre-Christian religions which was a proof of very careful research and prolonged thought; and in 1882 he brought his studies to a point in his lecture on "Confucianism," one of the St. Giles' Lectures on *The Faiths of the World*. This was a very fine effort, and it brought his name before the public in a new relation. The subject had evidently been growing in his mind, and he extended his studies, so that in 1892 he was able to publish a volume of considerable size and importance on the ancient religions. Its title, *The Distinctive Messages of the Old Religions*, indicated its purpose and its scope, and he was careful, in the preface, to make his intention perfectly clear. He says that his design was not to describe the old religions, but to photograph their spirit. "By the distinctive message of a religion," he says, "I mean not an enumeration of its points, but a selection of the one point in which it differs from all others. My design, therefore, is more limited than that of some volumes of equal

size. I do not seek the permanent element of
religion with the Bishop of Ripon, nor the unconscious Christianity of Paganism with F. D. Manvill,
nor the moral ideal of the nations with Miss Julia
Wedgwood : I seek only to emphasise the dividing
line which constitutes the boundary between each
religion and all besides."

The author introduces his subject by a lengthened
inquiry into the origin of religion, and its common
element.   From this he passes to a consideration
of the distinctive elements of the great religions of
the ancient world ; and in his concluding chapter he
considers the purpose of Christianity in relation to
these religions, and declares that its mission is one
of *reconciliation*.   It is in this that one sees the
value of the book.   From the point of view of Dr.
Matheson's biography it is a fresh proof of his own
message to the world, which also was one of reconciliation.   The religion of Christ was to his mind
the great ingatherer; in Him all "things stand
together," and in His religion he finds a meeting-
place for the messages of the nations.   The concluding paragraph of his book indicates what
to his mind these messages were, and also the
message of Christianity towards them.   The
religion of Christ, he believes, ought to have a
peculiar interest in the faiths of the past.

They are not to her dead faiths; they are not even
modernised. They are preserved inviolable as parts of
herself—more inviolable than they would have been if
she had never come. Christianity has claimed to be " the

manifold wisdom of God." In this ascription she has been candid to the past. She has not denied its wisdom; she has only aspired to enfold it. She has not sought to derogate from the doctrines of antiquity; she has only sought to diminish their antagonisms. China may keep her materialism, and India may retain her mysticism; Rome may grasp her strength, and Greece may nurse her beauty; Persia may tell of the opposition to God's power, and Egypt may sing of His pre-eminence even amidst the tombs: but for each and all there is a seat in the Christian Pantheon, and a justification in the light of the manifold wisdom of God.

A break of four years in Dr. Matheson's literary activity now intervened. It was the longest break, and for this very reason it may not be without its significance. Four years elapsed between the publication of *The Distinctive Messages of the Old Religions* and his next book, *The Lady Ecclesia.* It was in 1896 that he gave it to the world, and it made its entrance under the auspices of new publishers. For a number of years his books had been published by the Blackwoods. T. & T. Clark, James Nisbet & Co., Cassell, and James Clarke & Co., had also in turn published one or other of his books. With all of these firms he was on the best of footings, and maintained his friendly relations with them to the end; but he now became associated with Hodder & Stoughton, and the remaining volumes written by him, with the exception of one or two devotional books, were published by them. The break of four years, I have remarked, may be regarded as significant, for *The Lady Ecclesia* marks a new departure, and the books that he

subsequently wrote may be said to be but a
development of the lines which he in that volume
laid down. We now find him dealing with subjects
that are purely religious and personal. He had
advanced to the last stage in his literary development, in which he would seem to be drawn to
themes of universal import and to characters that
come into close touch with human life on every
side. Especially was he attracted by the central
figure in Bible history, Jesus Christ Himself.
The life and teaching of the Saviour became to
him the one theme worthy to be dealt with, and
the volumes that he wrote on this and kindred
topics were the most popular and influential ever
published by him. His progress, like that of the
apostle, was a descent. He began with subjects
of lofty thought; he contented himself at the end
with lowly themes, but these themes after all were
the only vital ones, for they were common to the
heart of humanity, and came into contact with
man's experience at every point. The last note
sounded by him was the same as that struck by
the angels : "Peace on earth, goodwill towards
men." Religion in common life came to be the
absorbing topic of his latest thought and writing.

The Lady Ecclesia is an allegory. For beauty
of thought, for chasteness of style, for sustained
interest, it would be difficult in its own class to find
its equal. Its subject is the development of the
Spirit of Christ in the Church and in the individual ;
a restatement in allegorical form of one of his

earliest books. Indeed, it might have as a sub-title, "The Christ of History and the Christ of Experience," and no one can read it without finding a world of light shed both upon the story of the Church, especially during its earlier struggles and triumphs, and upon his own Christian experience. Not only does it make plain different epochs in the history of the Church and in the struggles of the individual soul towards a fuller realisation of the spirit of Christ, but it also unfolds, sometimes with startling effect, the inner meaning of Christian doctrine, and gives a conception of Christianity as a whole which is certain to find an abiding place in religious literature.

Not its least significant note is the light which it throws upon his own life. The kingdom which *The Lady Ecclesia* has inherited from her ancestors, and which forms the background of the allegory, is an island, and the book abounds in descriptions of the great ocean which surrounds it. The sighing of the winds, the moaning of the waves, the passing to and fro of ships, and the infinite distance that lay beyond, are again and again referred to; and cause the reader to inquire, Whence come these allusions? what memories in the mind of the blind poet-preacher do they recall? The answer may be found in the following extract from Dr. Sime's reminiscences. It refers to the old Innellan days, to the times when Dr. Matheson sat in his manse overlooking the firth, and commanding a view of the sea opening wide in the distance. "At times," says the doctor, the moaning of the sea, with the sighing and sobbing of the sea breezes through the trees below, would come into his study where he was sitting, perhaps pierced ever and anon by the solemn monotone of the whistle of an ocean steamer passing along.

"I often listen to that music," he said one evening, shortly after my arrival, and as we stood together at the window. It was a breezy evening, the sun setting towards Arran, with a radiant shaft of light up the firth. White horses were racing athwart the sea and breaking on the shore with a muffled roar, and a black showery cloud hovered over the far-off town of Largs. Round Toward Point a brown-sailed barge, leaning well over with reefed, rounded sail, fled up the firth like a bird, and was quickly followed by the Wemyss Bay boat; whilst an ocean steamer glided majestically past Innellan through the white horses, the smoke of the steamer curling in the distance prettily, after its work was done. The music that was coming into the room was massive and grand.

"That weird music comes up here from the ocean like the far-off music of another world, a symphony of great Nature. How varied and multiform it is! I often listen to it, when sitting here alone, or perhaps sometimes in the depth of night; it puts one in reverie. And that? Listen! The monotone of that passing steamer, decisive and clear, how finely it blends with Nature's majestic music! What liner is it?"

"An Allan liner, I think, for Canada! The ships, the lights, the shadows, pearly edged distant cloudlets, the breezes,—are passing through the firth like thoughts through one's consciousness."

"Exactly! One's consciousness is more lasting than the firth itself, with a character of its own which we bring into the world, unfledged. It is an eternal fact, deeper than force or matter, and altogether distinct from either; for that alone I reverence and hope for the utmost wreck of a man that I meet. That passing syren-note of your passing steamer, faintly pealing through the breezes, is beautiful, is it not? It is a part of the massive music we hear, and perhaps the grandest. It reminds me of the story of Goethe when he was on the Alps. On the whole, it seems he liked best, not the mountains and their snowy peaks in the sky, but a manufactory in one of the valleys. The unceasing humming of the spinning-wheel sounded in his ears in such a place, as never before, as the Music of the Spheres. No wonder, then, that Carlyle so valued Goethe. It was unquestionably the harmony of the spheres he suddenly heard; and in the valleys, mind you; think of that! So is that symphony of Nature we are listening to, with the occasional syren-note; but in the most solitary clachan of our mountains and glens, you will sometimes see—I daresay you have already seen it— the sweet light and the unruffled life of heaven itself. Heaven sometimes begins here, and immortality."

The same year saw a fresh volume of Meditations from his pen, *Words by the Wayside*, which has been translated into German. A year later, in 1897, he published a small Christmas book, *The Bible Definition of Religion*, based on Micah vi. 8, and a larger volume, *Sidelights from Patmos.* This latter book he describes as "Flashes of modern suggestion from the ancient Apocalypse." Many of its chapters originally appeared as articles in *The Expositor*, and it was at the suggestion of the editor of that magazine that Dr. Matheson collected them, and, with some fresh additions to their number, brought them out in book form. He remarks: "I believe the design of St. John in Patmos was to state the principles which would regulate the good time coming. He wishes to indicate what in any world would be to him the

consummation of happiness. He does so sometimes in sober language, sometimes in allegoric
symbols. I have made a few selections both from
the sober language and from the allegoric symbols,
with a view of testing the adaptation of the picture to
our modern ideas of optimism. The other question I wish to consider in these, otherwise disconnected, chapters is, Whether St. John's ideal is
still our ideal; whether we should still accept his
principles as those which should regulate the good
time coming?"

The success of the volume was an assurance of
the author having answered the question, which he
put to himself, in a satisfactory manner. The
subject suited his mind; it was quite in keeping
with his own method; and the fresh light which
he threw on passages that had been a source of
difficulty to generations of readers, secured him
heartfelt thanks from every quarter. He received
many letters of gratitude, and with such an effort
he could very well close his literary record as
minister of St. Bernard's.

CHAPTER XI

DR. MATHESON AT HOME

ADMIRERS of Dr. Matheson will, in the days to come, seek out the house in St. Bernard's Crescent, where for twenty years he lived and laboured. It was the third which he occupied since he became a minister. For the first few years at Innellan he resided at Labrador House, until his manse was built, and during the whole period of his residence in Edinburgh, with the exception of a few weeks towards its close, 19 St. Bernard's Crescent was his home. The crescent itself is quiet and dignified, having a noble front of Doric pillars, which makes it one of the most distinctive buildings even in Edinburgh. The crescent, in and around which many men eminent in art and literature have resided, had an interesting origin. "Three-quarters of a century ago its site was part of the estate of the great painter, Sir Henry Raeburn. Walking one day with the owner, another great painter, Sir David Wilkie, suggested to him that he should build on each side of the double row of elms, a crescent, in the purest style of Greek architecture. Sir Henry took his brother artist's advice, and the result is perhaps unequalled in a range of private houses. Within the railed, grassy enclosure in the centre are the remains of the avenue of elm trees, now reduced to the sacred number of seven, whose branches are dotted in spring-time with the nests of cawing rooks; hence the local name, 'Craw Crescent.'" Among the famous men who at one time or another resided in the near neighbourhood were Sir James Simpson, the famous physician; Sir John Watson Gordon, President of the Royal Scottish Academy; the great Christopher North; Robert Chambers, the publisher; Horatio Macculloch, the artist; and Thomas Carlyle, the first eighteen months of his married life having been spent at No. 21 Comely Bank, hard by. The district had seen better days. Right beneath Dr. Matheson's study, which looked to the back, was a slum quarter; and his windows, which were double-cased, looked down upon a public-house, whose sign-board boasted of his own surname. But he chose the house for its spacious-ness, and for its proximity to his church and to his sphere of parochial labours. It suited him admirably in every respect until the end, when he migrated to a new house which he had bought in Belgrave Crescent, one of the finest residential districts in Edinburgh, but which, alas, he did not live long to occupy.

It is natural that many should like to know how Dr. Matheson, with his physical infirmity, was able to accomplish so great and so varied a work during the thirteen years of his active ministry at St. Bernard's.   The chief factor, undoubtedly, in his harmonious, successful, and marvellously fruitful life, was his sister, Miss Matheson.   The world will never know what she was to her brother during those years of incessant toil and strenuous effort.   She shielded him from the worries that are the lot of those who, as parish ministers, think and toil for their people.   In her hands he knew that his household affairs were safe, and his domestic peace secure.   In every movement of a congregational or parochial nature, where a woman's hand should be seen or felt, she took a leading part, and, in the social life in which he had to mingle, her tactful and gentle manner smoothed over every difficulty.   With this safe anchorage he could devote himself unreservedly to his own special work, in the full knowledge that, whatever happened, no trouble could disturb his dwelling.   During his residence in Edinburgh, his youngest sister, Ellen, formed a member of the family, and between the three there was such a perfect sympathy and understanding that ofttimes their happy moods recalled to the visitor the innocent joys of childhood. During his earlier years at Innellan his other sister, Mrs. Monteath, then unmarried, and affectionately known among the villagers, with whom she was very popular, as " Miss Maggie," occasionally relieved Miss Matheson of the management of his house.   The affection which

19

they had for him in his boyhood deepened with the growing years and contributed largely to the "happy life" which, he said to his eldest sister shortly before his death, had been his lot.

He was in the habit, as has already been pointed out, of taking full advantage of every minute of time; and without his careful arrangement of the day's labours, shielded though he was from every unnecessary interruption and worry, he would not have been able to get through his day's work, or to accomplish all that he was able to do in the world. He was greatly aided by the young men who from time to time acted as his private secretaries. They were naturally drawn to him, and he was able to inspire them with his own enthusiasm. They looked up to him with profound respect and reverence, and no task on his behalf was to them a labour. One of them, and not the least devoted, Mr. William Smith, who served Dr. Matheson in this capacity during the last ten years of his life, has furnished me with the following account of his daily routine. Mr. Smith came to him shortly before he was provided with a colleague in St. Bernard's, and the brief sketch which he contributes of his parochial duties does not give the entire measure of the work which Dr. Matheson performed when he had sole charge; but his description of his chief's method of work in the study is not only full but most interesting. Speaking of his parochial labours, he says:

When I took up my duties I began to put forth my

poor energies to assist him in his literary labours and the parochial round of St. Bernard's Parish, Edinburgh. Down in the Stockbridge vale he lived, and moved, and had his being. Select company had lived there before him ; it was a region sacred to the memory of the mighty dead. And was not this a worthy follower in their footsteps. Did he not dream in Carlylean philosophy, did he not picture in his pages those Bible heroes whose descendants look out upon us from the canvas of Raeburn ? It would seem that here, for him, those great ones had left an imperishable legacy behind.

A parochial round, I say—but no common task. For those were busy days. The numerous parochial organisations made their due demands. And then the baptisms and the marriages—usually performed at his own house at the mystic evening hour of eight ! How impressed I was—coming from the South—with the simplicity of these marriage rites, and yet with their solemnity, as, with his full resonant voice, he pronounced the words, "The Lord bless thee, and keep thee : the Lord make His face to shine upon thee, and give thee peace." It was thought a great thing to be married by "the blind minister," and even to be visited by him. But early in my day he was beginning to curtail the parochial visitation. Allied to the prolonged and constant strain of mental work, it was more than he could bear. At the expense of his own pocket, he secured the services of an ordained minister. And yet his day was full. Session meetings and other meetings remained ; the regular pulpit work, literary work, baptisms and marriages, were with him still. It was surprising how he got through so much and yet found time for the social hour—the hour of recreation.

Mr. Smith then takes us into the study and shows us the nature of the work that was done there, and the way in which Dr. Matheson utilised the time at his disposal. His method was much the same as that which he followed at

Innellan, but it varied in some important points, which are worth recording.

What was his day's routine? For his life was essentially a routine—a clearly defined programme essential to his happiness. He would descend about nine to his breakfast, which he took with his correspondence and the papers. Unless any letter's reply involved some theological question, I usually replied myself, in his name. But he liked all replies sent off practically by return of post, and he would scarcely rest till I told him they were despatched. When I had read to him his letters, I took up the morning papers. Notices of interesting literature were, on the whole, the most attractive feature; but his attention was by no means restricted to the book department. Politics, criminal trials, wars and rumours of wars, all held for him a certain interest. Particularly had he a penchant for the realm of criminal law. He often told me he would in other physical circumstances have studied for the Bar. Assuredly he had a remarkably logical mind, which, in this respect, enabled him to decide the question "Guilty or Not Guilty?" with, I have every reason to believe, absolutely unfailing justness. He ever had an interest, too, in prison methods and criminal reformation; he might have written *It is Never Too Late to Mend*. In the field of politics he did not evince very pronounced opinions. Matters of mechanism had for him a wonderful attraction. When I explained to him the nature of the turbine or the motor, or read to him of some accelerated service of train or steamship, he drank in the information greedily. He would speculate on their developments in the future, and, in this respect, he might have produced Mr. Wells' *Anticipations*.

From the papers he would pass to his studies in French and German. These were brief; but they were regular and remembered. He would often remark on some British slang as obviously derived from one or other of the modern tongues. And then he would read. Theology, philosophy, science, history, literature—these were his favourite lines. Usually a spell at some two such volumes. And then he proceeded to dictate for the press. This completed, he left me to attend to letters or any proof-reading I might have on hand, betaking himself to his work of composition. Leaving his world of books and shadows, he would retire into the realms of inspiration light.

This comprehended his day's serious work. In the afternoon I again read to him fiction. And in the evening I sometimes gave him his third daily repast— miscellaneous books *and* fiction. But what *was* his fiction? All kinds, if good. He admired the best—George Meredith. But, candidly, I think he preferred the lighter vein. Among living novelists, there were none he liked better than Braddon, Hall Caine, W. E. Norris, and, although so optimistic in himself, he thoroughly appreciated the genius displayed in the pessimistic pages of Thomas Hardy. He held strongly that fiction's province is to amuse, and though he perused the problems, thought they were problems out of place. Among other modern fiction writers in this country he favoured were, of course, George Eliot, Barrie, Anthony Hope, Humphry Ward, Merriman, and E. F. Benson. In America, he thoroughly enjoyed Gertrude Atherton, Mary Wilkins, and James Lane Allen. Of the school farther back, Thackeray, Dickens, Trollope, and Kingsley had his sympathy; while as to Scott and Lytton—well, he read them once, of course. He recently tried again, but could not persevere. The elephantine phraseology, just as is also the case with the bulk of translated fiction, was too much for him. But how he would laugh when fiction afforded a "good thing." I used to think that, could the writer have heard that laugh, he would have felt his labour had not been in vain.

After he had been some four years in St. Bernard's, Dr. Matheson acquired a knowledge of the Braille system of writing for the blind. Previous to that time all his sermons and books

and articles were dictated.   It is hard to measure
the strain which this put on his mind.   The last
work written by him in this manner probably was
The Spiritual Development of St. Paul.   Mr.
Smith makes very interesting references to the new
method, and also mentions Dr. Matheson's equal
mastery of the typewriter.

Let me now speak of his Braille.   Strictly speaking,
genuine Braille it was not.   It is true, he began the
practice of his peculiar system by learning the orthodox
Braille alphabet; but he soon played havoc with that
alphabet.   A large number of the letters he "improved
upon"; and he never even began to learn the Braille
method of contractions.   Largely his own letters, entirely
his own abbreviations—this system fulfilled its definite
purpose and no more.   That purpose was to act as a
private notebook.   But when I say "notebook," I do not
mean that he committed to his Braille characters the
mere outlines of his train of thought.   Every word—every
article and   conjunction — figured   in   that "notebook."
The public is indebted to that characteristic—a characteristic which enabled me to supply, word for word, a considerable amount of literary matter which, at his death,
existed only in the form of Braille "copy"; in other
circumstances the full beauty and rhythmic flow of this
particular writing would have been lost.   When he committed matter to his Braille, then, it was quite ready for
dictation for the press.   Ultimately, when it *was* transferred to black and white, I do not say that there was *no*
retouching; an occasional ambiguity was removed—a
too-oft-repeated word was exchanged; but very seldom
was the whole gist of any sentence altered.   And here
I may mention a point which has always struck me
forcibly—the remarkable absence in his writings of any
repetition, in the big sense.   And what a common failing
this repetition is!   And let me suggest how heavily in
this respect George Matheson was handicapped.   The

ordinary writer has no difficulty in the rapid scanning of his foregoing pages; but when Dr. Matheson had "written up" a sheet of Braille, he rarely reverted to it till time for dictating arrived. Once the sheets had been added to the pile, the difficulty of "skimming back" was so great that it was rarely, if ever, resorted to. And ultimately, even when dictating, the piecemeal character of the process was such as to positively court the danger of repetition, while by this time his mind was usually full of other work—other schemes. But no, his train of thought was far too clear to allow him to succumb to this common weakness; his inspiration went steadily forward—no stopping, no going back; it was like the river, flowing gently onward to the sea.

He occasionally evinced a certain dissatisfaction with his Braille concerning its shortcomings in the foregoing respect; but he ever admitted that its advantages greatly outweighed its drawbacks. Latterly, indeed, he regarded this apparatus as a kind of talisman or spiritualistic medium. I remember, once, he made some kind remark about my own literary qualifications. I scarcely took him seriously, though, for that matter, I find that the fittest have most sympathy for the unfit. At any rate, I repudiated his view of my "fitness." "Nonsense!" he replied, "get hold of something as I get hold of my Braille; my Braille to me is a regular 'planchette.'" It would almost seem that his physical affliction had produced positive helps to his intellect, that out of his stony griefs Bethel he raised.

His acquiring of this "blind" method of writing, dates only from some sixteen years back. Before that time his literary and sermon work must have been pursued with enormous difficulty. He never practised contemporaneous study and dictation; and I have often wondered how even his great intellect contrived to store the material till committal to black and white relieved the strain. I believe some lady friend suggested the innovation to him; we are indebted to her, for the old régime could not have lasted much longer, and we should have been less rich to-day. Usually, when the Braille matter was "written up" the original was destroyed; but he always kept a certain stock, comprising lectures, sermons suitable for special occasions, and the like. These were kept in a special cupboard in his study, so that he himself could get access to them at his will. This cupboard was indeed a sacred spot, and the periodical cleaning thereof was only effected under the strictest surveillance of myself. When travelling, he usually had occasion to carry a certain quantity of Braille matter, with a view to dictation at the journey's end. This was ever a cause of the keenest anxiety to him. "William," he would say at least six times on the road, "is that MS. all right?" An unhappy experience preyed on his mind; he had once had most of his "raised dots" flattened down on account of improper packing. He feared this awful event would recur. It did not recur—I took good care of that; nevertheless, like Rachel, he refused to be comforted.

Occasionally he would receive a Braille letter from some blind stranger—usually in England—who had heard of his preaching or his books, or who evinced an interest in his successful career. With his ignorance of the orthodox system, he never attempted to decipher such a letter himself. I used to transmit them to the Blind School at Craigmillar, Edinburgh, where the headmaster soon kindly procured a written interpretation of the same.

For some time after Dr. Matheson became permanently blind, he maintained ordinary penmanship. To aid him in this, he made use of a small frame crossed at intervals of about an inch with pliable catgut strings. In this frame the paper was fixed, the pliable strings enabling him to keep a fair alignment without placing too abrupt a check on his straying from the path. Whether this simple expedient was his own invention or whether it, too, was suggested to him, I never ascertained. Long before my day he had entirely discontinued penmanship— though to the end he performed his signature in the case of legal documents.

I must here state, however, that he acquired a knowledge of the typewriter. He had himself no particular wish to do this; but a friend was so convinced of its usefulness to him that he was persuaded to accept as a present a fine Remington. Mr. Illingworth—then head-master of Craigmillar Blind School—came periodically to give him lessons; and in a very short time he got on surprisingly intimate terms with the keys. He never practised regularly enough to acquire any considerable speed; and rapid working was also precluded by the preciseness and correctness that pervaded all his work. Often during my absence, he would in this manner answer his letters on his own account; and even at other times, when not too pressed with work, he would use his machine "just to keep his hand in." "I think I have forgotten that typewriter," he would say; and he would ultimately express much satisfaction when I told him his production needed little or no correction. But if on fairly intimate, he never got on affectionate, terms with this innovation. It did not really meet his felt want. He could not himself refer to the typed, any more than he could refer to the pencilled, lines; and for the practical purposes of his serious work, it was useless. With all its drawbacks, his boon and blessing was his Braille.

I have said that in the case of his literary work every word was committed to the Braille characters. This was not the case with his sermons. In his early preaching days at Innellan his sermons were entirely committed to memory, and they were preserved in their entirety in sermon books. But he forsook this policy—committing only the skeleton and enlarging extemporaneously thereon in the pulpit. These skeleton sermons were preserved in books just as were the complete ones, and, after his acquisition of the Braille, were committed to those char-acters also. He retained in this Braille form certain sermons suitable for special occasions such as anniversaries, so that, when occasion arose, he could work them up entirely on his own account. He treated in this way lectures, or, if he had time for such preparation, public speaking of any kind.

He was very impatient of interruption when his mind was in the actual flow of composition, and his anxiety to accomplish within the promised time

a task he had undertaken often brought him down
to his study in the morning long before anyone in
the house was astir.

If any event could give his mind a morbid turn, it was
an interruption during his working hours. Right into the
midst of our morning studies would come a servant with
a card. She might have brought a bombshell! "The
Rev. Melchizedek Howler," I would read, "Kamschatka!
it's really *too* bad!" he would exclaim as he rose from
his chair, "I simply *must* be left time for my work."
Presently, that laugh—that pervaded the house—and the
house next door! The cloud had passed! He would
return to me: "William, we must just stop there this
morning; mark the place"; and off again to his new
friend—new, I say, for, assuming he had failed to recognise
the name, he no more forgot names than he forgot voices.
It was the same with his tailor or his hairdresser. Faithful
to the moment would they come. But the great brain
had forestalled them and demanded their immediate
attention. A word—a gesture of impatience. But soon
again the joke, the laugh—diversion complete. Verily his
moods were varied and multitudinous; but very few were
sad.

These were the only clouds that even temporarily
darkened his life. Patient in his affliction—but impatient
in the hampering of the chariot wheels of his intellect.
An extra pressure of correspondence, an urgent request
for some magazine article which he did not like to refuse
—a spirit of intense impatience immediately possessed his
soul. I might try my best to curb this spirit; but all
efforts had little effect. "That article will do quite well
in a *week*." That article was usually done in half the
time. Often have I appeared for my duties in the morning
—to find *him* first in the field. He had prematurely
risen, descended the stairs, and commenced to work with
his beloved Braille—to the servants' consternation and
dismay. They might dust the foundations; they might
dust the roof; but they must leave him for the nonce in
his study—alone. "I could not rest," he would tell me;

"I must get this thing off my mind." But I had to rest —till the flash of inspiration had been duly recorded in his memorandum. This was his pessimistic vein—the magnifying of his responsibilities. "I'm over head and ears," he would say to his sister; "no one must bother me to-day." He evidently believed he had twelve hours work before him. His surprise and satisfaction were positively childish when he found he had finished in four.

When Matheson was at the height of his fame the demands made upon him to preach in almost every part of the United Kingdom were very numerous indeed. He had engagements made, nearly two years in advance. He had to refuse the vast majority of the invitations sent to him, but once a month he was in the habit of occupying the pulpit of another church in some part of the country, usually in the larger centres of population, and in no place did he receive a heartier welcome than in his native city of Glasgow. Mr. Smith makes amusing reference to the crowds that besieged the vestry on such occasions, and to the way in which Matheson was able to distinguish some old friend or admirer, whom he had not met perhaps for thirty years, by the tone of his voice.

In my early days with him he made a practice of preaching from home about once a month. I understand that neither in Innellan nor in St. Bernard's did he ever preach the same sermon twice. The preaching from home, however, usually gave him the opportunity of using an old discourse, especially as the occasion—often an inauguration or an anniversary—practically necessitated this. "Old sermons," I say; they were often presented with such utterly fresh illustration that many might hear them

again and think them new.   And how obviously gratified
he was when, as he and I emerged from the vestry
corridors, I said to him, in an undertone, "A very full
house."   I suppose "a full house" is inspiring to *most*
ministers; it certainly was to *him*.

He always found the actual travelling a great bore;
but, on the whole, he thoroughly enjoyed these week-ends
from home.   He was apt to be somewhat abstracted till
his work was done, but after that he was the very soul of
vivacity and merriment.   It is highly amusing to recall
some of the *preparations* for his week-end, especially in
cases where he was bound for a house which he had never
visited before.   To ensure a night's rest in his prospective
quarters, he deemed it best to make certain arrangements
some few days before leaving his own house.   Sometimes
in the train, to try and "pass the time" for him, I read
aloud a little, and I used to wonder if the operation were
more painful to him or to me.   He seemed grateful,
however; and really I used sometimes to think that,
by some telepathic means, he "saw" as much of the type
as I did.

Arrived at a strange abode, he liked early to secure the
general geographical idea of its principal apartments, and
in this kind of thing he seemed fully as clever as a good
many people with sight.   Also, if the church or lecture
hall were in the vicinity, he would express a wish to "take
his bearings" in that respect before the hour of service or
lecture arrived.   I used to conduct him up and down,
perhaps twice, to and from his prospective rostrum, and,
as he was somewhat prone to gesticulation, he was ever
anxious that no loose books, no glass of water, no gas
chandelier, should be within reach of his arm.   Whether
he *always* evinced such anxiety I do not know ; but I
understand that on one occasion a gas globe which pro-
jected from the side of the pulpit was smashed to atoms by a
wave of his hand.   He stopped and with amazing presence
of mind exclaimed, "Gather up the fragments."   But,
though he had this preliminary interview with his immediate oratorical surroundings, I made a practice of carefully
conducting him ultimately to his perch; and verily it

might oft have been said that "they climbed the *steep* ascent to heaven." I have known occasions when, after the service, the vestry was literally besieged; and particularly was this the case when preaching in the West. Old friends who had not met him for many years would push in their forms. "You'll not remember me, doctor!" A moment's hesitation, then a flash over the face, a beaming smile, and "Mackintosh!" Oh yes, it was Mackintosh, right enough—no mistake about that. Nothing wonderful perhaps; if men shut their eyes occasionally, it might open their ears.

It is also amusing to recall the intense interest he evinced in the personal characteristics of the new friends he had been brought into contact with—personal, I mean, with regard to physical appearance. There is no doubt that, as a rule, he formed a wonderfully accurate idea of their outward forms through the medium of their voices. On the road home, this subject usually cropped up; and the comparing of our notes often occasioned in him the most intense amusement and jocularity. In the mere matter of stature, he could be practically left to judge for himself; given a good light, he could actually discern objects in silhouette.

Mr. Smith, after referring to Dr. Matheson's recreations, speaks with tenderness and admiration of his chief's Christian heroism under his great affliction.

It would not be easy to say, however, what actually constituted Dr. Matheson's recreation, unless you applied this term to his every conscious act. He so obviously "revelled" in his every experience that it was impossible to discriminate between the effect of the one and the effect of the other. Did he laugh loud and long at some passing joke in fiction; he would also find "a good thing" in philosophy's sober tome. Did his countenance evince pleasure as, seated on steamer's deck, the Clyde's balmy breezes fanned his cheek; I have seen equally pleasurable expressions when, seated in his study chair, the flash

of inspiration came like manna from above. No, everything was recreation to Dr. Matheson; though barred
from the earthly light, more life and fuller was his portion.
I think I never knew a man who more thoroughly
"lived." I experienced an agreeable surprise at our very
first interview. But surprises greater were in store. I
naturally felt chary of making any intentional reference
to his particular physical affliction, even in the general
sense. I went further; I actually skipped over such
references when they occurred in books or papers I was
reading to him. To the end of my service I retained this
very natural delicacy; but I really think it was labour
lost. He was prone rather to joke about "the poor blind
man" than to treat such a subject with sympathetic
lament. "Pure pretence!" you will say. I do not know.
Dr. Matheson was not good at pretence. At any rate,
outwardly he bore his burden lightly, gallantly, on to
the end.

And yet I admit, though usually the most optimistic
of men, he impressed me at times with strange incon-
sistencies. I remember more than once that he told me
he never woke in the morning but with a feeling of regret
—regret that he *had* woke, that he had not slept on, into
that sleep which knows no waking. A brief moment, and
some scrap of news, some chance remark, some unexpected
visitant, would instantaneously change the key. His joke,
his laugh, his beaming face, were a living illustration of
the *joy* of living, of life for life's sake.

Ah, yes! the *pessimism* was the disguise—he could
not have played the opposite rôle so long—so long and
so successfully. You will find no pessimistic shadows in
his books; those who ever met him in the flesh will frame
him in an atmosphere of wit and geniality.

None could more effectually enter the heart of the
child. He had practically given up the Sunday School
work before my day; but I understand his addresses to
the little ones were masterpieces of their kind. He once
told me he thought he would write a book for children—
"wee things" he ever called them. Our little ones are
poorer than they might have been.

And he had another talismanic medium—his calumet
of peace. He certainly had faith in its more or less
imaginary influence. He ever restricted this indulgence
to the evening hour, and he has told me that it was to
him an hour of communion. Latterly, however, he became less meditative at this particular time of day, owing
to the fact that he took his pipe with his evening
reading. And he had great faith in the workings of the
subconscious mind. Often has he told me he has taken
his dilemma to bed with him, and has woke up—to find
the problem solved, the mists dispelled.

Dr. Matheson was in his home quite as interesting and inspiring as in the pulpit. Should the
visitor be an expected or invited guest, or should
he be an old friend who called at an opportune
moment, he was overwhelmed with kindness. The
hospitality of his house was probably unequalled
in the Church of Scotland, and the gracious welcome
offered by his sister received a double assurance
from him. His table-talk on such occasions was
the brightest, wittiest, and most humorous that can
be imagined. He kept everyone in the best of
spirits; and conversation, light, gay, and laughter-
provoking, made the visit memorable. At times
he might be in a silent mood, but that was the
exception, and the originality of his remarks, the
unexpected allusions, the apt quotations, and the
startling suggestions, acted like a tonic on the
spirits. Dr. Matheson's laughter was the Carlylean
laughter of the whole man. His nature for the
time being was absolutely under the control of the
humorous mood which possessed him. His animal
spirits reached their highest when he was delivered

from some great mental strain.   If a difficult piece of literary composition were completed, or some great effort, in the way of oratory, had been successfully accomplished, there was a strong reaction, and he gave himself up for the moment to that absolute *abandon* which possesses a boy when the first hour of his holidays has arrived.

It was in the study, however, and under the soothing influence of his beloved pipe, with the day's work of preaching or writing well over, that one discovered the man in all his moods.   On such occasions he freely unbent himself and gave to his visitor of his very best.   There were two outstanding facts which speedily impressed anyone who had frequent personal intercourse with him, and these were his remarkable memory and his acute sense of hearing.   A friend who had been on the most intimate terms with him for many years, and who by nature and training is of an observant nature, remarks regarding the first of these :

Dr. Matheson's extraordinary memory was, from the first, most striking.   He could quote by the pageful, not merely the Bible—which he had I think by heart —but any book which he was interested in, however solid or volatile.   Nor was it merely the literature that he loved that he remembered with exact precision, such as Wordsworth's, Shakespeare's, or Burns' poetry, and likewise the most abstract metaphysical disquisitions, but also the most ephemeral writings of the hour.   To my surprise, years afterwards, he used to quote, verbatim, whole sentences and even paragraphs of a paper of mine which, at his pressing instigation, I prepared and read at the village hall, with nervousness—a paper on

Burns. It was my first lecture and public appearance anywhere.

For the mere sake of revealing the extent of his retentive power, I tested his memory one evening. I took up a copy of the *Glasgow Herald* from the table, and twice over read slowly and as solemnly as I could, an entire line, column after column, from left to right, of an advertisement page, and then, in the same fashion, the second line. There was no connection whatever between the advertisements, and they ended abruptly and incoherently. Then we had half an hour's talk over our pipes, or " burnt-offerings," as we used to call them, about the Correlation of Forces or other subject, a whole universe away from a line or two of broken advertisements. Finally, again I took up the newspaper, and to my astonishment— for it looked like witchcraft or clairvoyance—my friend, laying down the pipe, deliberately repeated verbatim the incoherent fragments, just as I had read them. He had a memory, I told him, as sensitive and receptive as a photographic plate, and retained for a time good and bad alike, rubbish as well as diamonds, but ultimately only the diamonds and flowers, in the deepest valley of his memory. But he did not much prize mere memory, however necessary and valuable. He valued more highly observation, reflection, reasoning, insight, foresight, imagination. Imagination he prized as the highest power of man; he considered that its cultivation was too much ignored or neglected, and, very much too frequently, positively discouraged, in even the youngest children, much more so in boys at school and young men beginning life's work and responsibility; for not only was imagination one of the earliest of the great powers, but imaginative forethought through life was a gift of the gods, and covered far more than mere fairy tale or fiction or make-belief; it ranged still more effectively and richly over the hardest and sternest facts of life.

The other fact which, I have observed, speedily impressed anyone, who was on friendly terms with

Dr. Matheson, was his acute sense of hearing, regarding which the same sympathetic observer speaks as follows :

His sense of hearing was not merely most acute, it was observing, discerning, and thinking. I have never come across, even in the blind, a more delicately acute hearing. It was the one perfect avenue in which things external poured into his thoughtful mind. In conversation the minutest difference of tone, he at once detected. My footsteps on the gravel path of the garden he used to recognise long before I got into the Manse, or he was within earshot of my talk or laugh; and his friend's idiosyncrasies and many unknown people's peculiarities he diagnosed from their cough, their walk, their mode of blowing their noses.

Upon his sense of hearing he largely relied for his picture of character and mind. It was for him direct, first-hand knowledge. His knowledge of things visible— forms, colours, distance—was from memory or inferred and second-hand. Nevertheless, excluded as he was from all the visible beauty and harmony of life, he frequently said to me that he would rather be deprived wholly of sight than hearing. And perhaps it was not an unreasonable inference. The avenue of hearing is nearer than that of vision to the sensorium, or the central nidus of the soul, and disease in this direction or from the seat of hearing ends much more frequently in insanity itself, as in the great Dean Swift's case. To also lose hearing would have been for my friend, who relied on it so wholly for communication with the best around him, a complete eclipse. Not to hear the voice of his sister, who through life remained to him as his guardian angel, he told me; not to hear the thrilling tones of loved friends, or the silvery laughter of children at play, would have been to him in his blindness a blanker groping, than it was, for the Infinite. Well might he value hearing, for it was the one divine avenue for him from earth to heaven. His hearing was perfect, and he judged quickly and much from mere tone of voice. The mere tone and its quality and intensity had for him colour, form, expression, character, and infinite variety. It was for him as subtle a quality as the mind itself, and as characteristic as its colour to a ruby or emerald, or its brawling music to a Highland burn.

All subjects came to him with equal readiness, the latest fiction or the newest theology were alike known to him. His memory was unerring. The tendencies of thought in any theological volume or the characters in any novel, however far back they had been read, were never forgotten. His memory gave him a large store of subjects to draw upon, and his active, restless mind continually passed from one to another. He had endless enjoyment in humorous sallies, whether from himself or others, and he had an ecstatic way of expressing fun, or his appreciation of fun, in bursts of laughter. In conversation he seldom monopolised the first or only place. " Many times I should have pre-ferred," says Dr. Hately Waddell, who saw much of him at North Berwick, during the last few summers of his life, when he was on holiday there, "that he did, but he had no desire to hold forth and to lecture, and never asked anyone to sit at his feet. All the same, his presence usually domin-ated the conversation by reason of some vigorous statement of a view, remarkable, unusual, or con-troversial. He conversed usually in a graphic and fragmentary way. He did not mind that conversa-tion should now and then flag, or that it started too soon on some new theme. Only once do I remember a subject consistently discussed for any length of time, and that was the subject of 'Eternal Life.' "

Dr. Matheson naturally took the view that Eternal Life was not any divided portion of existence, separated from that which now is, but that it was already here in its true conditions, was continually expanding in new experiences, and would find death merely an incident in its course. Judgment, he said, was certain, but was not only retribution; it was simply a new phase of life in which we should be compelled to take a proper relation to our true self, and to God. All men who having misspent their lives here should find themselves compelled to live the opposite kind of life there. As to Christ's second coming, that also he said was continually on the way; it began at the resurrection.

When at Innellan I was in the habit of visiting him of an evening at his manse. I was at the time a student of philosophy, and he manifested great interest in the lectures of Professor Edward Caird, under whom I was studying. Caird was the greatest living exponent of Hegelianism, and I was struck by Matheson's intimate knowledge of the system. He was in those days a strong believer in Hegelianism, and discussed its merits with much enthusiasm. Years afterwards he declared that he had modified his views somewhat, but he never liberated himself wholly from the grasp of the master. He discussed on such occasions subjects like the " Higher Criticism," and he made no secret of his opinions regarding it. He would say :

I don't believe in it very much, from no mawkish feeling, for to tell the truth I am rather broad, but as a mere matter of historical fact I don't believe in it. My reason is that, from a minute study of the earliest prophets, Amos and Hosea, I am convinced beyond all question that there was a previous national religious law existing among the people. The very manner in which the prophets rebuked the people proves they were familiar with an existing code. Now, if the prophets had existed before that law their rebukes would have had no meaning. Then the whole question is, What are the factors or agents of evolution? Well, the answer of science is that there are really two factors in all revolutions, force and environment. I am willing to admit this, provided they will allow environment to include God Almighty. That makes all the difference in the world. Is God to be one of the agents in the process of evolution? My own opinion is that everything is produced by the combined action of force and environment, but in that environment I include not only earth and sea and sky, but also that great force which Spencer called the Unknowable, but which I call God. I quite believe that the revelation of Scripture is a progressive development, and that it grew out of historical surroundings of different ages. If the theory of the Higher Criticism was proved it would not in the least weaken my sense of the Bible's value. The real miracle of the Bible is, to my mind, the fact that out of a multitude of disconnected writings, originating from various sources and often proceeding from opposite tendencies, there has emerged as a result the picture of the Messianic life.

Another subject which cropped up in such conversations was "Evolution." "I wrote a book," he once said, "to show that evolution, if true, is quite compatible with orthodoxy, but I have since come to the conclusion that evolution is not true.

I have no more fear of it than I ever had, but I am quite convinced that in, say, twenty years it will be regarded as an exploded heresy. I am an unbeliever in Drummondism. Henry Drummond triumphantly waves his hand—you can almost see him do it—over what he thinks is the strongest point in evolution, namely, similar things that in you and me are not of the slightest use, but in animals are of great utility; his conclusion being, that we were animals first and that these things are survivals. My conclusion is not that at all; I would be driven to it if no other explanation were reasonable. But if I want to make another staircase in this house there are two ways in which I can do it. I can begin afresh from the ground floor or I can start at the first landing. I say that God Almighty always adopts the latter method, to economise space and time; He makes the new life start on the top of the old—not grow out of it; and that accords with the whole analogy of nature. The first stair cannot itself get beyond the first landing, but another stair may be built upon it. I believe in the eternity of species; that all differences existed from the beginning. I don't believe that first there was a trunk, and that this trunk broke up into branches. I believe the branches were first, and that they are gradually being welded into a trunk. I believe in individualism— individualism bound up into the life of God. I am convinced that in modern speculation the individual has not had justice done to him, and that the movement of the future will be towards individualism.

As might be expected, he frequently discussed "Novels and Novelists." Present-day romance had a wonderful fascination for him. He once remarked to his friend, Mr. M'Kenzie Bell:

"I like *Sir Richard Calmady*. It reveals a victory of mind over matter, even while at every moment the author is showing what a poor cripple Sir Richard is. Even that bad girl realises the influence of Sir Richard Calmady's force of character over his environment. One of my greatest dreads, when I was growing blind, was that thus I should lose affection—especially the affection of women —but I was wrong. In that way my blindness was a positive advantage, for it drew out their affection, though

I have never been in love. Dr. Robertson Nicoll is most persistent in trying to persuade me to write a novel. I could do the plot, the characterisation, and the pathos. But I think I should fail where every tyro would succeed. I should fail in giving vitality to the scenes in which a knowledge of the verities of sight became necessary." I did my very utmost to disabuse his mind of this fixed idea, urging in the strongest way in my power that photographic realism was not at all a necessary adjunct to fiction. But from his manner I saw clearly that my arguments had produced no impression.

I expressed my surprise that he, so great a prose poet, did not write more metrical poetry. Further, I pointed out that he, unlike a great prose poet, my friend Blackmore, had achieved in " O Love that wilt not let me go " and in a lesser degree in " God's Captive " the writing of noble verse-lyrics. He admitted to the full my contention that eminent poets of prose generally fail to become eminent poets of poetry. " My lyric ' O Love that wilt not let me go,' " he exclaimed, " is merely the exception that proves the rule. It came to me spontaneously, without conscious effort, and I have never been able to gain once more the same fervour in verse."

From novels in general it was an easy passage to the " Religious Novel " in particular. He had no hesitation in expressing his disapproval of this form of literature.

I am not in favour of it at all, for the simple reason that the novel with a purpose always conveys to my mind the impression that it is a sermon from the very outset, and the whole novel becomes a foregone conclusion. Now, I hold that the sole aim of a novel should be to amuse, as it should be the sole aim of the drama.

I fully admit the transcendent genius of George Meredith, but I do not consider that his works come up to my ideal of what a novel should be. I should be disposed to say that the test of the true novel should be: what do the public like, for it is for them alone that the novel is intended. And judging from their verdict generally, and from that point of view, I would place Miss Braddon at the head of the list. She is a great favourite of mine, and I think I have read every book she ever wrote.

Another subject on which he would converse was "Creeds and Confessions." He often said that he would never dream of altering these, but he would continue to fill them with new meaning. He frequently, says Dr. Waddell, discussed the subject with me at North Berwick. He held that

the best way of broadening the religious thought of the time was by working from within the Church, by leavening the lump. There was nothing at all timid in this; it was just his chosen method of bringing the Church into accord with the modern spirit. He knew that the people did not any longer completely believe in the old formulas, but he also knew that they clung to the old expressions, and he wisely resolved to disturb these expressions as little as possible, while his readers and hearers felt the breath of the new and wider meaning moving through them. He was, of course, essentially broad in his views, but he preferred that any broad interpretation of religious thought should filter gradually through old channels rather than it should burst the banks of traditional faith and bring commotion and destruction in its course. He believed the Church was saved in the present generation, not by the narrow-minded who forced others out of it for conscience' sake, but by the broad-minded who determined to stay within it for the same reason. Naturally, he also saw that once a hand is laid upon an historic creed no limit can ever be set to alterations. Within the historic creed you may permit a wise freedom of interpretation; without the historic creed you lose all common standard. What one Assembly alters another Assembly may continue to alter, and within a few years or generations all standards become movable. This he could not abide, and he maintained that the need of an historical document had not only been historically proved, but that the wise and prudent preachers would continue to uphold it. A widening of the "subscription-formula" was his method of freedom, rather than that of "creed-alteration."

It was not often that he referred directly in the conversation to the person of Christ. Like all great natures he was diffident of speaking about what he loved most, but talking on one occasion on Spinoza's conception of God he was led on to express his views on this supreme subject. Spinoza's conception of God as the underlying Substance of the universe was too remote for him and too shadowy. He hardly admitted that the unknown, the unknowable, underlying Substance might be a perfected harmony in the heaven of heavens, making for perfection through an infinite process of specialisation. No, he would say:

Not so much through a process of specialisation as through the Christ, the perfected Christ of Galilee. He and He alone is God made manifest to men, God's life, light, character, purpose brought very near to the heart of humanity, and through the utmost limits of thought itself.

Without the Christ in humanity, not as a mere ideal but as the spiritual quickening essence of God performing a miracle of transformation in man, Nature for him was dark indeed. He would sometimes say:

As a pure revelation of God Himself, the grandest the world has ever seen or ever will see, I bow down prostrate to the *Christ of Nazareth*. But for that revelation in Christ every thinking man or woman would be, I feel, a sad enough agnostic, and even without the reverence of Hume, the calm serene-minded thinker, so different a being from the witty Voltaire.

CHAPTER XII

LAST YEARS

WHEN Dr. Matheson had been eleven years
minister of St. Bernard's he felt that the burden
of his office was more than he could bear. He
had at that time been thirty years a minister of
the Church, and during the whole of that period
he had laboured with a constancy and a zeal which
it would be difficult to parallel. There was no
failing in his powers, no falling off in popularity,
no abatement in love for his work; but the constant wear and tear of congregational and parochial
duties began to tell. Besides, his increasing reputation as a preacher, and the requests of editors for
articles and publishers for books, drew him in
another direction; and the question came to be,
Which call was to be obeyed? Up till this time
he had met every demand. He was convinced
that he could do so no longer. He was not the
man to attempt what he could not accomplish, or
to neglect his immediate duty. He carefully considered which road he should now travel, what
work he could accomplish with satisfaction to him-

self and benefit to the public, and he decided that
the course which would be truest to himself and
in the best interests of all concerned was to resign
St. Bernard's and to devote himself to special
preaching and to literary effort.

It may be worth while to reflect for a moment
on the career in this relation of some of the most
popular preachers of recent times. Take his immediate predecessor as the first preacher in Scotland, Dr. John Caird. The distinguished Principal
of Glasgow University, when at the height of his
fame, deliberately and wisely chose those charges
in which he would have a minimum of congregational and parochial work. It is true that he
was once minister of a city charge, Lady Yester's,
Edinburgh, but he only remained in it for a very
short time. The constant demands that were made
upon him hastened his flight, and he chose the
quiet country parish of Errol where he could develop
his thoughts and mature his style in peace. When,
again, he determined on a more public sphere
of duty, he accepted a call to the Park Church,
Glasgow, at that time without a parish and amid
a population that made little call on his ministerial
activity. Caird, it should also be remembered, had
not up till this time published anything, with the
exception of a volume of sermons. The five years
during which he was minister of the Park Church,
he confessed to a friend, were more than sufficient,
and he was convinced that if he had continued much
longer under the strain he would have broken down.

Or take the great Chalmers. The world has
never ceased to hear of his parochial activity when
he was minister of the Tron and St. John's,
Glasgow. It may be true that he accomplished
more in this relation than any minister of the
Church of Scotland before or since. He organised
his Session; he manned his Parish; he founded
schools; he relieved the poor: but with the exception of his Session and the agencies necessary
for carrying on his educational work he had no
other organisations. Chalmers, so far as I can
gather, confined his visitation to his parish. When
the spirit moved him he would call upon the
inmates of a tenement, and now and again he
would gather them together to be addressed. No
one can deny his enormous labours, but they were
on the whole more congenial and less exacting than
Matheson's. Nor was he hampered in his work by
the multiplicity of agencies, which, however artificial
they might be, were a tradition in St. Bernard's;
and upon their success more than upon the dynamic
power of the pulpit some good people thought
the salvation of the church and parish depended.
Chalmers found eight years of Glasgow to be
quite enough, and he was glad to accept, at the
end of that period, an invitation to the Chair
of Moral Philosophy in the University of St.
Andrews.

It may not be without interest to cross the
Border and to allow our eyes to rest for a moment
upon one of the greatest preachers of a past genera-

tion, I mean Dr. Joseph Parker. Matheson had a sincere admiration for Parker. He told me on one occasion that Parker was the greatest preacher he had ever heard, and the tribute which, at his death, he paid to his memory in the columns of *The British Weekly* was one of the finest things he ever wrote. Nor was Parker without his influence on Matheson. It has always seemed to me that the minister of the City Temple was to a certain extent responsible for a change in Matheson's preaching which characterised his Edinburgh days. It was during his incumbency of St. Bernard's that Matheson delighted his hearers with graphic pictures, startled them with semi-humorous asides, and set their souls on fire with sudden and unexpected flashes of original thought. A certain spontaneity and freedom, which made the preacher's personality all the more attractive, marked Matheson's later preaching. It may have been Parker's style that gave him confidence. It was all there long before, but the fact of having found it in another may not have been without its effect in causing him to have respect for his own true self, and to allow the spirit that was in him to have free play. Well, what demands were made upon Parker as minister of the City Temple? They were purely of a preaching nature. He lived at Hampstead, miles away from what may euphemistically be called the scenes of his labours. He only appeared upon them about twice a week, on the Thursday and on the Sunday, when he delivered his sermons. He

had no parish to attend to, no calls upon him for
daily visitation and nightly services.   He was
master of his fate.   He was a great preacher, and
the conditions under which he worked were of such
a nature as to allow his special gift to be cultivated
without hindrance, and his message to be delivered
with a fervour unimpaired by harassing and dis-
tracting toil.

It will be one of the chief glories of George
Matheson that, while as a preacher and as a writer
he may claim equal rank with those great names
just mentioned, he at the same time, and for a
longer period than any of them, discharged faith-
fully and successfully the duties of a parish minister
in a congregation which at one time under him
numbered nearly two thousand members, and in a
parish composed for the most part of poor people
whose needs had to be ministered to.   And he was
blind!   They had every faculty unimpaired, but he
was denied the power of vision ; yet in spite of it
he toiled on, attending to every duty, discharging
every task which his office demanded, preaching
sermons Sunday after Sunday which drew admiring
crowds from far and near, and publishing books
which circulated over the world and were read by
thousands.   It is no exaggeration to claim this
as one of the most unique ministries, not only in
the Church of Scotland but in the Church of Christ,
not only in our generation but during the Christian
era.

Having thus determined on the resignation of

his charge, he addressed the following letter to the
Session Clerk of St. Bernard's :—

December 28, 1896.

I have long felt that I could do more good to the
Church if freed from special parochial work. I have
given the matter a very lengthened, a very earnest, and
a very careful consideration, and I have come at last,
with absolute conviction, to the definite and final resolution to resign the charge as at Whitsunday. I intend
that my ministry shall close on the second Sunday of
May—the eleventh anniversary of my incumbency of this
church—after which the supply of the pulpit will devolve
on the Session.

It is not too much to say that the news of
Dr. Matheson's intention fell upon the congregation
with a shock of surprise. Immediate efforts were
at once made to induce him to reconsider his
decision. Pressure was brought to bear upon him
from office-bearers and congregation alike. It is
well known that the matter weighed heavily upon
him and caused him great anxiety. His own desire
was to resign ; the earnest wish of his people was
that he should remain. They did not wish to lose
him as their minister, and they feared that if the
ties which bound him to St. Bernard's were severed
there would be a marked decline in membership.
After much hesitation, and somewhat unwillingly,
he at last yielded to the overtures made to him,
and at a meeting of Kirk Session, held on the
twelfth of January, he intimated that he withdrew his
resignation, and intended to apply to the Presbytery
for a colleague and successor.

The arrangement come to was, that he should be freed from all parochial duty, and set at liberty to devote himself to preaching and to literary work. This indeed was an arrangement that ought to have been arrived at long before.   He had on his own account, a year or two previously, engaged as his personal assistant an ordained Minister of the Church who relieved him of certain duties.   Had this taken place earlier, indeed from the very first, and with the full concurrence of his Kirk Session and the Congregation, his services would have been at their disposal for a longer period, and his life might have been spared.   The compromise came too late in the day.   The Church of Scotland had no place for a man like him.   He was compelled to conform to the use and wont of the parochial system, excellent in itself; but its very excellence when universalised is apt to destroy its efficiency. A good system is all the better when it is elastic, and leaves room for development on other lines than its own.

Dr. Matheson, in approaching the Presbytery, wrote as follows:

January 13, 1897.

After eleven years of laborious work as minister of the Church and Parish of St. Bernard's, and having regard to the physical disability under which I labour, I desire now to be relieved from all parochial duties and work, except preaching.   I am prepared to give up the whole stipend, retaining merely the endowment of £120.   Should the Presbytery not see their way to appoint a colleague and successor, I tender the resignation of my office of Minister of St. Bernard's.

The Presbytery appointed a committee to confer
with Dr. Matheson and the Kirk Session, with the
result that the committee reported that it would be
for the advantage of the congregation that Dr.
Matheson should continue their minister, and that
an assistant and successor should be appointed.
After sundry procedure the Rev. J. J. Drummond,
B.D., now minister of Jedburgh, was elected, and
appointed as his colleague and successor. The last
meeting of St. Bernard's Kirk Session, presided
over by Dr. Matheson, was held on the 3rd October
1897, Mr. Drummond's induction taking place on
the 23rd of the same month. Dr. Matheson was
fortunate in his new colleague, who had been brought
up under his own eye in St. Bernard's, and between
them, during the two years in which they worked
together, there was the greatest cordiality and
goodwill. Mr. Drummond, referring to his connection with Dr. Matheson as a student and a minister,
bears ample testimony to his high appreciation and
deep reverence for his friend and mentor. He says:

My first association with Dr. Matheson was when I
was a member of his Bible-class. The class met on a
week night, and was attended by young men, intelligent
artisans, and some divinity students. He lectured on the
opening chapters of Genesis. The lectures were eminently
suggestive and fresh, even for him. He was then at the
full maturity of his powers and at the height of his
popularity in Edinburgh. In these, my divinity student
days, he showed me great kindness. I was often in his
house, had many a smoke and a chat with him in that
spacious study, which was more like a business room than
a library, with the outlook into slummy Dean Street. He

did not care for any assistance in filling or lighting his pipe. He spoke always with great animation, mostly about theological or literary subjects. In 1891 I was elected to the parish of Longformacus, in Berwickshire. Two years afterwards Dr. Matheson preached at a special service there in my newly renovated church. The long summer afternoon we spent at the Manse, and I read aloud to him passages of Anglican theology.

During the following years I saw him only at rare intervals, but in July 1897 I was elected as his colleague in St. Bernard's. It was very far from my wish to exchange the pastoral simplicity and peace of a beautiful moorland parish for the work and worry of a city charge, but I was unanimously elected, and I knew that I could fit into his ways and make things easy for him as an entire stranger could not have done. It was eminently desirable that Dr. Matheson's services should be retained to the church, but this could not be unless he had a colleague in whom he had confidence, and who had some tact and understanding. He received me with the greatest heartiness and kindness; indeed, he rather overwhelmed me at the induction dinner with a eulogy far beyond the deserts, either of myself or of anyone who might have been elected as his colleague.

Then I started on the actual work of the parish. The arrangement was that we were to take the church services alternately. I was to be Moderator of Kirk Session, to teach the communicants' classes, Bible-class, etc., and do all the visitation and pastoral work. The arrangement worked out most harmoniously. Dr. Matheson seemed to have but one thought: to put me forward and to slip into the background himself.

The arrangement thus amicably entered into was cordially carried out for two years, but on the 15th June 1899 Dr. Matheson wrote the following letter to the Session Clerk of St. Bernard's :—

The pressure of other work compels me to sever the remaining thread which connects me with St. Bernard's.

I wish to take this opportunity of stating how cordial have been my relations with Mr. Drummond. We have lived on terms of unclouded affection, and we have never had a difference even of opinion. He has kept the church at the zenith of prosperity, and I leave it in his hands with perfect confidence. As I do not wish to resume the charge after the autumn holiday, I desire my resignation to take effect from the end of July.

A similar letter was written by him to the Clerk of the Edinburgh Presbytery. It was considered by that body on the 28th of June, and on the 26th of July 1899 the Presbytery accepted Dr. Matheson's resignation. Resolutions passed by St. Bernard's Kirk Session and Congregation, with reference to Dr. Matheson's resignation, were read. The Kirk Session testified to the most cordial relations that had existed between them and Dr. Matheson during his thirteen years' ministry, and to the great measure of prosperity that had characterised the congregation during that time. They earnestly hoped that he would long be spared in health to render further service to the Church. The Congregation likewise expressed in their resolution their deep regret at the loss they had sustained, their high appreciation of his services, and their earnest hope that he would long continue in the enjoyment of his well-earned rest. At the meeting at which these resolutions were read deputations from the Kirk Session and Congregation also appeared. Several of the members addressed the Presbytery, and the remarks of all were indicative of the warm relations that existed between Dr.

Matheson and his parishioners. One of the deputies said Dr. Matheson could not retire from the love, respect, and esteem of his people. Another, who was deeply moved, characterised their sorrow as too deep for words. A third said, he would like to inform the Presbytery of a single fact, and one that was very interesting for the members to know, namely, that during the thirteen years of Dr. Matheson's ministry in St. Bernard's he had never preached the same sermon twice to his congregation. The Presbytery in accepting his resignation did so with equal regret, which was somewhat mitigated by the hope that a man so gifted and so active would not altogether be lost to the Church.

The public press could not be silent on a matter that was of interest, not only to St. Bernard's congregation and the Church of Scotland, but to the Church of Christ at large. Numerous comments appeared in their columns on the event, and particularly on the fact that during the whole of his thirteen years' ministry Dr. Matheson had never preached to his congregation the same sermon twice. This was generally regarded as something very unique. And the same feeling of surprise was experienced when, a few months afterwards, Dr. Matheson delivered a farewell address to his congregation, which was held on all hands to be the most remarkable of its kind ever listened to. The gathering took place in the Freemasons' Hall, George Street, on the 17th November 1899. The spacious building was filled to its utmost capacity.

Farewell presentations were made to Dr. Matheson and to his sister, Miss Matheson. Dr. Matheson, after returning thanks in his own name and in that of his sister, said :

I come to bid you one of the most remarkable farewells that was ever uttered. Nearly all things that say "Good-bye" say it before starting. When the spring intends to leave us it presents us beforehand with a primrose; when the summer purposes to quit it sends us a present of short days. But *my* farewell has inverted the order. I have first gone away and then come back to say "Good-bye." I have come too late for leave-taking. I have brought my primrose to your completed year. Why have I done this? Through unfeelingness? Nay, through excess of feeling. I wanted to say "Good-morning" instead of "Good-night." I wanted to meet you when the first pain on either side was dulled by the passing hours. How could you think I was indifferent to you? Have I not been with you for thirteen years in sunshine and in shadow?—and the sunshine has been more than the shadow. Have I not caught the spray of your baptismal fonts? Have I not heard your marriage-bells? Have I not seen your courtships and your courtesies? Have I not brought the grapes of Eshcol to your hours of sickness? Have not your children in my presence flowered into manhood, into womanhood? Have not your middle-aged men grown white with the winters' snow? I have been with you in your Canas, in your Nains, in your Bethanys. The cord between us has been an unbroken cord, and it is still undissolved; therefore it is that I said not "Good-night" but "Good-morning."

. . . .

I came a taper amid the torches. My place was down in the valley—the Stockbridge valley. Do not think it was less onerous on that account. There, where the Water of Leith threads its devious way, you will meet humanity unveiled. There you will see man outside the stage, with the lights suppressed and the music silent, and the dancing ceased — man unconventional, man natural, man struggling hand to hand with life's poverty and toil. These were the masses before which I stood —an atom in the crowd. It was a tragic spectacle; it was blind Samson with his hands upon the gates of Gaza. The Philistines laughed; but I think I lifted these gates one inch. And I think that next to the strength of God, and next again to your kind co-operation, I was indebted to my own weakness. These sons of toil said, " Here is a man with an environment no less unfavourable than ours—barred by every gate of fortune, yet refusing to give in—overtaken by the night, yet confident of the morning. I say that such a spectacle was a spectacle fitted to stimulate the toiling Stockbridge masses: the appearing of a working-man who by his own hammer and by God's arm should cleave his way through opposing obstacles and plant his feet on a solid shore. This has been my Gospel, this has been my message; by this shall I stand or fall. My sermons may have flown over your heads like the bird of Paradise; but my life has been level with your own—an obstructed life, a circumscribed life, but a life of boundless sanguineness, a life of quenchless hopefulness, a life which has beat persistently against the cage of circumstance, and which even at the time of abandoned work has said not " Good-night " but " Good-morning."

Dr. Matheson's former assistants, eight in number, all of them now occupying the position of parish ministers in the Church of Scotland, determined not to be behind the congregation of St. Bernard's in showing their appreciation of their late chief. Towards the end of October they invited him to a luncheon in the Balmoral Hotel, and presented him with an illuminated address which testified to the kindness which he had shown them and the enthusiasm with which he had inspired them. Between them there had been the most cordial relations, and the fact that within the brief period of thirteen years the one succeeded the other so rapidly in their promotion to parishes, was a proof of his influence and of the readiness with which he exercised it. Indeed, there was no class more deeply attached to Dr. Matheson than the young ministers of the Church. He was always prepared to welcome them, and to give them every encouragement and assistance in their work. There are not a few who now occupy important positions who owe their promotion to him. The concluding paragraph of the address testifies to the whole-hearted devotion of his former assistants, and their admiration of his character and work :

But while we thus gladly recognise your widespread influence, we especially desire to acknowledge our own indebtedness to you as a teacher and a friend. When we came to you it was at a period in our lives when we were anxious to impart the truth we knew, but lacked the knowledge of how best we could do so. From you we received instruction and inspiration. You at once opened to us the wondrous possibilities of thought, and exemplified to us the attractive methods of expression. That we were privileged, during shorter or longer periods, to enjoy your pulpit ministry, your private and social intercourse, your kindly and helpful advice, we are grateful to the Giver of all good gifts.

The first-fruits of Dr. Matheson's retirement was his *Studies of the Portrait of Christ.* It marked a new and final stage in his theological development, and proved the most popular of all his books. The subject had long lain in his mind. It was one that many thought would have attracted him at a much earlier period of his literary life, but it was wisely ordered that he should take it in hand at a time when his thought was ripest and his experience most matured. He was fond of treating his themes and characters in the order of their development, and he himself, as has already been pointed out, was subject to the same law that he found governing others. It was only towards the close of his life that he came to the study of Him who is the Life; at all events, that he felt commissioned to give to the world the fruits of a study which, in very truth, was life-long. Dr. Matheson began as a theologian; he developed into the apologist. He thereafter took up the rôle of the biblical scholar and the historian of religious thought. In all his works there is to be found the imaginative glow which ever and anon blossomed into poetic song, and that devotional spirit which found expression in his series of Meditations; but it was only after he had traversed the whole course of Christian thought that he ended where many begin. The worship of Christ, which the young convert is asked to regard as the first step in the new life, was, in a sense, the last in the career of Dr. Matheson. I do not desire to be misunderstood. That worship pervaded his life, but it was only towards its close that it ripened into full maturity and took possession of his whole nature. If in his earlier years his ambition was to find in

Christianity a solution of the problems which vex
human reason, in his later years it was his absorbing desire to find in Christ Himself the solace of
the human heart and the satisfaction of the human
spirit. His own development, like that of his
Master, was also in its nature a descent. It
witnessed the fall of his spirit from the heights of
theology to the prosaic plains of religion; from the
effort to cleave the skies on the wings of thought to
the patient sitting at the feet of the Master. It
was there, at last, that he found perfect peace. The
Christ of Prophecy, the Christ of History, and the
Christ of Aspiration had become to him the Christ
of Experience.

The book was issued in two volumes; the first
appeared in the autumn of 1899 and the second in
that of 1900. In the Preface to the first volume he
said that if it proved a success he would continue
his studies to their close. Its success was, for a
book of the kind, almost unprecedented. Eleven
thousand copies were sold within the year. Its
reception by the press was equally hearty; the
reviews were enthusiastic. One or two complained
of the title of the book, and wished that he had
simply called it a "Life of Christ." But he had
good reason for his choice, and in the Preface to
the second volume he replied to the critics. "By
the Title of this Book," he says, "I do not mean
a study of the different Portraits which have been
drawn of Christ, nor even a comparison of the
Pictures drawn by the Four Evangelists. The

Portrait of Christ is to me the united impression produced upon the heart by these four delineations. My office is not that of a critic, nor that of a creator, nor that of an amender, but simply that of an interpreter ; I study the Picture as it is."

The first volume embraces that period in the ministry of our Lord which ends with the Feeding of the Five Thousand. This miracle the author very aptly characterises as the " First Communion," and it is the climax in the first stage of our Lord's work. That stage has as its keynote sympathy for the multitude. During it we see Christ giving Himself to man and finding joy in the giving. In the second period of His ministry, which closes with His death, Christ's aim was to induce the multitude to give themselves to Him. In His apparent failure to accomplish this lay His sorrow. The tragedy of His life is found in the unresponsiveness of man.

In filling in his conception of the ministry of Christ, as thus indicated, Dr. Matheson pays due heed to historical accuracy. It is quite true that he does not treat the records of the life of Christ after the manner of the modern historical school. His is no dry-as-dust production. He believes that the possession of ideas, as well as the knowledge of facts, forms a necessary equipment of a biographer. But he is careful that his ideas should illumine his facts, and not overcloud them. In the opening chapters the author deals, in an original and luminous manner, with such subjects as the " Messianic Hopes of the Jews " and the " Baptist's

Conception of the Christ." It is in the sixth
chapter, however, that he gets to the heart of the
subject. To the question, What is the plan of
Christ's life? he boldly replies Christ had no plan.
By this he means that our Lord did not arrange
beforehand the details of His ministry. He had in
His mind, from the very first, the aim to be the Holy
One of God. But He allowed each day and hour to
determine how that aim should be realised. God,
says Dr. Matheson, had a plan for the Son, and the
Son in yielding Himself to the will of the Father
carried out that plan without determining its
contents in advance. Its general scope, however,
the author would find in St. Paul's conception. of
Christ's work, which is recorded in the passage that
says, " Let this mind be in you which was in Christ
Jesus who, though in the form of God, thought
equality with God a thing not to be snatched at,
but emptied Himself, and took upon Himself the
form of a servant, and was made in the likeness of
men ; and being recognised in the fashion of man,
he humbled Himself and became obedient unto
death, even the death of the cross." This passage
gives the keynote to Dr. Matheson's conception of
our Lord's life. For he holds, in this matter, St.
Paul to be a better guide than Renan, Schenkel, or
Seeley. Such a philosophy of the life of Jesus, he
remarks, is the description of a ladder of descent.
In the chapters that follow he works out this conception in detail, not, however, in a hard-and-fast
manner, for that would be to reduce his work to a

piece of mechanism.   All the same he believes that
the sequence which the apostle sketches will be
found to follow, if not the steps, at least the
principle of the life of Jesus.   In each event which
leads up to the First Communion, with which the
volume closes, when our Lord's sympathy with the
wants of men received its full manifestation, the
human and philanthropic spirit of the Master is
seen to grow ever deeper and wider.

It is at this point that the second volume takes
up the story and continues it to its close.   The
pivot on which this period in the life of Christ
turns is the thought of His death.   This is the
point which Dr. Matheson selects as the central
theme of the volume, and he has shown a true
instinct in doing so.   Nowhere else can one find a
study of the "final catastrophe," as it has been
called, so fresh, so profound, and on the whole so
hopeful ; which indeed transforms death from being
a "final catastrophe" into a "final triumph."

It is impossible for the student of the life of
Christ to read Dr. Matheson's pages without
challenging a comparison between him and the
greatest of those who have treated the same
subject.   Since the day when St. Bonaventura,
early in the thirteenth century, wrote, outside of
the sacred canon, the first *Vita Christi*, more Lives
than can be numbered have been written of Christ.
But for the present generation two studies stand
out as of special interest—the *Ecce Homo* of Professor
Seeley, and *The Training of the Twelve* by Pro-

fessor Bruce. Each of these works, in addition to its great power as a whole, contains a single gem, which of itself would be sufficient to redeem it, supposing it needed redemption, which it does not. The gem of *Ecce Homo* is the story which describes the repentance of a woman—a story which has gone to the heart of Christendom, and which has given to Christian art the figure of the Magdalene. The gem of *The Training of the Twelve* is the anointing at Bethany. Severe though the test may be, Dr. Matheson in each case supplies us with a new gem which is worthy of being set beside them. Indeed, the book as a whole is richer than any that he ever wrote, in originality, in depth, and in beauty of expression. A spirit of calmness pervades it; there is a sureness of touch in the thought as well as in the style. It bristles with suggestions; it is bold and yet reverent, deep yet devotional. He might well call it *Studies of the Portrait of Christ*, for it is a veritable picture gallery in which one loves to linger. The Character, whose lineaments he traces, is depicted in every stage of His development, and in every form and fashion of His unique career. The lines may be few, but they are drawn by a master-hand. Each chapter introduces a fresh aspect and shows a new feature. Round the central Figure are grouped the leading members of the League of Pity; filling in the background are the sisters of Bethany, the sorrowing Magdalene, the scowling Pharisee, and the promiscuous crowd. Nineteen

centuries of thought and progress combine, in the
hands of Dr. Matheson, to re-create the first century,
and to give us back the Christ of religion, whom
the Christ of theology had taken away.

The hope was expressed by the members of the
Presbytery of Edinburgh, when Dr. Matheson gave
in his resignation as minister of St. Bernard's,
that his services as a preacher would not be lost
to the Church.   He amply fulfilled that hope.
One of the burdens of his office as the incumbent
of a stated charge was that he had, in addition to
his immediate duties, to meet the constant and repeated demands made upon him for special services
by ministers and congregations of nearly all the
Protestant denominations in the land.   He did his
best to meet their wishes, and he endeavoured
once a month to preach in other churches than
his own.   After he was freed from St. Bernard's

he responded to these requests more readily, and
for the first few years he was active in preaching
special sermons in different parts of the country.
There was one class in particular that loved to
hear him.   During the first year of his ministry in
Edinburgh he was invited to deliver inaugural
addresses to the theological students of three such
different Colleges as the Edinburgh University,
the United Presbyterian Hall, and the Free
Church College of Glasgow.   He was a prime
favourite with Scottish students, and if there was
one University city in which he was more popular
than another it was Aberdeen.   He visited it on

several occasions, and was always gladly welcomed.
The most important of these was when, at the
invitation of the University, he came to deliver one
of the Murtle Lectures. This was in December
1901, and Professor Nicol, who presided, has
furnished me with the following interesting account
of Dr. Matheson's address :—

I wish your request to say something about Dr.
Matheson's pulpit appearances in Aberdeen had fallen
into more competent hands. But I had a sincere admiration of his genius, and as a colleague for several years in
the Presbytery of Edinburgh I was proud to win his
friendship and to retain it to the end.

That he was exceedingly popular in Aberdeen was
shown by the large congregations which assembled to hear
him on the rare occasions when he fulfilled public
engagements in the city. His published works had made
his name familiar among all denominations, and among
Church of Scotland people he had long been known
through his charming meditations and poems and contributions to the Magazines. And of course his great
hymn, " O Love that wilt not let me go," had long been in
the *Scottish Hymnal*, and latterly had found a place also
in the *Church Hymnary*.

It was at one of our University Chapel Summer Services
in 1900 that I heard him first in Aberdeen. He had
officiated at least once on some public occasion before, and
had then been the guest of Professor Matthew Hay. So
attached had he become to Dr. and Mrs. Hay, and so
much did he feel at home with them, that on his later
visits to the city he took up his abode with them. And it
need not be said that the esteem he had conceived for
them was warmly reciprocated. There was a large
attendance of students, considering that it was summer,
when a much smaller proportion of them are at classes ;
and, with as large a representation of the general public
as our beautiful chapel could admit, he had a crowded
audience.

The preacher gave them of his very best. His opening prayer was very striking and uplifting, and, though it was short, it awakened reverence and aroused expectation. His text was in Romans v. 20, "Where sin abounded, grace did much more abound"; a subject wholly congenial to his own sanguine temperament, and on which he based an appeal to his student audience to cherish the optimism of youth as one of their dearest possessions. As he closed a remarkably fresh and impressive discourse, delivered with that action of the uplifted right arm so characteristic of his manner, he expressed his pride at being invited to preach one of the University Sermons, and showed how highly he esteemed the occasion.

His next appearance in Aberdeen was in December 1901, when he was invited by the University to deliver one of the Murtle Lectures. These Lectures are five or six in the course of each winter session, and are delivered in the Mitchell Hall, Marischal College. Among the Lecturers of recent years have been Moderators and past Moderators of the Presbyterian Church, the Bishops of Salisbury and Stepney, Canons Scott Holland and Hensley Henson, Professor Margoliouth of Oxford, the late Principal Rainy, and the late Dr. John Watson (Ian Maclaren), and even laymen like Professors M'Kendrick and our own Sir William Ramsay. For one labouring under Dr. Matheson's physical limitations a lecture, usually occupying a full hour or more, must have been a trying ordeal, but to the end he held on his way with the ease and lucidity and brilliance which marked his briefest meditation. His subject was "The problem of Job's patience." There was a crowded attendance in the large Hall, every seat being filled, and many standing in the passages, and even without in the adjoining picture gallery. When the great congregation joined in singing, as they did with unusual heartiness, the hymn "O Love that wilt not let me go," one could see that the preacher himself was moved. When the lecture began, the subject which in less experienced hands might have become commonplace was opened up with an originality and power which at once arrested the audience. The preacher found in the literature of the world four typical notes of despair,—first and deepest that of Omar Khayyám, next that of the Book of Ecclesiastes, then that of Pascal in his *Thoughts*, and finally that of the Book of Job. To expound the significance of this last, he set himself with a wealth of illustration the most effective, and at the same time left the impression upon some of his hearers that the most pathetic touches were derived from his own experience. It was an effort worthy to be ranked among the most successful delivered under the auspices of the Murtle Bequest.

The relations established between Dr. Matheson and the University of Aberdeen were of the most cordial character. He had been nominated by the Senatus for the Gifford Lectureship, but had declined. In 1902 the Senatus conferred upon him the degree of LL.D., an honour which gave him immense gratification. When he died, in the course of last year, we felt that there had gone from us a unique personality, and one of the greatest ornaments on our Roll of Honorary Graduates.

His friend, Professor Cowan, wrote a letter to Miss Matheson on the evening on which the address was delivered, in which he says :

> Your brother was in excellent form and voice, and gave us a brilliant lecture. The Hall was crowded, including the passages filled with standers, and a large number who came fairly punctual had to go away, owing to the failure of standing room. The audience listened with rapt attention.

Dr. Nicol refers to two special honours conferred on Dr. Matheson by the University of Aberdeen. They offered him, in 1899, the Gifford Lectureship, and in 1902 they conferred upon him the degree of LL.D. It was a disappointment to many when he declined the Lectureship. It was the greatest gift in the hands of the

22

Senatus, and one that is only bestowed upon
the most distinguished men. Many wondered
why he declined this honour. I remember
speaking to him about it at the time, and expressing the general regret at his inability to
deliver the lecture. He replied that the reason
was one of health. His doctor had forbidden
him. This was the very year in which he had
resigned St. Bernard's. He may not have been
aware at the time of any failing of health, but
there is no doubt that this fact may have had not
a little to do with his determination to relinquish
his charge. The great strain under which he
had worked for so many years, and the worries
attendant on the arrangements which led to the
appointment of a colleague, told upon him, and he
now began for the first time to realise that
physically he was not the man that he used to be.
The question of the lectures themselves could
not have seriously troubled him, for he had
already in manuscript a full course on the very
subject on which he would have had to speak.
This volume was evidently meant for publication,
but it has never seen the light; it is on Natural
Religion.

The other honour conferred upon him was the
degree of LL.D. He was greatly gratified at this
recognition, especially on the part of a University
that was not his own. But to do Glasgow justice,
it was an open secret that the Senate had resolved
that very spring to bestow upon him the same

degree, but it was anticipated by Aberdeen, much to the regret of the Professors, for they felt that his own University would honour itself in honouring him. Principal Story, in particular, was anxious to make every reparation for Glasgow's tardiness, and if both had lived but a little longer it was the intention of the Principal to propose Matheson for the degree of D.D. Many years previously, in 1890, he had been made a Fellow of the Royal Society of Edinburgh, so that at the comparatively early age of fifty-nine he was the recipient of all the Academic honours that his native country could bestow upon him.

The other occasion on which Dr. Matheson appeared to greatest advantage as a special preacher was when, in October of 1903, he delivered the annual sermon in Brunswick Chapel, Leeds, in connection with the Wesleyan Missionary Society. This was not by any means the first occasion on which he had appeared in an English pulpit. He had previously preached at Bradford and other places; indeed, he was as much sought after by congregations across the Border as in his own land. The hold which he had upon the members of other communions was most remarkable. He was as popular with other denominations as with his own. There was no church, for example, in which he preached more frequently than in Free St. George's, Edinburgh, and for Dr. Alexander Whyte he had the greatest admiration and regard. The esteem was mutual. They were the two outstanding ministers of Edinburgh. For originality of thought and freshness of treatment they had no equal. Dr. Whyte, on the appearance of the *Studies of the Portrait of Christ*, sent the following letter to Dr. Matheson :—

BALMACARA, LOCH ALSH, N.B.

DEAR DR. MATHESON,—On the last day of my Loch Alsh holiday, a cold wet day, I have read your brilliant *Portrait of Christ*, at a long down-sitting and pen in hand. And now I sit down to put my notes of your book in order for future inspiration and use. It is a true test of a work of genius that its touch fertilises the mind of the reader, and my mind and my heart have both been fertilised to-day over your deep and beautiful book.—With warm love and honour,   ALEXANDER WHYTE.

In a communication from Dr. Whyte, he says : " I never heard Dr. Matheson preach, though more than once he took my place in my absence; but always when he preached for me, there was an outburst of praise among my people, most unanimous and most thankful. I never could account for the extraordinary kind words he would employ about myself, or rather, I always accounted for them as the outcome of his extraordinary deep and warm heart."

His discourse at Leeds was on the " Boundlessness of the Bible," based on 2 Timothy ii. 9, " The Word of God is not bound." It was a Missionary sermon, and one of the most characteristic that he ever delivered. " The attraction of a great preacher and the power of the pulpit," says a correspondent, " were shown on Wednesday evening,

when, in spite of pouring rain, people came from
all parts to hear the annual Missionary sermon in
Brunswick Chapel. The sermon was an extraordinary deliverance, in treatment as in manner.
Dr. Matheson's striking delivery and vibrant voice,
added to his original way of dealing with his
subject, at once arrested attention and kept it
undiminished till the close." The Wesleyan
Church, as a whole, had a great regard for Dr.
Matheson. One of its leading ministers has
written to the effect :

> I thought probably you would be.pleased to know, in
> so strenuous a Church as the Primitive Methodist Church,
> Dr. Matheson was greatly loved and read. I was sur-
> prised to discover how strong was the devotion in our
> Church to this prophet-seer, and it has given me no little
> joy that there is the clearest evidence that Matheson's
> soul has passed into many souls in our Church, and he
> lives again in lives made better by his presence.

In 1901, the year following the publication of
the second volume of his *Portrait of Christ*, he
published two books, *Times of Retirement* and *The
Sceptre without a Sword*. The first was a volume
of meditations, the second a Christmas idyll. I
well remember the inception of his *Times of Retirement*. Some eighteen months before its
appearance I happened to be on a visit to him.
It was at the time when I was making preparations
for my editing of the Church of Scotland weekly
journal, *Saint Andrew*. He took a deep interest
in the venture, and as I was leaving he asked to
be excused for a moment, and on returning he had

in his hand a brown paper parcel, carefully bound up, and with evident delight he handed it to me and said, " There's my Christmas present for *Saint Andrew.*" On opening the parcel I discovered that it contained twenty meditations. When they had appeared he sent me fresh instalments. When they too had run their course in the magazine, the series was published in volume form, with a brief " Biographical Sketch of the Author," written by me at the request of the publishers. These valued contributions were a free gift from him and a mark of his friendship, and he continued to write regularly for the journal until his death, and on the same terms. Indeed, the last book published by him, *Rests by the River*, first saw the light in *Saint Andrew*, a fact which he is careful to note in the very first line of his Preface. It was also a book of devotional meditations, and was published in the spring of 1906. *The Sceptre without a Sword* is a charming booklet, based on the vision of Daniel, " I saw in the night visions, and, behold, one like the Son of Man came with the clouds of heaven. . . . And there was given Him a kingdom" (vii. 13). Dr. Matheson interprets the vision of the old Hebrew seer in the light of the history of the world since the coming of Christ. He argues that the secret of the difference between ancient and modern times is the influence of Christmas Day ; in other words, the fact that the hearts of modern men have been dominated by a Man of sacrifice—simple motives setting in move-

ment great forces, the wheels of time quickened by
the heart finding impulse and inspiration in the
sublime events associated with Christmas-time. In
this helping of man by man he finds the hope that
differences which now separate men will be
hushed, and the notes of a common Hymnal
drawing all together in that meridian hour of
Christmas Day when the last vestige of difference
shall be removed.

His contributions to periodical literature during
this period were not numerous. It is true that in
1901 he wrote a series of eleven articles to *The
Expositor* on "Scientific Lights on Religious
Problems." He now regarded the old war between
science and religion as at an end, and he himself
was an important factor in bringing the strife to so
happy and fruitful an issue. He now calls in Science
as the handmaid of Religion, and in these articles he
shows how the great doctrines of the Christian
Faith can be interpreted by it. In the previous
year, 1900, he wrote an article to *The London
Quarterly Review* on the "Characteristics of Bible
Portraiture." It was a preparation for his next
important book. In this article he promulgates
the views which he afterwards embodied in his
Portrait of Christ and *The Representative Men of
the Bible.*

It was in the autumn of 1902 that the first of
his striking books on Bible characters appeared.
He published it under the above title, *The Representative Men of the Bible.* "By this," he says,

"I mean the men of the Bible who represent phases of the Bible, irrespective of place and time, and I consider them only in those incidents in which they are representative. These studies," he continues, "are not historical, they are not critical. They are an analysis of the portraits as we see them, without any attempt to inquire how or when they came." He follows the method which, for a brief study of any human character, is always the most illuminating; he adopts a point of view. He looks, so to speak, at the individual whom he intends to sketch; focuses the incidents of his life and the features of his character, and allows himself to be impressed by the idea which is then produced. This he regards as the soul of the man, the mental or spiritual fact represented by him; and it is what he pictures. No one was more capable of excelling in a work of this kind than Dr. Matheson. His point of view may to the prosaic mind seem at times a little far-fetched. As occasionally happens, when this method is adopted, violence may be done to certain features which do not harmonise with the image that the artist has in his mind. But taken as a whole it is a suggestive method, one which lifts its subject out of the crowd of details which obscure the character in place of revealing it. Matheson pondered each "Representative Man" in turn. He allowed the subject for the time being to possess him; he brought his own creative genius to work upon it, and the result is a portrait gallery of Bible characters which has few equals in Christian literature. The three volumes which he published, two on the Old Testament and one on the New, are as certain to live as anything he ever wrote. The first volume was received by public and press with much enthusiasm. In a short time it reached a fourth edition. These volumes, along with his *Studies of the Portrait of Christ* and his *Meditations*, have had the largest sale of all his works, and give every hope of continuing to attract readers for many a day. One feature common to them all is the devotional note with which each chapter ends; and the following interesting letter from a missionary of the Presbyterian Church in Japan bears striking testimony to Matheson's far-reaching influence :—

MATSUYAMA, JAPAN,
May 12, 1906.

DEAR DR. MATHESON,—My wife and I were of some help to a Japanese military doctor who was very sick during the late war with Russia, and upon his recovery to health he asked me many things about Christianity, and especially about prayer. I am teaching English in a Government school here in Matsuyama, and asked one of the English-speaking Japanese teachers to translate into Japanese the prayer which follows on your study of David in *Representative Men of the Bible*. This doctor said that the prayer is comprehensive, and he used it every day. While not yet baptized, I think the Lord has been guiding him by this sickness to the truth. I thought perhaps you might be interested to know that your prayer has had an influence even in Japan, and thus the scope of your work has been enlarged more than you might think. I thank the Lord that He has qualified you for being such a help and comfort, to many like myself, through your printed works. I have had such pleasure in reading your books, and in feeling through them the warmth of your spiritual nature. I hope you will still have many years of being the teacher of God's comfort to others, even as He has taught you of His comfort.—Yours very sincerely,

A. V. BRYAN.

To this Dr. Matheson replied :

14 BELGRAVE CRESCENT,
June 13, 1906.

Please accept my very best thanks for your very kind communication! It is my greatest joy in life to learn that my poor effort affords help and comfort to my fellow-man. It is truly good of you to send me such a high appreciation of my work. But specially am I rejoiced to know that my words have influence outside the Church of Christ; this is indeed a thing of which one may be justly proud. But, for that matter, I have the greatest admiration for the Japanese nation ; and I firmly believe that, in the main, they live the Christian life. I cannot but think that that life will yet shape itself in the form of a creed which will inspire them with the hope everlasting, and stimulate the duties of earth by the light of heaven.— Yours very sincerely, etc.

Hearers of Dr. Matheson's sermons were well aware of the variety of his intellectual and literary interests. He appeared in the pulpit with a Divine message, but one that was lit up and illustrated by the fruits of his multifarious reading. His books, treating for the most part of theological and religious subjects, fail to give the same impression of his wide culture. In truth, however, he was quite as much interested in secular literature as in sacred, and his knowledge of the one was almost as extensive as his knowledge of the other. It was a surprise to many when, in the spring of 1905, an article by him appeared in the *Glasgow Evening News* on the "Modern English Novel," showing an acquaintance with the popular authors of the day quite as extensive as and much more informing than that of the professional novel reader ; and the surprise of others was almost as great when in the previous year, at the annual dinner of the Edinburgh Ninety Burns Club, he delivered his remarkable oration on the poet. Dr. Matheson's friends were well aware of his admiration for the national bard. His enthusiasm broke out now and again in the pulpit, and in one instance he made a happy use of a famous passage in the life of Christ to illustrate and in a sense to justify the poet's character. In his *Portrait of Christ*, remarking on an incident which he says has transfixed the attention of the world, the contrasted attitude of the Pharisees and of Christ in the presence of an unfortunate woman, there is the following striking passage :—

This particular kind of sin was precisely the one from which a Pharisee was apt to be free. There are cases in which Satan casts out Satan ; there are men and women who are exempt from certain vices simply through the presence of other vices. A cold, phlegmatic nature would never commit the sins of Robert Burns. This does not justify Robert Burns ; but it shows that one disease may be cured by another disease. It is a matter of daily experience that the advent of a new ailment may cause an already existing ailment to subside ; there are forms of physical illness which cannot live together. There are forms of moral illness which are also mutually antagonistic. I cannot imagine that the typical Judas Iscariot could ever have been guilty of that form of sin which char-

acterised this woman. The man who could carefully
count out thirty pieces of silver as the price of his Lord's
betrayal would never have committed the miscalculations
of her who squandered life, reputation, respectability, on
the sensuous passion of an hour.

So much for Dr. Matheson's conception of the
character of Burns; it reveals at once his insight
and his charity. In his Edinburgh address it is the
poetry of Burns that forms his subject, and the two
notes which, to his thinking, distinguish it are its
sympathy and universality. He aptly illustrates
the former by a reference to Burns's poem on the
Daisy. "Did it ever occur to you to ask," he
exclaims, "why he speaks of the flower as 'crimson
tipped'?—

Is it not the fact? you say. Of course: but I doubt
very much if that is why Burns said it. Burns is not the
maker of an almanac. He never records facts just because
they are facts, he has always a reason beyond. And if I
am not greatly mistaken he had a reason here. He has
been calling the daisy "modest." What is the expression
of modesty? Is it not blushing — blushing crimson.
Could any two epithets come together more beautifully,
more harmoniously? Crashaw once wrote a poem on
the Miracle of Cana of Galilee; he wrote it in one line
—"The Conscious Water knew its Lord, and blushed."
Burns, I think, had the same thought about the daisy. It
grew upon the mountain-top and saw the glory. And
it blushed before the glory. It felt its own inherent
nothingness and the crimson dyed its face.

In referring to the second note of Burns's poetry,
its universality, Dr. Matheson remarks:

This man is an instrument of ten strings — of all
possible strings. He wears the garb of Scotland but he

is the poet of Humanity. His accent is provincial but his
speech is cosmopolitan. He sings in a national dialect,
but he delivers a message to man. The hands are the
hands of Esau, but the voice is the voice of Jacob. We
claim him as the property of our separate land, but in
truth he has made our land universal. This man, in a
literary sense, has soared above principalities and powers.
He is neither Jew nor Greek, barbarian nor Roman, bond
nor free. He is neither Scotch nor English; he is neither
French nor Italian; he is neither Dutch nor German: he
is neither, and yet he is all these—he is human. It is on
this we base his claim to immortality. Nationalities will
die. Even though the foot of an enemy should touch
them not, time changes their countenance and disrobes
them of their vesture. The nationality of Scotland itself
has faded in the ever-increasing assimilation to her
wealthier sister. But Burns has not faded. He stands
on the mountain-top in full vision of that Canaan where
the immortals dwell, and his eye is not dim nor his natural
strength abated.

The great annual break in Dr. Matheson's life,
when he was minister of St. Bernard's, was his
summer holiday. He took two full months, August
and September, and during them he would preach
for no one. For the first fifteen years of his life
in Edinburgh he spent his summer vacation on the
west coast, chiefly at Craigmore, Skelmorlie, or
Largs. He did a certain amount of work each day,
and enjoyed being read to as usual, but he took
frequent sails on the river steamers and long
drives into the country. Latterly, however, he
preferred to go to the east coast, and for several
summers in succession he spent his holiday at
North Berwick. The quiet of the place, its
bracing sea-breezes, its variety of carriage drives,

and its congenial society, all appealed to him. It
was there that he made the friendship of Dr. Hately
Waddell, and the two had frequent intercourse
together. Dr. Waddell, who had a great admiration for his friend, has communicated to me certain
impressions which are particularly accurate and
interesting. He remarks, for example:

> Dr. Matheson was in the habit of saying, in his
> paradoxical way, that blindness was not the want of sight
> but in reality too much sight. He was blind, he would
> say, not because he saw too little but because he saw too
> much. Blindness was excessive light, and the time of
> revelation for him was in the night; then he saw clearly.
> He was fond of expressing himself in paradoxes, and it
> was difficult sometimes to know how far he was in earnest
> in statements of this kind. But certainly no other form of
> words could so well have described his temperament
> either as a writer or a preacher. All his work, written or
> spoken, was a transcription of what he mentally saw.
> Truth came to him as a vision; he did not reason it out.
> He had a vivid picture of it complete at once, and its
> certainty was more or less tested by the vividness of the
> form it assumed in his mind.

What chiefly struck Dr. Waddell was Matheson's
impressionist temperament, which, he says,

> gave such force to his preaching and such vividness to
> his writing. His power lay in holding up to others the
> same living impression of a subject which he himself had
> experienced. His preaching was not so much the
> elucidation of a text or of a theme as the re-telling of
> a series of graphic impressions which the subject had
> already made on the preacher, each of which seemed to
> absorb for the time the whole truth of life. Hence also
> his writings, even his earlier works, assumed chiefly a
> descriptive rather than an argumentative form, and

finally became by preference a series of portraits or picture studies.

But while his genius was thus poetical, pictorial, and imaginative, and while he proclaimed himself to be an idealist,

he never allowed either poetry or imagination to run away with him. His work was all of an exact and practical kind. Whether for pulpit or press his ideal conceptions were reduced to the actual necessities of the occasion. The most poetical themes and exalted views of life and history became real and persuasive to those who listened or read. No great man is vague in his thinking, and Dr. Matheson shared this characteristic of true greatness: that he worked out all his thought to its legitimate conclusions and left a large and complete picture of it on the imagination and memory. The truths of religion and history he regarded as universal, and the differences of time, or thought, or nationality, merely incidental. He would have held himself as defrauded of an inalienable right had he been forbidden to translate the teaching of the Bible into all the varied conditions and vernacular of to-day. His chief mission, he latterly thought, was just this form of translation of Bible truths into modern conditions. Not necessarily the illumination of antique formulas but, certainly, the reconstruction of them by modern ideas.

Dr. Waddell is in doubt as to whether he was more theological or devout in his nature, whether he was more reasoning or emotional in his habit of thought. He thinks both tendencies were fairly well balanced, and that in his writings there is a unique combination of both. " It is true," he adds,

that his more reasoned themes had a great influence on current opinion, especially perhaps *The Old Faith and the New*, which Tennyson is said to have recommended to the late Duke of Argyll, and which Sir Andrew Clark recommended to many friends as the best antidote to atheism. But the most of these works were the outcome of his historical and theological reading, and are not so peculiar to his genius as his more individual meditations on devotional subjects. I should say that naturally his temperament was more that of the preacher than of the author, and that subjects which were treated from the standpoint of the preacher were both more congenial to himself and more helpful to his readers.

Referring to his most abiding mood, during his later years, he says :

The truth of Christianity, which chiefly appealed to him, was not any dogmatic definition of its special purposes and aims, but the broader revelation it contained of the immanence of the Divine in the human, of the eternal in the temporal, of the spiritual in the natural. Nothing indeed appealed to him more than this Christian consecration of the natural and commonplace, of the apparently common and unclean. This was the Gospel of his later years: the immanence of the Divine in the human, in all life and in all conditions of life. This, too, was the ever-recurring theme of his conversation, it was not so much a philosophy as simply a spiritual conviction, learned direct from Christ.

Wherein, asks Dr. Waddell, lay Matheson's chief value to the Church of his generation ? Putting aside his literary work, he would find the answer in his fresh, spontaneous, unconventional personality.

He was a living rebuke to all formality, to all ministerial mannerisms, to all outworn proprieties. He had a unique character, and it ruled all his clerical functions. Like his conversation, these were absolutely unconventional. His sermons and his prayers were things by themselves ; they were sometimes startling, but always fresh and forceful. He chose his own methods, but he had strength to make them successful. He broke away from clerical customs, but he did not need their support. And in days of advancing ritual he thought the Church might perhaps stake too much upon forms and proprieties. Much will be accepted from one who lets his own religious individuality have its full swing. This was the advice he gave as to ministerial training. He had great faith in human nature when consecrated to an ideal, and had no patience with anything artificial or unreal.

Speaking of a well-known trait in Dr. Matheson's character, his frank outspokenness and free criticisms of men and things, he remarks :

A strong humanity ruled all his social views, though at times his criticisms of individuals were severe. That, however, was but one side of his criticism, for the next moment he would find something in the same character worthy of the highest praise ; indeed, he passed from blame to praise without delay and without grudge. It was his nature to be constantly in extremes, and no one would have dreamed, least of all he himself, of taking these sudden valuations of character as prearranged judgments. His whole conversation was ecstatic and unpremeditated, and rose and fell with quick succession of varied feelings. It never was commonplace.

He had the same rapid and careless way of flashing out quotations on what might seem dangerous occasions. For when the application appealed to him he could not restrain a good-natured criticism or comparison, however pungent. But, as one said who knew him well, "These things all came and went in a moment." He took for granted always a hearer of judgment and tact, who could sympathise with and understand the sudden transitions of a quick-moving mind. A Homeric simplicity ruled all his character. The most sacred and profane equally appealed to him. The unity of God's great world gave worth and meaning to everything, even to things which religious society, with its conventional judgments, abandoned or condemned.

23

It was when on holiday at North Berwick, in the autumn of last year, that he took suddenly ill and died. I had seen him in Edinburgh at the beginning of June, and I was very much distressed at the change which was perceptible in his appearance. It is true that he was just recovering then from a serious attack of influenza, but it seemed to me that the hand of Death was upon him. I understand he recovered with surprising rapidity, and it looked as if he had many years still before him. The one object of interest to him, in those last days, was the beautiful new house which he had bought at 14 Belgrave Crescent. The last letter I ever received from him was one from North Berwick, assuring me of the welcome which he would give me in his new abode on his return home. Mr. William Smith, his secretary, has kindly furnished me with the following details regarding Dr. Matheson's health during the closing years of his life :—

"First, I did indeed notice that some two or three years before his death he was not in a physical sense the George Matheson I had met some seven or eight years before. He first, I fancy, realised his failing health on the occasion of a trip to Leeds, where he preached a great sermon to the Wesleyan Methodists. From that time he became increasingly averse to travel, and he declined, right and left, invitations which involved travel ; and before long he declined invitations to preach, whether they involved travel or not. It was not that he feared the preaching itself; he merely objected to being any length of time from his own house. The last occasion on which he preached was in Morningside Church, Edinburgh, on the 14th of February 1904. That sermon, I admit, appeared to call from him a great physical effort. I remember, when disrobing him in the vestry afterwards, he was positively wet with perspiration. What I mean is, that he evidently anticipated this effort, judged by what I recollect was an unusual amount of anxiety, for him, for some time before the event was due. I do not remember his text, I only remember that Morningside Church was filled that day, and that I was rather concerned about his physical condition. I remember, too, having an inkling myself that he could not preach again. Whether he had such an inkling I do not know; I should say not; and, for that matter, he was destined to make another public appearance, on the occasion, in November of 1904, of one of the annual services of the Life Boat Saturday Fund Service. He delivered a very fine prayer on the Sunday evening at the Empire Theatre. Even that occasion caused him a great effort, especially as he had committed the prayer to memory—a practice he was latterly much averse to. And yet I do not think that up to this Empire appearance, nor indeed till much later, if even then, he himself realised that his bodily health was giving way. His naturally optimistic disposition could not permit him any despondency.

"He manifested during the last years of his life symptoms of that trouble which in the end proved fatal, and his increasing shortness of breath made him more and more reluctant to take bodily exercise. But he was told that driving exercise was the thing for him, and, latterly, he often took this driving exercise when he would much rather have stayed at home. The very work of getting in and out of his carriage became more and more difficult. Realising this myself, I latterly volunteered to personally assist him when he returned from his two hours' drive. 'Ah!' he said one day, when I had assisted him from his carriage to his study, 'this is very good of you. I am a poor creature, and I don't think you will have me long.' This happened, I should think, about three weeks before his death. But that mood did not prevail till the end. During our working hours together he seemed as cheery and vivacious as ever. Those pleasantries to which he was accustomed were always in evidence, and his laugh was something in his old style. But if any instance struck me afterwards, as having been of a premonitory nature, it was the fact which occurred only some four hours before his apoplectic seizure. After an hour's read —from 8 to 9 p.m. on August 27th—which was commenced upon the Napoleonic vol. (vol. iii. or iv., I forget which) of the Cambridge Modern History, and finished upon the lighter diet of one of W. E. Norris' novels, I was considerably 'staggered' by, 'You might give me that Braille, William; I

think I'll do a little work.' I should not have
been 'staggered' by such a request three or four
years earlier; but not for a very long time had he
been in the habit of 'writing up' anything so late
in the day. I took it upon me to remonstrate with
him—gently but firmly. 'But I must get on with
my book!' [*Representative Women of the Bible*;
published after his death] he argued. 'An old adage
tells us not to "put off till to-morrow what we can
do to-day"'—a saying rather suggestive, I think.
At all events Dr. Matheson could not have finished
his book that day, and it is perhaps just as well
that I prevailed on him not to attempt it.

"Personally, I have not much faith in pre-
monitions; but that looked remarkably like something of the sort. But allowing that these somewhat gloomy forebodings really found root in him,
his skies were of a singularly alternating nature.
He assuredly never thought the end was *so* near.
I am sure that, not more than a day or two before
his death, he was making plans regarding his new
house—how he would entertain during the then
coming winter. Then, during his drive on August
27th, lasting about two and a half hours, I understood that he was in exceptionally good spirits.
So the premonition did not altogether weigh him
down. It is some years ago now, but he once
told me—in a not *altogether* jocular way—that he
thought he should '*never* die'! The fact is, his
abnormally active intellect could not conceive that
intellect in a state of passivity."

His sister, Miss Matheson, speaking of the last
visit to North Berwick, remembers her brother
saying to her then, as he had often said before, "I
have had a happy life." "He also told me he thought
he had a new note in his voice, which made me
think he was strong; and I did think he was seeing
better. One day he asked the doctor if there was
anything organically wrong, as he felt not so well.
The doctor said, quite decidedly, 'No.' My brother
replied, 'I would like to live to do a little good.'
Surely God had more important work for him to
do." "He was very happy," she continues, "at
North Berwick, and full of bright plans for the
future. He enjoyed driving with my sister Nellie
and me on the 27th, and was busily engaged in
writing his last work that day. He retired to rest
at 11.15, and bade me his usual affectionate good-
night. At 1.30 in the morning I heard a slight
moan. My sister Nellie and I rushed downstairs,
and found he could not speak. He was quite
conscious, however, and smiled with a restful, satisfied look to us both, showing that he knew us
well and was glad we were near. I was told
not to go to his room, as the doctor wished him
kept very quiet. He thought he would recover,
as he had a fine constitution. I did go once, however, and when he heard my voice his face lit up
with a lovely, beaming expression, full of joy and
peace. I shall never forget it, and I feel that no
photograph could ever depict that radiant glow.
He passed most peacefully away; there was no

suffering. As the doctor said, ' He had an abundant entrance.' "

The news of Dr. Matheson's death came as a shock of surprise, and produced a profound feeling of regret. It was so sudden and so unexpected, and, so far as age is concerned, he had not long passed the meridian of life. It was known that he was more disinclined than ever to preach, but this was not put down to any special physical weakness ; and a fresh volume by him having appeared, so recently as the spring, gave everyone the hope that he would be spared for many years to instruct and to comfort the Church of Christ. Long and appreciative notices of him appeared in almost every newspaper in England and in Scotland, indeed throughout the British Empire and America. Special references were made to him from almost every pulpit in his native land on the Sunday after his death ; and, by a unanimous desire, his famous hymn was sung on the same day by most congregations. The two leading Presbyteries of the Church, those of Edinburgh and Glasgow, and the Royal Society of Edinburgh, minuted special resolutions of regret and sympathy, copies of which were sent to his family. But more significant than any of these, and a stronger testimony to his work and to his influence, were the letters that his sister received from admirers in different parts of the world, and in particular from those, like himself, who suffered from dire physical calamity, and whose life his example had inspired and whose suffering his faith had mitigated. Indeed, under Providence, his special gift to the world may, in the end, prove to be, the encouragement which his noble life will give to those who, like himself, may be subjected to a life-long physical affliction. Let me give two such letters.

SURREY,
September 2, 1906.

DEAR MADAM,—Will you pardon me, a stranger to you, if I seem irreverently to intrude in your unspeakable sorrow.

I only desire to convey to you a humble and an affectionate acknowledgment of the endless debt I owe to the late Dr. Matheson, whom having not seen I love.

He who writes to you is a young clergyman of the Church of England, and a Scotsman. My eyes have been permanently injured by illness for many years now,—but after long darkness they partially recovered.

So your dear brother has been to me, by his heroic life, a constant example in my ministry, and in times of difficulty I have gone to his books for light and inspiration.

I had for some time wished to write to him, but hesitated to intrude.

May I now, and especially under the circumstances I have named, be forgiven for sending these simple words of deep gratitude to you?

If so, I hope this letter will reach you.—Yours most sincerely,   M. A.

DEAR MISS MATHESON,—It was with feelings akin to shock that I learned of the sudden death of your beloved brother, and I desire on behalf of my wife and myself to offer to you and all the mourning relatives our sincerest sympathy. May you realise, in a very special degree, the comforting presence and consoling companionship of Christ in your great sorrow.

I cannot tell you how much your highly gifted

brother was to me. Like him, I too lost my sight very
early in life, but through his magnificent example I was
induced to enter the ministry, in which I have been
labouring for these eleven years. It is somewhere about
seventeen years ago since one of my fellow-students
introduced me to Dr. Matheson, and well do I remember
our first meeting. I have met him more than once since
then, and I have corresponded with him frequently. He
was always kind and gracious, and supremely hopeful and
inspiring. It may interest you to learn that my wife had
just finished " The Glory of the Morning" in *Moments on
the Mount*, when her eye caught the sad announcement
of his death in the newspaper. The eternal youth of
which he writes so beautifully in this meditation is now
for him not an inspiring vision but a glorious reality.

He died at Avenell House, North Berwick, on
Tuesday, 28th August 1906, and he was buried in
the family vault in Glasgow Necropolis on the following Saturday, September 1st. His remains
had been previously brought to his new house at
Belgrave Crescent, which, alas ! was only to know its
owner in death. There service was conducted in
the presence of the family and of those specially
invited to the funeral. On reaching Glasgow a
large concourse was found waiting the arrival of
the cortège.

How the sun did shine on his funeral day! Its
rays poured with a steady brilliance, that made men
wonder. It was not a day on which one could be
sad—it was a day of light and creator of gladsome-
ness. Many may have thought of this as they
crossed the Dean Bridge, or walked along one or
other of the terraces, on their way to the funeral.
Joy, not sorrow, the very heavens seemed to de-

clare, ought to be the prevailing note in the service and the feeling in the heart. For the day had a message. It flashed the thought, that to him who had been surrounded with outward darkness all was now bright; that to the miracle of the New Birth which gives sight to the eye of faith had been added the miracle of the New State in which we "shall see Him as He is." Nor did the sun lose one ray of its lustre all that day. It followed the cortège with its glad message of hope to Matheson's own city, the city in which he was born and bred, and round which clustered many of his fondest recollections. Glasgow was proud of him while he was in life, and it will ever cherish his memory in death. Many of its leading clergy and citizens met and accompanied the bier to its last resting-place in the noble Necropolis. The ancient Cathedral, with a look of perpetual youth on its venerable walls, spoke as they passed of the "glorious resurrection." Around the open grave the mourners stood in sad dejection; and when all was over, and the last words of farewell and hope were spoken, they still stood as if expecting something more—they knew not what. That "something more" will be revealed to them, also, when "Death is swallowed up in victory."

INDEX

CPSIA information can be obtained
at www.ICGtesting.com
Printed in the USA
LVHW092150280621
691419LV00001B/2

9 781165 733651